Francis A. Drexel
LIBRARY

Books For College Libraries
Third Edition

Core Collection

PRAEGER LIBRARY OF U.S. GOVERNMENT DEPARTMENTS
AND AGENCIES

The Bureau of Labor Statistics

PRAEGER LIBRARY OF U.S. GOVERNMENT DEPARTMENTS
AND AGENCIES

Consulting Editors

ERNEST S. GRIFFITH

Former University Professor and Dean Emeritus, School of International Service, American University; former Director, Legislative Reference Service, Library of Congress; and author of *The American System of Government* and *The Modern Government in Action*

HUGH LANGDON ELSBREE

Former Chairman, Department of Political Science, Dartmouth College; former Managing Editor, *American Political Science Review;* former Director, Legislative Reference Service, Library of Congress

The
Bureau of
Labor Statistics

Ewan Clague

FREDERICK A. PRAEGER, *Publishers*
New York · Washington · London

FREDERICK A. PRAEGER, Publishers
111 Fourth Avenue, New York, N.Y. 10003, U.S.A.
5, Cromwell Place, London S.W.7, England

Published in the United States of America in 1968
by Frederick A. Praeger, Inc., Publishers

© 1968 by Ewan Clague

Library of Congress Catalog Card Number: 68–30832

This book is No. 13 in the series
Praeger Library of U.S. Government Departments and Agencies

Printed in the United States of America

Dedicated to the staff of the
BUREAU OF LABOR STATISTICS
for their devoted public service

Preface

The writing of this book has been a labor of love derived from my long association with the Bureau of Labor Statistics (BLS). However, I have tried to bring to bear upon the history and accomplishments of the Bureau the same objectivity I endeavored to maintain in my work within the Bureau. To assist the reader, who must judge both attempts, I am outlining here the nature and extent of my connections with the Bureau over the years.

When I finished my graduate work in labor economics at the University of Wisconsin in 1926, I had the good fortune to obtain my first professional statistical job in the Bureau of Labor Statistics. The Commissioner of Labor Statistics, Ethelbert Stewart, had sent a telegram to my major professor, John R. Commons, asking him to submit the name of a young graduate student who might go down to Washington to make some statistical studies for the Bureau. Professor Commons selected me, and I went. Technically, I was appointed as a commissioner of conciliation in the U.S. Conciliation Service of the Department of Labor, and I was on the payroll of that service, but I was detailed to the Bureau of Labor Statistics in order to make studies of "labor productivity."

The cost of living had become stabilized by the mid-1920's, and the unions no longer could use rising costs as an argument for wage increases. With widespread mechanization in American industry, union representatives turned to the productivity argument in their negotiations. The Conciliation Service, having encountered this new approach, thought it desirable to have some statistics on the subject.

The Bureau of Labor Statistics had already made some special studies of certain remarkable cases of the effect of mechanization, as in glass-bottle blowing. Although spectacular in their way, these studies were of limited significance to the economy as a whole. The Commissioner assigned me the task of devising measures that would be both comprehensive and continuing. This assignment was the origin of the annual indexes of productivity for specific industries, which the Bureau began publishing in late 1926. They were the forerunners of the indexes of productivity that the Bureau issues today.

The next year, the Commissioner negotiated a special study of the iron and steel industry. Three of us—Meredith Givens, who had been a fellow University of Wisconsin graduate student, another BLS staff member, and myself—spent six months in the field collecting information on trends in output per man-hour in blast furnace, open hearth, and Bessemer operations, measuring the performances of the mid-1920's against the prewar period of 1911–14. Unfortunately, only one small publication came out of the study. In the summer of 1928 (the end of the fiscal year), the available money gave out, and Givens and I were laid off.

My next connection with the Bureau came in 1933–34, when I served as a member of the Committee on Government Statistics and Information Services (described in Chapter I of the text). I was selected as one of the fifty-seven economists and statisticians who were to spend more or less time in Washington during the functioning of that committee. Meredith Givens was secretary of the Committee, and I was assigned responsibility for reviewing the statistics of the Labor Department, including the Bureau of Labor Statistics. Isador Lubin, who had just been appointed as the new Commissioner, gave us enthusiastic cooperation, as did other officials of the Department. There were many accomplishments in those years. Perhaps the most significant was the thoroughgoing revision of what was then called the Cost of Living Index.

In 1936, I joined the staff of the Social Security Board, where I became Director of Research and Statistics. Because the statistics required for social security purposes, especially those relating to unemployment compensation, impinged directly upon the employment and payroll statistics of the Bureau of Labor Statistics, I continued to have numerous contacts with the Bureau. Thus, although I was neither at that time nor later, during World War II, directly connected with the BLS, I always knew a great deal about its work.

My third and final connection with the Bureau began in 1946. By that time, I had been appointed by the Social Security Board to be director of the Bureau of Employment Security, which administered the federal-state program of unemployment insurance. One Saturday (then a regular working day), I received a telephone call from Professor Edwin Witte of the University of Wisconsin. He asked to come over to lunch with me at the social security building, insisting that it was urgent that he see me before he returned to Wisconsin. As soon as we sat down, he said to me, "I want you to be Commissioner of Labor Statistics. Now, don't say 'no' until I have a chance to explain."

I promised and I listened. He explained that he had been offered the job, but he wanted to spend the remainder of his professional career at the University of Wisconsin, writing and teaching on social security. He felt that the Bureau needed a younger man, one who had had extensive experience in government as well as in relations with labor and management. He urged me to see Secretary of Labor Lewis B. Schwellenbach.

Schwellenbach and I had been classmates at the University of Washington and graduates of the class of 1917. Although I had certainly known of him at the University (among other accomplishments, he was the champion college debater on the West Coast), he had not known me. However, Mrs. Aryness Joy Wickens, the Acting Commissioner of the Bureau of Labor Statistics, had been a student of mine at the University of Washington in 1919–20, when I was a young instructor in political science. Undoubtedly, she supplied Schwellenbach with highlights of my professional career. In addition, Schwellenbach felt a strong sentimental attachment to the University of Washington and to the state. He was warmly sympathetic to Professor Witte's ambition for me.

I was extremely reluctant to leave the Social Security Board. I had a civil service position, I was doing work I enjoyed, and I was devoted to the whole social security program. Furthermore, I had no political strength in the Senate, and the commissionership required Senate confirmation. Schwellenbach said he would take care of that. Consultations with friends within the Bureau convinced me that my appointment would be warmly and enthusiastically received by the staff. The challenge of the job appealed to me, and I was still young enough to tackle new problems. In the end, I became Commissioner and served from August, 1946, until October, 1965, with an interruption of one year.

When I was confirmed for a fifth term, in August, 1963, Secretary of Labor W. Willard Wirtz and I reached an agreement that we should be on the lookout for a successor. When Professor Arthur M. Ross of the University of California at Berkeley, one of the names on our joint list, became available in the summer of 1965, I submitted my resignation, and Ross was appointed Commissioner. He resigned the post in June of 1968. A successor has not yet been named.

A good many of the accomplishments, and many of the failures, of the Bureau occurred during my administration. I do not attribute the successes to myself. The reader will learn from Chapter I, on the early history of the Bureau, that it was a great organization long before I became connected with it. It will continue to be. Today, the Bureau of Labor Statistics ranks as one of the finest agencies in the U.S. Government, with a tradition of high standards, consistently maintained. Its staff members have, in general, been dedicated people. It is they who have made the organization what it is. I am fortunate to be able to tell their story.

EWAN CLAGUE

Washington, D.C.
July 1, 1968

Contents

Charts

A section of photographs follows page 64.

The Bureau of Labor Statistics

I

Samuel Gompers Recognizes
a Wholesome Effect

The first federal bureau of labor statistics began as the Bureau
of Labor in the Department of the Interior. Four years later,
the Bureau itself became the Department of Labor, an independent agency but without Cabinet status. After fifteen years
of independent existence, it reverted again to being the Bureau
of Labor, this time in the Department of Commerce and
Labor. Then, in 1913, when Congress created today's full-
fledged Department of Labor with the Secretary a member of
the Cabinet, the Bureau of Labor became the Bureau of Labor
Statistics, known also as the BLS. Despite these changes of
name and status, the Bureau has maintained a continuous existence since its first commissioner was appointed, in January,
1885.

LABOR SEEKS A VOICE IN GOVERNMENT, 1865–85

When the growing American labor movement began to flex
its economic and political muscles in the tumultuous period
following the Civil War, the unions set out to obtain a department of labor that would develop and support legislation and
government policies beneficial to working people. What they
did obtain was a fact-finding agency dedicated to statistics and
research on labor problems, which refrained from taking positions on legislation and economic policies.

By the end of the Civil War, the labor unions had begun to

take a new look at government. The war, by speeding up the industrialization of the American economy, had introduced enlarged opportunities for labor organization. Efforts were made to form a nation-wide labor movement—the National Labor Union. At the second annual convention of this organization, in September, 1868, a resolution was adopted containing these paragraphs:

> WHEREAS, there is no department of our government having for its sole object the care and protection of labor, and the various enterprises and undertakings of workingmen, having for their object an equitable distribution of the products of industry, and the elevation of those who labor; therefore be it

> RESOLVED, that the president of this body, and four others to be appointed, shall constitute a committee, who shall prepare a petition, to be by them presented to Congress, asking the creation of a new department at Washington, to be called a "Department of Labor."

Various bills were introduced in Congress to establish such a department, but none were passed.

The drive for labor representation in government was successful first in the states. The initial break-through occurred in Massachusetts in 1869. Success there was due to a political combination of the trade union movement and the intellectuals of the New England Reform League, which was supported by liberal ministers, church groups, and middle-class people with a humanitarian interest. The reformers were deeply concerned about child labor and women workers in the textile mills, about long hours of work and low wages, and about drink, slums, poverty, and family destitution. The middle-class liberals and philosophers supported a 10-hour movement in the interest of improving the living conditions of working people, while the unions promoted an 8-hour movement in pursuit of economic betterment in the form of higher wages.

State legislative commissions had investigated labor problems over a period of several years but invariably had arrived at the conclusion that reduction of the 12-hour day to an 8- or even 10-hour day was uneconomic. However, the plight of child workers deprived of education had aroused widespread public sympathy, and a law was passed providing that children between the ages of ten and fourteen should receive six months' schooling each year. Then, a mild business recession in 1867, coupled with the introduction of new technology, threatened to create unemployment among the shoe workers and induced the Massachusetts legislature, in 1869, to create a Bureau of Statistics of Labor

> . . . to collect, assort, systematize and present in annual reports to the legislature . . . statistical details relating to all departments of labor . . . especially to the commercial, industrial, social, educational and sanitary condition of the laboring classes, and to the permanent prosperity of . . . productive industry.

The new bureau embarked on a stormy career quite early. Its first chief was nearly seventy years of age, a member of a famous Massachusetts family, who had been a teacher, a cotton mill operator, and state treasurer. His deputy was a young man in his early thirties, a forceful and successful labor leader. Both had been prominent in the labor reform movement. But being active proponents of reform, they considered their statistical studies to be geared directly toward the development of legislation. Furthermore, they were not statisticians, and their early questionnaires to employers in Massachusetts were not well conceived. The surveys were poorly conducted; the eventual reports, more promotional than factual. Conflict between research and policy-making increased, and adverse employer reaction and growing legislative opposition threatened the existence of the bureau, which was eventually faced with possible abolition.

In this crisis, Governor William B. Washburn decided, in 1873, that "the remedy for complaint . . . must be sought, not in discontinuing the investigation . . . but in lifting it to a higher and broader level, making it more thorough, and conducting it with larger aims." When the terms of the original officers expired, the Governor appointed State Senator Carroll D. Wright as chief of the Bureau. At the early age of twenty-four, Wright had achieved the rank of colonel in the Civil War, and he had been a teacher and a lawyer before being elected state senator. He had never been directly associated with the labor movement or its problems, but he was sympathetic to labor and to the reform movement in Massachusetts. Coming to the conclusion that there must be a clear-cut separation between research and policy, he turned for advice to the leading economist of the day, Francis A. Walker, President of the American Statistical Association and Director of the Census of 1870. With Walker's help, Wright brought statistical *expertise* to bear on the studies conducted by his bureau, concentrating on the development of facts concerning two of the most crucial issues of the moment—wages and the cost of living. His statistical reports on these and other subjects received widespread attention and commendation, and the Bureau became a permanent feature of the Massachusetts state government.

The example set by Massachusetts in establishing its Bureau of Statistics of Labor led to the creation of similar bureaus in other states. Pennsylvania established such a bureau in 1872; Connecticut, in 1873; Kentucky, in 1876; Ohio, in 1877. By the end of 1884, a total of fourteen state bureaus had been established, including those in New Jersey (1878), Illinois, Indiana, and Missouri (1879), and New York (1883), and Iowa and Maryland (1884).

Commissioner Wright was not only the senior state labor commissioner; he was also dean and leader of the group. It is significant that the National Convention of Chiefs and Commissioners of Bureaus of Statistics of Labor in the United States, held under his leadership in 1884, unanimously adopted the following resolution:

> RESOLVED, that the best interests of the State Bureaus of Statistics of Labor, and of the industrial forces of the Country, demand that such bureaus should be administered without reference to political influence; and that all officers of such bureaus should be selected for their fitness for statistical work, and not on account of allegiance to or services rendered any party.

This emphasis upon nonpolitical appointments in government was the result of the assassination of President Garfield in 1881 by a disappointed office-seeker. The unfortunate event was an important factor in the passage of the Federal Civil Service Act, in 1883. Later, when Wright became U.S. Commissioner of Labor, he succeeded in applying the act's principles in the federal Bureau, but very few states managed to maintain such a good record.

BREAK-THROUGH IN WASHINGTON

The establishment of numerous state bureaus or departments of labor took some of the political heat off the federal government, although legislation to create a department of labor continued to be introduced in the Congress throughout the 1870's and the early 1880's. But, in the summer of 1884, the pressure upon Congress to create a federal agency was stimulated by the economic situation. The deep and prolonged post–Civil War depression, which had begun in 1873, had finally ended with the resumption of the gold standard in 1879. There followed a 4-year period of prosperity, which was ended by a business downturn in 1883–84. Political activity of trade unions generally becomes stronger in times of business depression, and this time it was bolstered by developments in the labor movement itself.

One important development was the creation, in 1881, of the Federation of Organized Trades and Labor Unions, which became the American Federation of Labor in 1886. At the 1881 convention, Samuel Gompers, representing the New York Cigarmakers Local, had urged the establishment of a national bureau in these terms:

> We recognize the wholesome effect of a bureau of labor statistics as created in several States, and we urge [on] our friends in Congress the passage of an act establishing a national bureau of labor statistics, and recommend for its management the appointment of a proper person identified with the laboring classes of the country.

Another was the rapid growth of a new and frankly political labor organization, the Knights of Labor, in the early 1880's. Terence V. Powderly, the Grand Master Workman (President) of the Knights, had long advocated the establishment of state bureaus of labor statistics, and later, in 1887 he was to throw the support of his organization behind a proposal to create a department of labor.

Finally, the Presidential election of 1884 gave promise of being an exceedingly close one, making Congress more receptive to pressures of many kinds.

At any rate, in June, 1884, Congress passed an act to establish a bureau of labor in the Department of the Interior, to be headed by a commissioner of labor. The assignment given the commissioner was to "collect information upon the subject of labor, its relation to capital, the hours of labor, and the earnings of laboring men and women, and the means of promoting their material, social, intellectual, and moral prosperity."

Unexpected difficulties arose over the appointment of the commissioner. Immediately after he signed the bill, President Chester A. Arthur, who had succeeded to the office after the assassination of Garfield, sent over to the Senate the name of a prominent labor leader, and the appointment was immediately confirmed. However, the President later discovered that his appointee had favored Senator James G. Blaine for the Republican Presidential nomination. He therefore refused to issue the commission, and the office went unfilled for six months.

In those days, the second, so-called lame-duck, session of Congress began in December and ended on March 4, when the Presidential transition took place. With the risk of facing inquiries from Congress concerning the Commissionership, President Arthur sought another man. Although the Republicans had lost the Presidential election, they still controlled the Senate, and an ample supply of political candidates was available. Perhaps because President Arthur was finished as a political figure, he made the decision to appoint a statistician. At that time, the most reputable labor statistician in the country was Carroll D. Wright of Massachusetts, who had steered his state bureau through a dozen years of successful operation. There was one hitch, namely, that the appointment as Commissioner was for a term of four years. The new President, Grover Cleveland, a Democrat, would take over on March 4. But apparently some negotiation took place with President-elect Cleveland, because Wright accepted the appointment in January, only about six weeks away from the political change-over.

So what seems to have been mostly political accident turned out to be of momentous consequence to the development of labor statistics in the United States. The appointment of a statistician instead of a political figure firmly established the new bureau as a statistical and research agency. Furthermore, the nonpartisanship of the Commissioner began a tradition that has continued unbroken. Commissioner Wright served five full terms of four years each during periods of frequent political changes in the Presidency.

Despite the appointment of Commissioner Wright, the pressure for the establishment of a larger department of labor continued. In 1888, again just before a Presidential election, Congress amended the law creating the bureau and established a Department of Labor,

> . . . the general design and duties of which shall be to acquire and diffuse among the people of the United States useful information on subjects connected with labor, in the most general and comprehensive sense of that word, and especially upon its relation to capital, the hours of labor, the earnings of laboring men and women, and the means of promoting their material, social, intellectual, and moral prosperity.

However, this was a department without Cabinet status. The only organizational effect was to remove the Bureau of Labor from the Department of the Interior and set it up as an independent agency. Commissioner Wright was reappointed and the new "Department" continued to function as a research and statistics agency.

Since it was the onset of a depression that had triggered the creation of the new federal Bureau of Labor in 1884, it is not surprising that the Commissioner first directed his attention to that economic problem. His first annual report was on industrial depressions. He made a historical survey of the years 1837–86 in four European countries and in the United States. It is quite likely that the prolonged strikes in Chicago in 1888 led him to the subject of his third annual report, on strikes and lockouts. The next year, he moved on to a survey of the labor of women and children, and he also began a survey on the cost of living. The speedy success of the new bureau can be attributed in large measure to the timeliness and importance of the problems the Commissioner undertook to survey.

In pursuit of his objective of making the federal Bureau of Labor into a reputable fact-finding agency, Commissioner Wright spoke and wrote cogently on his ideals and principles. In a letter to his chief, the Secretary of the Interior, he set forth his views on the policy of the new bureau:

The positive policy of the Bureau of Labor is that this office makes its initial work that of pure fact; and any desire on the part of individuals or associations of individuals, whether of labor or of capital, seeking more or less than this policy indicates, must be considered as their wanting the work of the Bureau to conform to adopted theories or to be influenced to shaping special ends. . . . I assure you that no other policy can bring success. . . . A bureau of labor cannot solve social or industrial problems, nor can it bring direct returns in a material way to the citizens of a country, but its work must be classed among educational efforts, and by judicious investigations and the fearless publication of the results thereof, it may and should enable the people to more clearly and more fully comprehend many of the problems which now vex them.

Those principles governed the operation of the Bureau during the two decades of Wright's leadership. The tradition thus established was honored by succeeding commissioners, and it continues today as the guiding principle of the Bureau of Labor Statistics.

ACHIEVEMENTS OF THE WRIGHT ADMINISTRATION

Commissioner Wright's policy of unbiased and imaginative research won widespread congressional support. When a subcommittee of the Senate Finance Committee conducted an investigation of imports and tariffs in the years 1890–91, its members called upon Wright and the staff of the Bureau of Labor for assistance, thereby launching the Bureau into a comprehensive survey of the prices of domestic and imported commodities. The expert economist of the subcommittee worked with the Commissioner to develop an index of wholesale prices (that is, the prices of commodities in primary markets). This study eventually became the focal point for the Wholesale Price Index, which the Bureau of Labor Statistics produces today.

In 1893, the American economy was afflicted again with a

sharp and deep economic depression. In 1894, Congress responded to the unemployment crisis by adopting a joint resolution directing the Commissioner of Labor to

> . . . investigate and make report upon the effect of the use of machinery upon labor and the cost of production, the relative productive power of hand and machine labor, the cost of manual and machine power as they are used in the productive industries, and the effect upon wages of the use of machinery operated by women and children; and, further, whether changes in the creative cost of products are due to a lack or to a surplus of labor or to the introduction of power machinery.

In conducting this survey, the Commissioner and the Bureau's staff made a comprehensive and detailed comparison of the time requirements and labor costs of the machine methods of the 1890's as opposed to the hand methods of production a quarter- to a half-century earlier. This seems to have been the first comprehensive survey of mechanization and productivity conducted anywhere in the world. The results were published in a two-volume report of the Commissioner of Labor entitled *Hand and Machine Labor*. The productivity studies and productivity statistics produced by the Bureau of Labor Statistics today stem from this original survey in the 1890's.

DEPARTMENT OF COMMERCE AND LABOR, 1903–13

In 1903, Congress passed legislation establishing the Department of Commerce and Labor, whereupon the Department of Labor (without Cabinet status) again became the Bureau of Labor in the new department. Farmers had won special representation with the establishment of the Department of Agriculture, in 1889. Now, business interests wanted representation, and the labor movement was continuing to press its case for recognition at the department level. One factor that may have influenced the decision to create the new department was the rising importance of industrial disputes, especially the great coal strike of 1902, in which President Theodore Roosevelt had eventually felt impelled to intervene. He had appointed a Presidential commission on the strike, and the federal government exercised an influence on the final outcome, namely, recognition of the Miners Union. Wright played an important part in the work of that commission and in framing the eventual agreement.

However, in the Department of Commerce and Labor, the labor movement did not get even half a loaf. The Secretary was a businessman, and the labor position was represented by Commissioner Wright. He continued to conduct his bureau on the same principles as before—as a research and statistics agency. The Commissioner did go on record in opposition to the new arrangement, but, apparently, he made no effort to mount a political fight. He continued to serve out his term to January, 1905, when he retired to become president of Clark College, in Worcester, Massachusetts.

The next Commissioner was an appointee in the Wright tradition. Professor Charles P. Neill had earned his Ph.D. at Johns Hopkins University and was a professor of political economy at Catholic University in Washington. From time to time, he had made studies for the Bureau, and he was well acquainted with its work and its philosophy. The major change that took place during Neill's administration was a gradual shift from special studies and reports over to more continuous series of statistics. For example, in 1907, the Bureau began to collect annually the local union wage scales in scores of cities. It continued the collection of food prices in approximately 150 cities throughout the country—a program that had been initiated by Commissioner Wright in the closing years of his term. Commissioner Neill also launched a regular series on strike statistics.

Meanwhile, relationships between the growing labor movement and the federal government were becoming more troubled. A major problem arose over the application of the Sherman Antitrust Act to labor unions. The basic case became popularly known as the Danbury Hatters Case. The hatters' union conducted a strike against a Connecticut firm in 1902. As part of its strike strategy, the union organized a boycott of the company's hats, which were made in Connecticut but marketed in New York City and other parts of the country. In 1903, the company sued the union under the Sherman Antitrust Act. The case percolated through the courts until 1908, when the Supreme Court remanded the case back to the lower courts with the instruction that the union's boycott constituted a conspiracy in restraint of trade. As a result, the union was assessed triple damages. It was practically destroyed—and the effect was to strike a blow at union actions affecting interstate trade. There were other cases also, such as that of the Buck's Stove and Range Company, which involved a court injunction against a proposed boycott by a union. The impact of these court decisions intensified the pressure of the labor movement for legislation to protect union activities.

The culmination of the union drive for labor representation in government came in 1913, when Congress passed a law creating a department of labor with Cabinet status. President William Howard Taft signed the bill as one of his last official acts before going out of office on March 4, 1913.

This time there was no half loaf. The new Secretary of Labor, William B. Wilson, was a former secretary-treasurer of the United Mine Workers Union, and a congressman who, as Chairman of the Committee on Labor, had steered the bill through the House of Representatives. The chief clerk of the new Department was Samuel Gompers, Jr., son of the famous labor leader. The Department immediately became active in pressing for labor legislation, including the Clayton Antitrust Act of 1914, which was hailed at the time as the "Magna Carta of Labor." The act exempted unions from the Sherman Act governing restraint of trade, and it also limited the issuance of injunctions by the federal courts in labor disputes. Other labor legislation followed in the next several years.

THE BUREAU OF LABOR STATISTICS, 1913–33

With the creation of a new department, the Bureau of Labor now became the Bureau of Labor Statistics. Commissioner Charles P. Neill was reappointed for a third term in 1913, but he resigned on May 15, only six weeks after the new Department was created. The record is not clear as to whether he was reappointed on condition of an early resignation or whether he preferred not to continue under the new administration.

In any event, the next Commissioner, appointed in August, 1913, was Royal Meeker, who had been assistant professor of political economy at Princeton University from 1907 to 1913. Woodrow Wilson, as President of Princeton, was undoubtedly well acquainted with Professor Meeker and his work. The record shows that the Commissioner and the Bureau were given important new functions and responsibilities during the Wilson Administration, due partly to the domestic problems of World War I.

Commissioner Meeker took steps to enlist the services of his professional colleagues in the work of the Bureau of Labor Statistics. In 1914, Professor Wesley Mitchell of Columbia University was commissioned to make a study of wholesale price indexes—those of the Bureau of Labor Statistics, some private indexes in the United States, and some in other countries. Professor Mitchell endorsed the statistical methods used by the Bureau of Labor Statistics but recommended certain improvements—more price quotations, more markets, and more accurate definitions of commodities. (His work was published as BLS Bulletin No. 173, later revised and enlarged as Bulletin No. 284, published in 1922.)

The most outstanding development for the Bureau in this

period was the creation of the Cost of Living Index, during World War I. As has usually been the case in the history of the Bureau, this new development grew out of a burning economic problem.

The outbreak of the war in Europe created a heavy demand for war production and munitions in the United States. Workers were attracted from the rural areas and from other industries by the high wages in the munitions and shipbuilding industries. However, the excess of consumer demand sent prices skyrocketing, and labor disputes cropped up in the big manufacturing centers and in the port cities. The high cost of living ("old h.c.l.," as it was called in the press) became a major issue. When the United States entered the war, in 1917, the government felt it essential to avoid strikes, so various boards and commissions were established to deal with price and wage problems. Early in the war period, Chairman V. Everett Macy of the Shipbuilding Wage Adjustment Board asked President Wilson to arrange for the preparation of a reliable, scientific index of the cost of living, which could then be used to fix wages. The President instructed the Commissioner of Labor Statistics to develop a cost of living index, which would relate the current levels to prewar costs, and which would measure the changes occurring during the war.

In cooperation with the Shipbuilding Wage Adjustment Board, the Bureau of Labor Statistics investigated the cost of living in various cities throughout the country. Family expenditures were obtained from about 12,000 wage-earner and clerical-worker families during the period July, 1917, to February, 1919. The purpose of this survey was to determine relative weights of various goods and services in the average family's living costs. In 1919, the Bureau began publishing indexes for thirty-two large shipbuilding and industrial centers, with the base period 1913 = 100. That index survives today as the Consumer Price Index, one of the most important sets of statistics in the determination of national economic policies.

In 1920, Commissioner Meeker resigned his position in order to accept what he regarded as a more important one in the League of Nations, in Geneva, Switzerland. His departure opened the way for a career appointment. Commissioner Ethelbert Stewart, who had been a journalist and newspaper editor, had joined the staff of the old Bureau of Labor in 1887. He had worked his way up through the Bureau's organization until he was appointed chief statistician. He was not an academically trained statistician, but he had acquired a working knowledge of statistics through his bureau experience. Eventually, he became a Fellow of the American Statistical Association.

The catastrophic collapse of prices in the depression of 1921 put an end temporarily to the high cost of living as an issue in wage disputes. In fact, the decline in the Cost of Living Index lent weight to employer demands for wage decreases. In casting about for an alternative issue, the labor movement revived the concept of productivity, which had been dormant since the 1890's. However, this time the unions used a different argument. They stressed productivity not as a cause of unemployment but as a factor producing higher profits—in which the workers wanted to share.

The spectacular technological developments in American manufacturing in the 1920's constituted some evidence in support of the argument. Accordingly, in the mid-1920's, Commissioner Stewart inaugurated a series of comprehensive special studies of particular industries—glass-bottle blowing, longshoring, and steel making. In addition, he stimulated the development of industry productivity indexes relating output per man-hour in the 1920's to a prewar base in 1914. Those annual productivity indexes have been continued down to the present day. They constituted the forerunner of the over-all economy-wide and sector indexes, which today provide the foundation for the wage guideposts of the Council of Economic Advisers.

The onset of the Great Depression, in 1929, brought new problems to the Bureau and its Commissioner. Conflicting employment statistics within the Department of Labor caused trouble for the Bureau. The result was a growing coolness between the Secretary and his Commissioner, aggravated by the growing criticism throughout the country of the government's employment and unemployment figures.

Meanwhile, Commissioner Stewart had served beyond the federal retirement age. He was already over seventy years of age when he was reappointed for his third term, in 1928. During 1930–31, he was given two one-year extensions, but he was not reappointed when his term ran out in the summer of 1932. The Bureau's chief clerk became Acting Commissioner, and no new appointment was made until the Roosevelt Administration took office in the spring of 1933.

THE NEW DEAL IN STATISTICS, 1933–39

The Great Depression brought government statistics under fire from all directions. There was criticism of the lack of data, inaccurate data, misleading data, misinterpretation of data, etc. There were even suggestions that the public would be better off without any data at all.

The main fire was directed at the unemployment figures. During the 1920's, the federal statistical agencies, primarily the Census and the BLS, had developed some reasonably good statistics of employment and payrolls, based on reports from employers. But there were no unemployment figures—merely estimates derived from the difference between the employment and the estimated total labor force. With regard to the 1930 Census, Congress authorized the taking of a special unemployment count, which would at least provide a benchmark for estimates of unemployment trends.

However, the Census statistics landed in controversy before they were published. A dispute arose among the statisticians themselves as to whether certain workers should be classified as employed or unemployed. What about a worker, for example, who has just been laid off by his employer with instructions to report back, say, in two weeks? Or a worker who is not working, but who has the promise of a job on the first of the month? In 1967, both of these people would be classified as "unemployed." When Harry Hopkins was operating the Work Projects Administration (WPA) in the late 1930's, he considered such cases as "with a job, but not at work" and not eligible at the moment for government relief-work jobs. In the 1932 census controversy, the director of the special unemployment census insisted that they be classified as unemployed. When the decision went against him, he resigned with a blast at the Administration. With the 1932 election in the offing, this action threw statistics into the political campaign.

When Franklin D. Roosevelt took office, in March, 1933, his Secretary of Labor, Frances Perkins, opened up the subject by requesting the American Statistical Association to establish an advisory committee to review the statistics of the Department of Labor. Her action stimulated other Cabinet officers, so that eventually about a half-dozen of them joined in similar requests. The Social Science Research Council sponsored a project with the Rockefeller Foundation for the appointment by the American Statistical Association of the Committee on Government Statistics and Information Services to review the statistics of the federal government and make recommendations for their improvement.

The work and achievements of this committee constitute a landmark in the history of U.S. Government statistics. The Committee recommended better coordination than had previously existed among the agencies and set up the machinery for achieving it, which is now located in the Bureau of the Budget (Office of Statistical Standards). In addition, the Committee made a number of recommendations for changes in the location and organization of the various government statistical services. Many of these changes were adopted by government departments.

The activities of this committee were of profound significance to the development and utilization of statistics for public policy purposes. The Committee's recommendations not only established the continuing administrative machinery of coordination, but they also suggested the procedures through which future growth and improvement could emerge. The Committee laid the foundations for the use of statistics as instruments of public policy. (During World War II and later in the postwar readjustment period, statistics were used as guides to government policies by the Council of Economic Advisers, the congressional Joint Economic Committee, and many other government agencies.)

The Bureau of Labor Statistics was one of the beneficiaries of this growing interest in, and use of, statistics. Upon recommendation of the Committee, the Bureau's employment and payroll statistics were revised. The Cost of Living Index was given a complete overhaul. Partly by means of a WPA work project, large-scale surveys of family expenditures were made in 1934–36 for the purpose of revising and updating the "market basket," or the compilation of consumer costs used for the index. The work of revision occupied several years and was completed just in time for the index to be used as a guide for wage and price controls in World War II.

A new dimension was added to wage statistics during the depression years by the enactment of minimum-wage legislation of several kinds. In 1931, when public works became one of the programs designed to speed up business recovery, the Davis-Bacon Act was passed, requiring the payment of prevailing wages in all public construction supported by federal funds. The Secretary of Labor was given responsibility for enforcing that act. In 1936, the Department of Labor became the administrative agency for the Walsh-Healey Act, which authorized the Secretary of Labor to set minimum wage rates for government contracts. Finally, in 1938, the Fair Labor Standards Act was passed, establishing a statutory minimum wage rate applicable to interstate commerce. Responsibility for this act was also located in the Labor Department, which then established the Wage and Hour and Public Contracts Divisions.

The significance of these developments for the Bureau of Labor Statistics was that the Bureau became a service agency for fact-finding and statistical reporting. The Bureau's regular wage surveys acquired new uses and importance. In addition, the Wage and Hour and Public Contracts Divisions provided funds to the Bureau to pay for special studies and reports.

In the meantime, Secretary Perkins had selected Isador Lubin, from the Brookings Graduate School in Washington, D.C. (now the Brookings Institution), as her new Commissioner of Labor Statistics. Lubin was one of the outstanding young economists and statisticians of that day, a man eminently qualified to lead the Bureau to new responsibilities and achievements. He collaborated actively with the Committee on Government Statistics and Information Services in the revision of the Bureau's own statistics. In addition, he found new opportunities for the Bureau to serve other government operating agencies such as the Works Projects Administration, the Social Security Board, the Public Works Administration, the National Recovery Administration, and the White House itself. In fact, when World War II broke out, he was transferred to the White House, and he served throughout the war as adviser to President Roosevelt. Assistant Commissioner Ford Hinrichs became Acting Commissioner and directed the work of the Bureau through the critical years of the war.

THE BUREAU IN WORLD WAR II

At the onset of the war, new emergency agencies were created to supervise war production, price controls, wage controls, manpower controls, etc. Many reorganizations took place; regular peacetime agencies were transferred out of their departments and into emergency agencies. Old-line statistical agencies such as the Bureau of Labor Statistics retained their former status but were financed to perform research and statistics functions for the emergency agencies. Thus, the Bureau's Cost of Living Index served as a guide to the Office of Price Administration and to the War Labor Board, while both these agencies employed the Bureau to make special studies for them. At the same time, many normal peacetime functions required additional service under wartime conditions. Under such circumstances, it is not surprising that the Bureau's staff rose from about 600 in 1939 to about 1,700 in 1945, and a regular prewar budget of about $1.8 million became a wartime budget of nearly $7 million.

The Bureau had many adventures during World War II— significant achievements and a few failures—but the event that dominated the Bureau's life during the closing years of the war and profoundly influenced its later history was the wartime controversy over the Cost of Living Index. This controversy is more fully and more technically described in chapters IV and XIII, but it is necessary here to outline the nature of the controversy and its effect upon the Bureau.

In exchange for no-strike pledges, the unions were given assurance that wages and working conditions during the war would be reviewed by the War Labor Board. Collectively bargained contracts as well as unilateral employer wage and salary adjustments had to be approved by the Board. The basic statistic for this purpose was the Cost of Living Index. Workers should not suffer a loss in living standards, while neither should any group profit from the war.

During the defense period 1940–41, wages and prices were held in check by the substantial volume of unemployment carried over from the Depression. At the beginning of 1941, the unemployment rate was 14 per cent of the civilian labor force, and, even after a year of tremendous industrial expansion, at the time of Pearl Harbor, it was still quite high. But, in 1942 and early 1943, prices zoomed upward, reaching a level of about 125 (1935–39 = 100) when price control was established by legislation in March, 1943. At that time, the unions had little complaint, for wages rose with prices and increased employment generally yielded higher incomes. But, when price control began to bite (the index rose only about eight points in the next two years), wage gains also were restricted by the War Labor Board.

The real issue was between the War Labor Board and the unions, but the BLS was caught in the cross-fire. The Board was using the index to hold down wage increases, so the unions attacked the index. As will be explained more fully in Chapter XIII, President Roosevelt appointed a committee of experts who vindicated the Bureau and devised a formula to ease the basic conflict over wages. The Bureau's reputation was enhanced, but all official contact with labor union statisticians was broken, and other consequences followed later.

POSTWAR RECONVERSION AND INFLATION

When the war ended suddenly (and, one may surely add, quite unexpectedly) in August, 1945, the official government outlook, with some dissenting voices, was for a major reconversion depression, with perhaps 8 million to 10 million workers unemployed. At the same time, there was widespread apprehension about "the inflationary gap," which had been steadily building during the war when people were not able to spend as much as they were earning. These surplus earnings had been absorbed in war bonds and other forms of saving, but the return to a civilian economy seemed certain to produce explosive consumer demands supported by great volumes of dammed-up purchasing power (government savings bonds were cashable after sixty days).

The government's reconversion program was to abolish wage controls and return to the 40-hour week, so as to spread the work and facilitate the absorption of the unemployed from war industry. A labor-management conference was convened by the Department of Labor to work out a suitable wage policy for the transition. In the meantime, price controls were maintained in effect in order to set limits to an employer's capacity to concede wage increases in bargaining.

The combination of wage decontrols and price controls proved unworkable. The breakdown came through union action, but the genesis may have come from the average housewife. Take a typical family, with the breadwinner earning at that time $1 an hour and, with overtime, $52 for a 48-hour week. All at once, he suffered a reduction to $40 for a 40-hour week—a decline in family income of nearly 25 per cent. At the same time, there was no decrease in the cost of living. In fact, the index began to creep up. Naturally, the workers and their union representatives set about achieving wage increases that would compensate for the reduction in hours and thus maintain the purchasing power of the weekly wage.

With the employers backed against the wall of price controls and, therefore, resistant to excessive wage increases, the impasse broke open in 1946, the worst strike year in American industrial history. After nine months of battering, price controls began to give way in the summer of that year. They were taken off, reinstituted, and then taken off again, while prices began to boil. Postwar inflation got under way. In two years, the Cost of Living Index rose over 30 per cent and the Wholesale Price Index nearly 50 per cent.

During this reconversion, the Bureau of Labor Statistics was having internal crises of its own. The death of President Roosevelt, in April, 1945, brought a Cabinet change in the Labor Department. Frances Perkins resigned after serving for twelve years as Secretary of Labor, and Judge Lewis B. Schwellenbach, a former senator from the state of Washington, was appointed by President Truman. Schwellenbach's first pronouncement as Secretary reopened the wartime controversy about the Cost of Living Index, but this issue was finally resolved by the decision to change the name to the Consumer Price Index (CPI) (see Chapter XIII).

In February, 1946, the third term of Commissioner Lubin, who had been overseeing BLS affairs from his office in the White House for six years, came to an end. Secretary Schwellenbach offered to appoint him for a fourth term, if he would return to the Department and assume active direction of the Bureau. But Lubin decided to go into private industry, and the position remained vacant. In May, 1946, Acting Commissioner Hinrichs came to the conclusion that he would not be appointed, so he resigned, and the leadership of the Bureau devolved upon Mrs. Aryness Joy Wickens, a career employee, the Bureau's assistant commissioner for operations. Then began the quest for a new Commissioner, which ended in my being selected.

The Bureau soon encountered stormy seas. In the elections of 1946, the Republicans had captured both the House and the Senate. President Truman looked like a one-termer. An Executive and a Congress of different political parties always cause difficulties for government agencies, especially in the first year of the split. It was the first time since 1930 that the Republicans had controlled Congress. They embarked on a campaign of budget-cutting in which the Bureau was one of the heaviest losers. In the spring of 1947, the Congress cut the fiscal 1948 budget of the Bureau by 40 per cent. In a period of a couple of months, the Bureau had the unpleasant task of laying off about 700 employees out of 1,700. It was a devastating blow, not only to the newly planned programs, which were all lost, but also to the existing programs, many of which had to be slashed or even abolished. Some of the best and most promising employees were lost to the Bureau. There was no opportunity to be selective in the slightest degree.

Nevertheless, the Bureau retrenched its programs and adjusted to the new budget level. But the storm wasn't over. In

the spring of 1948, the House cut the Bureau budget by another 40 per cent, which would have wrecked the basic continuing statistical programs of the Bureau had not the Bureau
been saved by an industrial relations "miracle"—or so it
seemed to the staff. On May 24, 1948, the newspapers
throughout the country headlined the new two-year contract
negotiated between General Motors and the United Automobile Workers Union. To appreciate the tension of those days,
one must recall that 1946 had witnessed a bitter and prolonged
automobile strike. Two years later, the public was apprehen-
sive that industrial warfare would break out again. The collective agreement was headline news. But, for the Bureau, the
surprise was that, for the coming two years, the wages of the
auto workers would be moved up (or down) every three
months in accordance with the changes in the Consumer Price
Index of the Bureau. After that, there was no need to press the
argument that it was unwise to cut the budget of an agency
that was so important to peaceful labor-management relations.
The Senate restored the funds; the House backed down; and
the Bureau's fortunes changed.

One of my first objectives as Commissioner was the restora-
tion of working relationships with the labor union statisticians.
With members of that group, our staff worked out a plan for a
formal labor research advisory committee (later called a council) to meet several times a year. Next, arrangements were
made with the National Association of Manufacturers and the
U.S. Chamber of Commerce to sponsor a business research advisory committee of economists and statisticians. Both have
functioned successfully to the present (see Chapter X). It is
possible that the GM-UAW escalation contract of 1948 owed
its origin in part to the confidence of both management and
labor in the Bureau, derived from the functioning of the two
advisory councils.

In June, 1948, Secretary Schwellenbach died, and Maurice
Tobin, formerly Mayor of Boston and Governor of Massachu-

setts, was appointed in his place. In view of the dismal election outlook for the Truman Administration, the joke around the Department of Labor was that "Mr. Tobin would be the shortest-term Secretary in Department history." But everyone (possibly even including Secretary Tobin) was surprised when President Truman was re-elected, and Tobin became a labor secretary with a future. He was now ready to build up the Department—and the Bureau provided him the first opportunity.

The Bureau staff had become deeply concerned about the price indexes during the inflation of 1946–48. Both the wholesale and the consumer index were built upon prewar weights and patterns of family expenditures, modified to some extent by wartime surveys. Furthermore, a rapid and prolonged rise in prices can seriously distort a price index. Prices were already leveling out in 1948. The Wholesale Price Index reached its peak early in the year, and the Consumer Price Index reached its high in August. The outlook was for a period of comparative price stability. So, with the election over, the Bureau proposed a program of index revision. Secretary Tobin not only accepted the idea; he put the full prestige of the Department behind it. The Bureau's budget for the next fiscal year was opened up, and a special fund for a three-year program of revision of the CPI was added. The Bureau as an agency had hit bottom; it was now on its way up.

THE KOREAN WAR AND THE FOLLOWING YEARS

The Bureau's plans for a quiet period of index revision were shattered by the outbreak of fighting in Korea. New problems arose for the Bureau in its public services and responsibilities. The automobile industry's wage escalation contract of 1948 had attracted a great deal of attention on the part of management, labor, and the general public. But there had been very few followers. In fact, there was some doubt in the spring of 1950 that the contract would be renewed, in view of the facts that the index was lower than it had been two years earlier and the auto workers had taken a loss of a few cents an hour on the cost of living (more than offset, however, by the increases in the annual improvement factor). Nevertheless, the contract was renewed in May, 1950, for a term of five years—one of the longest major contracts in collective bargaining history.

Then came Korea. That crisis broke so suddenly that people overreacted. They rushed out to buy the goods that they recalled had been scarce during World War II (tires, sugar, etc.). The price indexes began to move up fast. Many unions took a new look at the escalation idea, and scores of contracts were reopened to provide for it. By autumn, several million workers had been added to the coverage.

In the meantime, the government was deeply concerned about the danger of a new inflation. Price and wage stabilization agencies were established, and controls were under discussion. But the administrative machinery for operation and enforcement had to be created, so the actual imposition of controls did not occur until March, 1951.

However, the Bureau was notified that the CPI would be needed for stabilization administration, and it was urged to develop a good measurement of price changes from the prewar month of May, 1950. Thus, it became imperative to introduce an emergency revision of the index pending the completion of the revision program. So the Bureau met its public responsibilities by introducing the Interim Revised CPI early in 1951. This served as a guide for price and wage controls for the duration (see Chapter IV).

Then trouble erupted on another front. Several of the labor union research chiefs who had produced the critical report during World War II decided on a repeat performance. They developed an index of their own and released it to the press and the public. It was accompanied by a vigorous attack on the CPI (see Chapter XIII).

The Education and Labor Committee of the House of Representatives decided that Congress should conduct a "friendly investigation" of the index and the Bureau. Special subcommittee hearings were held for about ten days in May, 1951. There was an outpouring of support for the Bureau from both labor and management. The subcommittee's report was a complete vindication of the Bureau and its work:

> On the basis of all the testimony presented to the subcommittee, we believe that the Consumers' [*sic*] Price Index of the Bureau of Labor Statistics is an excellent index and that it enjoys widespread confidence among labor and management groups and the general public. The fact that more than 3 million employees and their employers have tied wages to the Consumers' Price Index in contracts arrived at by collective bargaining indicates its widespread acceptance as a fundamentally sound index. . . . The subcommittee was impressed with the competence and integrity of the staff of the Bureau.

As the time for the introduction of the fully revised index neared, the Bureau was faced with some unforeseen problems. The 1951 interim revision had produced a series of index numbers on a 1947–49 base $= 100$. But the Old Index, on a 1935–39 base $= 100$ (which resulted in a different set of numbers), continued to exist. Despite the efforts of the Bureau to persuade labor and management to shift their contracts to the Interim Index, many contracting parties failed to do so. The Old Index continued to be used in contracts. The Bureau decided that, with the introduction of the New Revised Index for the month of January, 1953, the Old Index would positively be discontinued as of December, 1952. Once again, a number of the parties failed to take any action on their contracts. On top of everything else, there was a change of administration, with President-elect Dwight D. Eisenhower taking over on January 20.

An attempt to resolve the impasse was made by the White

House. The Bureau had already dropped the Old Index and closed out the reporting machinery. But delegations of both management and labor appealed for another chance. So the Bureau was supplied with funds and instructed to revive the Old Index. This was done in February by reopening contacts with the reporting stores and collecting January prices retroactively.

But this step only prolonged the impasse. The Old Index was to be continued for six months only—through June. Throughout that period, the Bureau was pressured to suggest the specific month when the shift should be made. However, the Bureau insisted that the choice of the month was a matter for the contracting parties. All that it did was to issue a convertibility table showing for each month for the past several years the fraction that would convert the Old Index to the Revised Index. Some contracts came to an end during the grace period; others had to be readjusted by the parties when the Old Index was discontinued as of June, 1953.

The secretaryship of labor was the last Cabinet post to be filled by the incoming Eisenhower Administration. There was great relief among the BLS staff when the President finally named Martin Durkin, a Democrat from Illinois. Durkin had been state Commissioner of Labor in Illinois; in 1952, he was national president of the Plumbers Union. But it was not primarily his political affiliation that pleased Department employees; it was, rather, his knowledge of the work of the Department and the Bureau. So far as the Bureau was concerned, Secretary Durkin gave the Commissioner a completely free hand.

In September, 1954, Secretary Durkin suddenly resigned, and there was a brief gap in leadership until October, when Assistant Secretary James P. Mitchell of the Department of Defense became the new Secretary of Labor. Once again, the staff was happy with the appointment. Secretary Mitchell had served with the Defense Department during World War II and was both personally and professionally well acquainted with the Department of Labor and its personnel.

My second term as Commissioner expired in August, 1954, and Secretary Mitchell proposed my renomination to the President. However, an unexpected block developed (described in Chapter XII) and not until a year later was I confirmed for a third term. Until August, 1955, Deputy Commissioner Aryness Joy Wickens served as a very competent administrator. My eventual reappointment demonstrated once more that the office was nonpolitical—and, when my term came up again in 1959, I was confirmed by acclamation within five minutes.

The next major change in the Bureau's functions and fortunes occurred in 1959, at which time the Department of Commerce and the Department of Labor agreed upon readjustment of the statistical responsibilities of the Census and the Bureau of Labor Statistics. In brief, the statistics of housing, which had been developed by the Bureau of Labor Statistics back in 1920, were transferred to the Census, while primary responsibility for the monthly reports on the labor force, employment, and unemployment was assigned to the Bureau. This move turned out to have momentous consequences for the Bureau a few years later, but, at this point, it is sufficient to trace the background of the 1959 agreement.

In the early 1950's, the Census Bureau was conducting labor force surveys as a part of its program of current population surveys. Every month, it reported on the total labor force, employment, and unemployment for the U.S. economy as a whole. The BLS reported on employment, weekly hours of work, and weekly earnings for hundreds of individual industries. The two agencies issued their reports separately. The results for the month were sometimes quite different—one series up; the other, down. There were valid reasons for such discrepancies, but these were difficult to explain to nonspecialists. For one thing, the Census reports came out first each month, because the figures were collected earlier in the month and the

Census had organizational unity in compiling the figures. The data were being issued by two different departments, and differences in interpretation confused the public.

The problem came to a head in 1953–54, when even the Council of Economic Advisers found itself baffled by contradictory data as it was attempting to appraise the emerging business recession. The congressional Joint Economic Committee also raised a protest about the state of the government's employment and unemployment data. In response, the Eisenhower Administration worked out a coordinated system in which the two sets of statistics were released at the same time and jointly by the two departments. An interagency technical committee was set up under the chairmanship of the Office of Statistical Standards of the Bureau of the Budget, with representatives of the Bureau of the Census, the Bureau of Labor Statistics, and the Bureau of Employment Security. The function of this committee was to review all the data and to compose a press release that would appropriately interpret the employment situation. The release was then issued to the public jointly in the names of the Secretary of Commerce and the Secretary of Labor.

Although these joint administrative procedures worked moderately well for five years, they were cumbersome and awkward. Within the government, the two sets of figures continued to be reported by the respective departments. The joint press release had to be cleared separately with the two department heads, who sometimes suggested changes that had to be cleared back through the mechanism. In addition, there were press problems, since two different departments were responding to questions from newspaper reporters. The situation became more acute when unemployment increased substantially in the business recession of 1958. This particular problem was solved by the 1959 agreement in which the Bureau of Labor Statistics assumed responsibility for obtaining the necessary funds to conduct the surveys. It contracted with the Bureau of the Census for the collection of the labor force data in the field by the Census Bureau's field agents and for machine tabulation of the results. The Bureau of Labor Statistics became responsible for the analysis, interpretation, and publication of the results.

THE BLS IN THE KENNEDY AND JOHNSON YEARS

The unemployment statistics became an issue in the 1960 campaign, when the Department of Labor was charged with holding up the publication of the figures until after the election —an episode described in Chapter XIII. Publication was, in fact, made on schedule two days after the election, but the criticism was that the figures might have been made available the day before, if special efforts had been made to do so. Had the unemployment rate been favorable (that is, lower than expected), hasty publication would have left the Department open to the opposite charge. Since it was somewhat unfavorable, though not surprisingly so, the criticism stuck. Secretary of Labor Arthur J. Goldberg solved that problem by having the Bureau of Labor Statistics announce a year in advance the schedule of publication dates, and no similar issue has arisen since.

A much more serious matter for the Bureau, the Department, and the Kennedy Administration broke out in the autumn of 1961, when a magazine article attacked the BLS for its handling of the unemployment statistics (see Chapter XIII). The result was the appointment of the President's Committee To Appraise Employment and Unemployment Statistics, which did a major job of reviewing the work of all the agencies. The Committee vindicated the integrity and competence of the agency staffs, including the Bureau of Labor Statistics, and then went on to propose continuing research on problems of measurement. As a consequence, an enlarged and more comprehensive set of labor force statistics was issued in January, 1967, with revisions back to 1947.

In October, 1965, Arthur M. Ross of the University of California at Berkeley became Commissioner. Ross had been a professor of industrial relations at California and was also a well-known arbitrator. He had previously served in government during World War II and again as a member of the Wage Stabilization Board during the Korean War. No major public problems arose during Ross's administration, although one of its difficult tasks was internal reorganization in accordance with a plan by a private management organization following a survey of the Bureau's operations.

Perhaps the most significant accomplishment of the last two years has been the completion of the work on standard family budgets. In November, 1967, the Bureau released the first bulletin describing and pricing the budget for a city worker's four-person family at a moderate standard of living. The budget has been priced in twenty-three cities, in four metropolitan areas, and for the U.S. average. Eventually, the Bureau expects to develop data for a budget for a minimum standard of living (lower than the moderate) and an "American" standard of living (higher than the moderate). There will also be a series of similar standard budgets for an elderly couple living in retirement. These studies mark the beginning of a more detailed and intensive analysis of the varied living conditions of American families in many sections of the country—and, perhaps, a new era for the Bureau of Labor Statistics.

II

BLS Organization Today

The Bureau of Labor Statistics is one of the key agencies in the Department of Labor (Chart I). The Commissioner of Labor Statistics is both the statistical and the economic adviser to the Secretary, and he reports directly to him and the under secretary of Labor, as do the four assistant secretaries. However, the Commissioner is one step lower in rank than the assistant secretaries, being in the classification known in government language as Subcabinet 5, while the assistant secretaries are in Subcabinet 4.

In terms of manpower, the Department of Labor is the smallest of the Cabinet offices. It has only about 10,000 employees altogether. However, it has an influence on the American economy far in excess of its size. For example, the Bureau of Employment Security, which includes the U.S. Employment Service and the Unemployment Insurance Service, furnishes 100 per cent of the administrative funds for the operation of the state employment security agencies, which, in turn, administer the local employment offices and unemployment insurance offices, manned by 63,000 employees. Through the office of the Bureau of Work Programs, the Manpower Administration has responsibility for the thousands of young people employed in the Neighborhood Youth Program. The Wage and Hour and Public Contracts Divisions administer federal minimum wage legislation involving millions of Americans, and

Chart I
THE DEPARTMENT OF LABOR

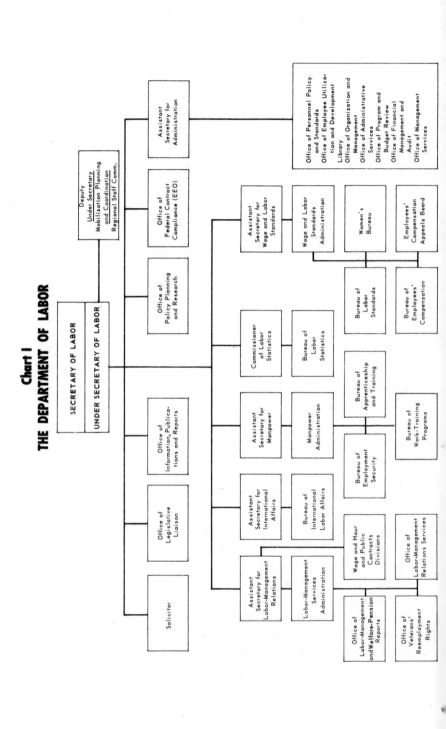

the Bureau of Employees' Compensation administers the workmen's compensation systems for federal employees and for longshore and harbor workers. Undoubtedly, the work of the Department of Labor touches all of us in one way or another.

The organization of the Bureau of Labor Statistics is portrayed in Chart II. The Commissioner is assisted by a chief statistician, a chief economist, a director of publications, and a director of administrative management. In addition, there are five program offices: Wages and Industrial Relations; Manpower and Employment Statistics; Productivity, Technology, and Growth; Prices and Living Conditions; and Foreign Labor and Trade. There is one operational office—the Office of Data Collection and Survey Operations, which is responsible for the collection and tabulation of the vast amounts of data necessary for the Bureau's programs. In the field, the Bureau operates through eight regional offices: Boston, New York, Philadelphia, Dallas, Atlanta, Chicago, Kansas City (Missouri), and San Francisco.

Before World War II, the Bureau operated solely through its Washington office. Field agents were sent out as needed, to collect statistics and obtain reports. Questionnaires were mailed whenever possible. For the large program of employment, hours, and earnings statistics, the Bureau furnished report forms to the state labor departments, which collected the information from employers, used it themselves, and then forwarded it to Washington.

During the war, however, the Bureau found it necessary to expand its activities, especially in price and wage statistics, in order to serve the needs of the Price Administration and the War Labor Board. It was then that the Bureau established regional offices closely connected with the regional offices of those two war-born organizations. After the war, despite the cutbacks that took place at the time, the Bureau continued its regional offices.

Until the advent of Commissioner Arthur M. Ross, in 1965, the Bureau operated its statistics-collection programs through its respective program offices. For example, the agents who collected price statistics for the Consumer Price Index were supervised through a regional representative who reported directly to the Office of Prices and Living Conditions in Washington on all professional and technical questions. This system had advantages and disadvantages. One advantage was that there was a close professional and operating tie between the program offices in Washington, which analyzed and published the figures, and the field agents who collected the data. A disadvantage was that the field agents became specialists in their respective programs and were not readily interchangeable within the region.

As a result of a survey undertaken by a private management firm in 1966–67, the Commissioner reorganized the Bureau. (Chart II shows the Bureau as it is today, after this reorganization.) A major change was the establishment of the Office of Data Collection and Survey Operations under an assistant commissioner, who reports directly to the Commissioner. Previously, there had been a chief of data tabulations, with lower rank and more limited responsibilities than are now encompassed in the office. The Office of Data Collection and Survey Operations now assumes full responsibility for the supervision of the staff in the field and the statistical specialists in the program offices in Washington. The effect of this change was to concentrate in a single office the collection and processing of the wide range of statistical data used by the various program offices within the Bureau.

The program offices themselves are responsible for the analysis, any associated research that may be undertaken, and publication of the results. Five of the program offices are headed by an assistant commissioner, who reports directly to the Commissioner, and a deputy. The assistant commissioner of For-

Chart II
BUREAU OF LABOR STATISTICS

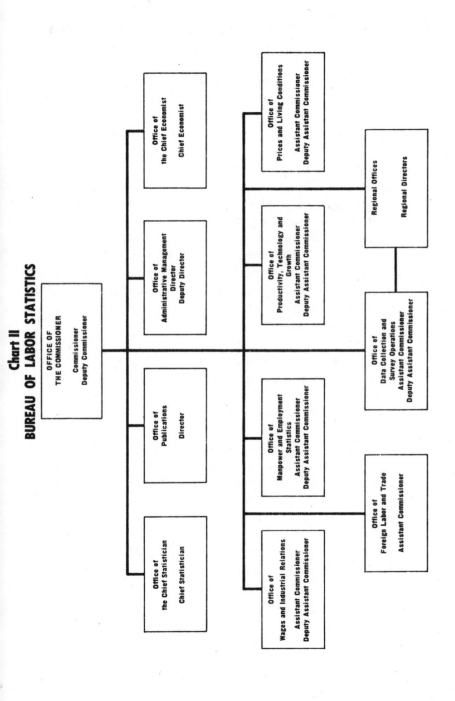

eign Labor and Trade has no deputy. Generally, the areas of responsibility are as follows:

The *Office of Wages and Industrial Relations* is responsible for conducting statistical surveys to establish wage and earnings yardsticks. In addition, this office is responsible for cataloguing and analyzing strikes, collective bargaining agreements, and corollary labor statistics (including, but not limited to, wage statistics) that measure the labor-management situation.

The *Office of Manpower and Employment Statistics* is responsible for conducting statistical samplings of manpower—the critical economic indicators of employment and unemployment—and administering a clearinghouse for its findings.

The *Office of Productivity, Technology, and Growth* is responsible for devising indexes that measure product output against man-hour input for the economy as a whole as well as for major sectors and industries.

The *Office of Prices and Living Conditions* is responsible for maintaining the Consumer Price Index, which measures the cost of living for wage- and salary-earners; the Wholesale Price Index, which measures farm and business prices; and the family budgets, which measure the living conditions of the workers.

The *Office of Foreign Labor and Trade* is responsible for developing statistics on foreign labor, manpower, cost of living, and all other economic or labor-related facts useful to the United States, to the industrial nations of Western Europe, and to developing nations around the world.

Under the 1966–67 reorganization, the *Office of the Chief Statistician* was upgraded from its former level. The chief statistician is now responsible for developing statistical standards and improving techniques, as well as for developing and increasing the use of improved computerized data systems.

The *Office of the Chief Economist* is responsible for the BLS program's planning and evaluation, as well as for special studies of economic and social issues, and for policy direction in the Bureau's program of economic analysis.

The *Office of Publications* not only is responsible for all the Bureau's publications, both periodic and special, but also maintains a close liaison with the Department's Office of Information, Publications, and Reports and advises the Commissioner on the Bureau's public relations.

The *Office of Administrative Management* is responsible for budget, personnel, office services, and general management.

To Have or Not To Have a Deputy

A much debated issue in federal government administration is the use of deputies. Under one theory of administration, every director of an office, division, or branch should have a deputy—a permanent and direct substitute for the chief, when necessary. The opposite theory is that each chief should supervise a limited number (three to five) of subordinates of the same rank, who, in turn, supervise similar numbers in the next rank. The issue takes on bureaucratic importance if (as is frequently the case) the deputy's job has the effect of pre-empting a classification grade and thus keeping the next-level subordinates in a lower grade.

Perhaps the best answer is that there is no uniform rule of good administration. Certain kinds of positions—and certain kinds of administrators—may require deputies, whereas others may not. A competent administrator can supervise effectively from three to five subordinates, provided he gives his full time and attention to the job. The case for a deputy arises when the administrator himself has other important duties besides the administration of his own organization. From this point of view, the Commissioner of Labor Statistics certainly needs a deputy.

The Commissioner himself must testify from time to time before congressional committees, participate in Department of Labor policy meetings, attend interdepartmental committee meetings, and have frequent contact with the public—labor, management, and citizens generally. Every month, he holds one or more press conferences to announce and interpret the Bureau's statistics. He is called upon to make speeches before organizations in many parts of the country. Because so many people use the Bureau's statistics, these public appearances are imperative.

In addition, the Commissioner of Labor Statistics is always designated to attend the international statistical conferences of the International Labor Office in Geneva (see Chapter IX). The Bureau cooperates closely from time to time with the statistical office of the United Nations in New York, and, in 1958, the Commissioner of Labor Statistics was appointed by the Secretary-General of the United Nations as the U.S. Government representative on the U.N. Expert Committee on Post Adjustments. This committee is responsible for guiding and supervising the cost-of-living studies that govern salary differentials of U.N. employees in headquarters cities throughout the world. (After my retirement as Commissioner, I was reappointed to this committee for a term ending in 1969, and, at its 1968 annual meeting in Geneva, I was elected chairman for the following year. Thus, at this writing, a retired employee of the Bureau of Labor Statistics supervises the statistical staffs of the United Nations and the International Labor Organization in the conduct of the world-wide cost-of-living studies.)

In my opinion, because of the demanding circumstances of his job, effective organization of the BLS requires that the Commissioner have next to his own office a competent deputy commissioner who can operate as his alter ego in the supervision of the Bureau's staff. It was my good fortune to have two excellent deputies—Mrs. Aryness Joy Wickens, for the first ten years of my term as Commissioner, and Robert J. Myers, for the last six. Both were fully qualified to have been appointed Commissioner.

DEPARTMENT RELATIONSHIPS

The Bureau of Labor Statistics has direct working relationships with practically all the bureaus, offices, and divisions within the Department of Labor. In the field of manpower, for instance, the Bureau of Labor Statistics has a cooperative arrangement with the Bureau of Employment Security for sharing the employment, hours, and earnings statistics obtained through reports from employers throughout the country. Since the Bureau of Employment Security operates through the state employment security agencies, joint action with state agencies is required. This federal-state relationship will be more fully described in Chapter XI. The BLS Office of Wages and Industrial Relations performs research and statistical service that is of direct use to the Labor-Management Services Administration, while the Wage and Hour and Public Contracts Divisions of the Labor Department delegate to the Bureau of Labor Statistics the statistical data-collection required for administration of the minimum wage laws. The BLS Office of Prices and Living Conditions provides data for the Labor Standards Bureau and the Women's Bureau, and the BLS Office of Foreign Labor and Trade furnishes research and statistics support to the Bureau of International Labor Affairs.

All these and other functions of the Bureau of Labor Statistics, how they have evolved, and to what purposes they are directed are explained in more detail in the chapters that follow.

III

Manpower and Labor Force Statistics

The story is told that, when President Warren G. Harding's Conference on Unemployment met in September, 1921, to look into the unemployment problem, the question came up as to how many workers were unemployed. Various numbers were suggested—3 million, 5 million, 7 million. The question was put to the members for a vote. How many think it is 5 million? 3 million? The final decision was 3.5 million to 5 million, and that guess was incorporated in the report.

The point of the story, of course, is not that the Conference members took haphazard action but that there were no statistics at all on unemployment in the American economy in 1921. They had to guess.

For more than a century, the American economy had been experiencing periodic depressions accompanied by severe unemployment—in 1817, 1837, 1857, 1873, 1893, 1914, to list only the worst years. Yet, throughout that period, the only information available on the nation's work force was data collected by the Bureau of the Census on the occupational status of the "gainful worker" population. A gainful worker was defined as one who followed an occupation that yielded some earnings or their equivalent, or one who assisted in production (that is, an unpaid family worker). There were no questions on actual employment or unemployment. The unemployed generally reported themselves as "gainful workers" because they had earned or expected to earn money by working. Furthermore, these data were available only every ten years, and then not until two or three years after the national census had been taken.

EMPLOYMENT, UNEMPLOYMENT, AND CONFLICTING DATA

Employment statistics on a current basis began to be collected by several state labor statistics bureaus shortly before World War I. A simple questionnaire was sent to a sample list of employers, mostly in manufacturing industries, asking for a report on the number of workers on the payroll in the middle week of the month and the total amount of dollars paid to these workers in that week. Later, the total number of hours worked was requested, and from this it was possible to calculate average earnings per hour for the work force on the payroll.

In 1916, the Bureau of Labor Statistics inaugurated a similar program for the economy as a whole. To avoid duplication, the Bureau worked out a cooperative program with those states that were already collecting such data. The result was a nation-wide statistical network, which provided a monthly or quarterly picture of changes in employment and in workers' earnings in manufacturing as a whole, in each of the larger manufacturing industries and in some nonmanufacturing industries. Such figures were available to Harding's Conference on Unemployment in 1921, but they covered only a fraction of total employment in the nation and contained no information on unemployment.

In the business recovery of 1922–23, employment expanded, and unemployment ceased for the time being to be a problem of public concern. There were flurries of renewed attention during the moderate business recessions of 1924 and 1927, but the complaints were minor until after the stock market collapse of 1929. Then, in the spring of 1930, the nation became acutely aware of unemployment.

The federal Bureau of Labor Statistics and the cooperating state bureaus of labor statistics had expanded and improved their employment statistics program during the 1920's. There were moderately good national statistics for manufacturing as well as for some nonmanufacturing industries, and a few states —New York, Wisconsin, California, Massachusetts, and Ohio among them—had good data. When the Great Depression struck, the first diagnosis of President Hoover and his Administration was that it would be a brief recession, like the preceding ones in the 1920's, and that the policy of the U.S. Government should be to encourage private industry to stem any business decline and restore prosperity as soon as possible. Firms were urged not to cut wages, and the public utility industries promised to expand their construction expenditures in 1930. The Secretary of Commerce of 1922, who had recommended public works as an antidepression program, had become the President of 1930, and he firmly believed that the best contribution the federal government could make would be to balance its budget. Income taxes were raised.

Now, conflicting employment statistics came into the picture. The U.S. Employment Service, which had been established during World War I to assist in moving labor to harvest crops and man war industries, had been drastically curtailed after the war, but a modest program remained, and the Service had public employment offices in some of the nation's larger cities. There were also a number of state employment services, but there was no cooperative arrangement between federal and state offices. The federal offices, in addition to carrying out their placement work, sent back to Washington every month a summary report on the employment situation in their districts, including a short-run forecast on the outlook. It was not a formal statistical report; rather, it was based upon conversations, mostly on the telephone, with leading employers in the community, who were asked to estimate their employment two months ahead.

In retrospect, it is obvious that this system contained a reporting bias—the good prospects happily reported, but the poor ones either failed to report or else concealed their pessimism. Few downturns were projected. The employment-office officials were not statisticians, and, in any case, the complexities of statistical sampling were not well understood in those days. (Some readers may recall the *Literary Digest*'s misinterpretation of data in the 1936 election.) Invariably, the reports were optimistic. The Secretary of Labor showed them to the President, who confidently proclaimed that "prosperity is just around the corner." This false hope may well have been a case less of wishful thinking than of reliance upon what then appeared to be good evidence.

These U.S. Employment Service reports came into Washington quickly, soon after the first of each month. In the meantime, the slower, more comprehensive reporting systems of the BLS and the states were grinding out their precise statistics garnered from many thousands of employers. By the time these were processed and published, six weeks had passed. The cold and unpleasant figures had already been superseded by another hopeful first-of-the-month prospect from the Employment Service. The discrepancy eventually became clear to the statisticians, but recognition of it did not penetrate into top government circles.

It was, however, well noted in the states. At that time, New York State constituted an excellent 10 per cent replica of the United States as a whole. Students of employment and economic conditions could often use New York trends to represent the United States. Frances Perkins, then Commissioner of Labor of New York, was quite aware of the true facts concerning employment. Eventually, the federal government was criticized for distorting and misinterpreting its own employment statistics, and Miss Perkins, as soon as she became U.S. Secretary of Labor, in 1933, requested the American Statistical Association to establish an advisory committee to counsel her on how to improve the statistics of the Department.

THE UNEMPLOYMENT STATISTICS IMBROGLIO

The unemployment question in the 1930's also triggered another statistical controversy. There was little public confidence in the figures to begin with, and, furthermore, the census of the unemployed in April, 1930, was of limited value by 1932 or 1933, to say nothing of the later years of the decade. A number of private estimates were developed—by the economists of the unions (AFL), by some business research services, and by individual economists. All had to follow the same general technique—namely, to make an estimate of the total labor force from the employment data available from the BLS and, finally, to subtract the number of employed from the total labor force to get the unemployment estimate. There was general similarity in the ups and downs of the different estimates, since the only up-to-date information was the monthly sample employment data. But they differed quite widely in level—at the bottom of the Depression in the winter of 1932–33, one estimate hit a high of 14 million unemployed at the same time as another reached only 10 million.

The catastrophic unemployment of those years created a volume and depth of destitution scarcely comprehensible to later generations. Unemployed families had to continue to buy food, but they stopped buying clothing and other necessities, and, eventually, they stopped paying rent. Mortgage foreclosures undermined the banks and finally led to the bank shutdown of March, 1933. There was no unemployment insurance to tide workers over short-run unemployment, nor any old-age insurance to support older workers who had to retire from the labor market. The only community resources were private charitable organizations and local public welfare agencies, which provided aid to widowed mothers with children, aid to the blind, and general relief for families in need—usually the chronically ill and households without employable members.

Already stretched thin in meeting the needs of the destitute in normal times, this feeble welfare system was soon overwhelmed as though by an avalanche. The burden shifted from the private to the local public agencies, then to the states, and finally to Washington. One of the first acts of the Roosevelt Administration in the spring of 1933 was to establish the Federal Emergency Relief Administration (FERA) to help the states and cities care for the destitute. A vital second step, taken in 1934, was to appoint a committee on economic security to work out a more orderly, long-run system for meeting people's needs.

Meantime, FERA Administrator Harry Hopkins decided that work for the unemployed—government-made work—was preferable to grants of relief funds to families. So, a major welfare step was taken in 1935, when the federal government assumed responsibility for providing jobs for all employable persons on the relief rolls. Under the Works Progress Administration (WPA), these people were put to work on government projects (mostly state and local, supported by federal funds) to earn enough money to support their families on at least a relief level. Conversely, the federal government turned back to the states and localities the responsibility for unemployable persons. The passage of the Social Security Act, in August, 1935, offered the prospect that the needy aged, mothers with children, and the blind would be eligible for federal matching grants to the states. But there was no provision for federal aid to other needy families, who could not qualify under programs for the aged, the blind, or children. The nation's welfare set-up has been handicapped ever since this unfortunate division of responsibility was made.

Hopkins' work program again raised, as a matter of public policy, the question of how many workers were unemployed. What size work program was needed? There were no figures and no systems for getting them. The first idea proposed was to get the unemployed to declare themselves. A plan was worked out to have questionnaires available in the post offices across the country and to persuade all the unemployed to pick them up and fill them out. Help was available, if needed. A survey based on these questionnaires was made in November, 1937.

Apart from the many weaknesses in the procedure itself, the limited value of a one-shot survey was soon plain. Seasonally, November is one of the months of low employment, but without the additional midwinter unemployment that appears in January and February. Moreover, a rather sharp new business recession began at the end of 1937, and additional heavy cyclical unemployment appeared early in 1938. One survey could not reflect the problems of a constantly changing situation. To illustrate, the number of workers on WPA rolls in the autumn of 1937 was approximately 1.5 million, according to *The WPA and Federal Relief Policy,* published by Russell Sage Foundation in 1943. One year later, according to this source, it was 3.25 million. In the autumn of the next year, 1939, the number was back down to about 1.75 million. These numbers do not represent the total volume of unemployment at the time, because not all of the unemployed were immediately eligible for WPA work; but the comparative WPA employment constitutes clear evidence of the 1938 shift in the business situation and the need for more up-to-date information on unemployment.

BLS AND CENSUS BUREAU HOUSEHOLD SURVEYS

When Harry Hopkins asked his statisticians to provide an answer to his welfare budgeting problems, they came up with one of the most significant statistical inventions in the social sciences. They proposed that a program be set up for selecting at random a small but representative sample of families throughout the country and for visiting these families to get information on who was employed, who was looking for work, and who was not in the labor force at all (homemakers, school children, disabled, retired). By relating this sample to the total population, the statisticians could estimate the total labor force in the economy, divided into the employed and the unemployed. These two groups could be subclassified into men and women, white and Negro, older and younger, and in terms of any other details for which the sample was large enough to provide satisfactory figures.

Ironically, by the time the statistical procedures had been worked out and put into operation, World War II was on the horizon, and the WPA was being phased out. Fortunately, the statistical achievement was not lost. The Bureau of the Census took over the household survey project in 1942 and kept it alive during the war years. Then, when postwar readjustment brought the Employment Act of 1946, this statistical series became one of the key guides to economic policy in the United States. Today, the unemployment rate is watched every month for signs of business recovery and recession.

The Council of Economic Advisers was created by the Employment Act of 1946. When it began operations, the immediate postwar unemployment threat had faded. The inflation of 1947–48 became the Council's primary concern. Even the recession of 1949 did not entirely stop economic expansion; the construction and automobile industries plowed right ahead. Then came the Korean War, with labor shortages and wage and price controls. It was the post-Korea readjustment in 1954 that first thrust the Council into the unemployment problem. That development, too, was sparked by statistical discrepancies.

As noted earlier, knotty administrative and public relations problems had emerged over the years from the lack of coordination between the Department of Commerce and the Department of Labor in the field of employment statistics. The 1954 recession intensified existing problems and then spawned a new one, which temporarily dwarfed the others.

The problem arose over the Census Bureau, which had requested funds in the 1953–54 fiscal year's budget to expand and update its sample of households. However, funds were trimmed to a level that made it impossible to carry out the full revision program that had been approved by the Bureau of the Budget. The Census Bureau decided to go ahead anyway, but the result was that a marked discrepancy appeared between the figures of the old sample and those of the new. The Council of Economic Advisers was disturbed; the congressional Joint Economic Committee called for action; and out of the contretemps came coordination between the Commerce and Labor departments for the joint release of employment and unemployment statistics—the system that lasted until 1959, when the Secretaries of Commerce and Labor agreed upon a major readjustment of functions. In this plan, the program and financial responsibility for labor force, employment, and unemployment statistics was assigned to the Bureau of Labor Statistics, and the BLS as noted earlier, then contracted with the Bureau of the Census for the collection of the data. This joint operations system of the BLS and the Census has proved happily cooperative, efficient, and effective to the present time.

FIGURES TROUBLE IN THE 1960'S

The unification of employment and unemployment statistics in the Department of Labor did not, however, put an end to criticism of the figures themselves and of the Department's procedures. One controversy over the release of the unemployment statistics prior to Election Day in November, 1960 (see Chapter XIII), was resolved when Secretary Arthur Goldberg instructed the BLS to select for a year in advance the monthly dates on which the figures would be released to the public. In the years since, there has been no further criticism on that point.

The other major public criticism (also treated more fully in Chapter XIII) was the charge that the BLS, in the summer of

1961, was inflating the unemployment figures in order to promote the Labor Department's programs. The congressional hearings and the appointment by President John F. Kennedy of the Committee To Appraise Employment and Unemployment Statistics quieted these complaints pending the outcome of the Committee's findings, which, after a year of study, were made public in the autumn of 1962. The Committee's report, "Measuring Employment and Unemployment," has had such a noteworthy effect upon labor force statistics that it is worthwhile here to outline the main conclusions and recommendations.

First of all, the Committee quickly disposed of the charge of lack of integrity:

After careful investigation, the Committee has unanimously and categorically concluded that doubt concerning the scientific objectivity of the agencies responsible for collecting, processing and publishing employment and unemployment statistics is unwarranted. The Committee remains highly impressed by the professional qualifications and the scientific integrity and objectivity of those responsible for the system of reporting the official data on employment and unemployment. . . . the Committee fully shares the conclusion recently reached by the Subcommittee on Economic Statistics of the Joint Economic Committee that there is "no basis whatever for doubt as to the integrity of the Bureau of Labor Statistics and the other Government agencies involved in planning and carrying out our employment and unemployment statistics programs."

The Committee then proceeded to make a substantive list of recommendations for the improvement of these statistics, which, it said, "are of vital importance to the economic health of the Nation." Among these recommendations, the most important was that the agencies concerned with the labor force as a whole should undertake research and experimentation to test the validity and the accuracy of the survey methods being used. In response to this suggestion, the Bureau of Labor Statistics, in cooperation with the Census Bureau, established a special test sample of households—a survey completely independent of the regular sample, which yielded the current labor force, employment, and unemployment figures. The test sample was used for varying the usual questions, checking the responses, modifying the definitions, and, in general, probing more deeply into the work experience of the members of the surveyed households. Over a period of several years, this test sample produced important new information on the employed, the unemployed, and those not in the labor force, and reaffirmed confidence in BLS methods. The results of the tests were incorporated in the revised figures issued by the Bureau of Labor Statistics beginning in January, 1967.

One important revision was the decision to drop the fourteen- and fifteen-year-olds from labor force statistics. This had the effect of reducing total employment by about 1 million persons, and unemployment by about 60,000. The argument in favor of this decision was that such youngsters consisted primarily of occasional and part-time workers such as newsboys, babysitters, and unpaid family labor—for example, boys and girls who worked on their parents' farms or in family stores—and that, in addition, child labor laws greatly restrict the job opportunities of youngsters under sixteen years of age. Statistics on this younger group continue to be collected and analyzed, but the official labor force figures were revised back into the past in order to eliminate them from the labor force data.

In introducing the revised statistics to the public, the BLS made the following statement in a publication entitled *Employment and Earnings and Monthly Report on the Labor Force, February, 1967.*

The sample has been expanded to 52,500 households, the lower age limit has been raised from 14 to 16 years, the definition of unemployment has been sharpened and clarified, the reporting on other items such as hours of work and self employment has been improved, and, finally, a considerable body of new information is being developed for persons not in the labor force.

The Committee acknowledged that no single measure of unemployment would satisfy all users of the statistics but did see a need for more precise boundaries between the unemployed and those not in the labor force and for more detailed classification within each of the two groups.

The changes in definitions and procedures that have been adopted will increase the accuracy of the statistics and will clarify, but not substantially alter, the underlying concepts.

DIFFICULTY OF ACCURATE MEASUREMENT

One of the limitations of the household survey was that the family sample was too small to provide reasonably accurate state and local data. This limitation was overcome to a degree when the Bureau was able to obtain the funds necessary to add the 1965–66 test sample of 17,500 households to the 35,000 in the regular sample. This enlargement of the sample made it possible to reduce the margins of error in the statistics for the larger metropolitan areas of the country. The Bureau chose the twenty largest standard metropolitan statistical areas and fourteen of their central cities. These metropolitan areas ranged from the largest (New York, Los Angeles, Chicago) to the smaller ones (Buffalo, Milwaukee, and Cincinnati).

Local area surveys in a few of the larger cities have thrown more light on the employment and unemployment situation in some of the problem sections of each central city. For instance, the twenty metropolitan areas selected for this sampling in 1967 accounted for one-third of total U.S. unemployment and 42 per cent of nonwhite unemployment. The two largest areas of the sample, New York and the Los Angeles–Long Beach area, together accounted for 9 per cent of the total unemployed in the country. From these tabulations, the Bureau has been able to develop more precise data on the nonwhite unemployment problems of the large cities. This program of special surveys, particularly in slum areas of major cities, is being enlarged, and new detailed information on six of the twenty cities should be available in 1969.

While the data for the individual areas have a wide margin of error in any one month, the accumulation of monthly figures over the year materially reduces the incidence of error. An over-all picture of the labor force in the United States during any year is determined by the annual average for the twelve preceding months. (Each month represents a cross-section for just one week at the middle of the month.) But, there are two important variables—the steady growth of the labor force and its seasonal variations. More youngsters enter the labor force in their teens than older workers die or retire. In recent years, the labor force has expanded by about 1.5 million workers per year. This growth tends to be concentrated in the early summer, when many high school and college students leave school and go to work. Additionally, there is a large seasonal increase in the labor pool by the summer peak in June or July, when farm work is in full swing, when construction is at a peak, and when many recreational industries are hiring summer workers. In contrast, the labor force is at its lowest point of the year in February, when work in many industries is slack, and when many young people are in high school or college classes.

Both these variations—growth and seasonality—can be detected in the following year-end figures for 1967:

	January	June	December	Annual Average
Civilian Labor Force	75,320,000	79,020,000	78,057,000	77,347,000
Employed	72,160,000	75,391,000	75,338,000	74,372,000
Unemployed	3,160,000	3,629,000	2,719,000	2,975,000
Percentage unemployed	4.2	4.6	3.5	3.8

The labor force increased by 3.7 million persons from January to June; there was an increase of about 3.2 million in jobs, and there were about 0.5 million more unemployed. By December, the labor force had shrunk by about 1 million, nearly all from the unemployment bracket, which declined from 4.6 per cent of the total civilian labor force to 3.5 per cent.

It is interesting to note that, in any one month, about half the unemployed have been out of work less than five weeks (that is, approximately a month or less). Only about one-quarter were unemployed more than fifteen weeks. In the last ten years or more, this group, sometimes called the hard-core unemployed, has consisted mostly of the unskilled, untrained, and poorly educated. Because of past deficiencies in education and training, Negro workers of all ages are heavily represented in this disadvantaged group. (In 1965, recognizing that the Negro unemployment rate was approximately twice that of whites, a White House conference, "To Fulfill These Rights," was held to study economic opportunities for Negroes. As a service to the conference, the Bureau of Labor Statistics prepared a study on the economic status of the Negro. The following year, the Bureau revised the study and published it as a bulletin entitled *The Negroes in the United States: Their Economic and Social Situation*. This study included not only the basic demographic and labor force statistics on Negroes but also other economic and social statistics drawn from a wide variety of sources. In 1967, the Bureau published Report No. 332, further updating and adding to the information available in the basic bulletin.)

Generally, the statistician's difficulty is that the monthly labor figures do not represent the same persons month after month, or even day by day. Continually, employed workers become unemployed, the unemployed get jobs, new workers enter the labor force, and other workers retire, returning to the home or to school. The high school student may seek a summer job in June and return to school in September, a housewife may work in the canning industry during the summer months, or in retail trade during the Christmas shopping season. Periodic surveys by the Bureau have shown that more than 12 million persons participate in the labor force during the year than are to be found during the peak summer months.

This constant turnover and large-scale movement of people in and out of the labor force make accurate measurement more difficult. For instance, when a student in April is actively seeking a job for the summer, when school will be out, is he unemployed? When the summer job has ended in the beginning of September and the young man has planned to register for college three weeks later, is he unemployed in the middle week of September? When a housewife worked in a store over the Christmas rush and was laid off in January, did she become unemployed? When a middle-aged, able-bodied man states that he is not working or looking for work, is he unemployed? He is classified as being out of the labor force, but one wonders whether he is living on his savings or income from investments or is discouraged by the job prospects in his locality.

During recent years, the Bureau has conducted studies designed to throw more light on the reasons for entering and leaving the labor force or for nonparticipation in the labor force. In September, 1966, the Bureau conducted a test survey with a representative nation-wide sample of 13,000 households. The purpose was to draw a distinction between the voluntary nonparticipants—those who had no intention of working—and the involuntary nonparticipants, who wanted a regular job but were not looking for work. The results of the survey provided some significant answers to the question of why some men, women, and young people are not in the labor force or do not expect to enter in the immediate future. At the same time, there were significant numbers of persons who, while not interested in work at the present time, were expecting to enter sometime within the next year. The Bureau is now collecting this information on a regular, continuing basis, with analysis of the results scheduled for the fall of 1968.

EMPLOYMENT, HOURS, AND EARNINGS STATISTICS

Labor force statistics obtained through the household-survey method are valuable as a picture of the economy as a whole. If the sample is large enough and good enough—and, as done today, it is—we can obtain reasonably accurate estimates of the total labor force—the employed and the unemployed—classified by age groups, by men and women (and teenagers), by white and nonwhite (mostly Negroes), by full-time and part-time workers, etc. The disadvantage of the household survey is that it is expensive to conduct, since it requires Census field agents to visit every family in the sample every month. Consequently, although it has been applied to major metropolitan areas, it has not been applied to states, or even to major regions of the country. Of course, it would be possible to use the household-survey method to obtain current and continuing state and local data, provided governments were willing to spend enough money. Apart from the work that the BLS is now able to do with its limited funds, nothing much is being done in those areas.

One reason for this hesitancy to invest government funds in household surveys is access to the mountains of information on employment, hours, and earnings that are available from employers' reports. Every employer who conducts a business of some kind must keep payroll records for his employees. It is a relatively simple matter for him to report the number of employees on his payroll for any pay period, as well as the total amount of money paid to those workers. Most employers also report the total number of hours worked by their employees during the pay period. With the advent of the Social Security System (old-age insurance and unemployment insurance) in the late 1930's, by law employers were required to keep rec-

ords reporting the individual quarterly earnings of their employees. Since the coverage of the Social Security System is so
widespread, the majority of all employers—large and small—
are now included. (Even the housewife is required to keep social security records for any domestic workers she employs.)

In 1967, approximately 150,000 employers voluntarily reported data every month on approximately 25 million employees to the state agencies and through them to the federal
government. The federal Civil Service Commission supplies a
complete monthly count of federal-government employees, as
do enough state agencies and local governments to account for
about half of the 9 million state and local employees in the
country. It is from these employer reports that the government
obtains the most detailed figures on employment in the American economy.

Although certainly useful, social security data become
available only after a wait of sometimes a year, allowing time
for the lagging returns to filter in. Such data are useless for
quick, up-to-date monthly figures but valuable as benchmarks
with which to check and correct the past trends in employment
shown in the sampling survey. A single report from an employer furnishes data on total employment, production-worker
employment, hours of work of production workers, and total
weekly payroll for such workers. These data contribute to
the analysis of the state employment picture and to that of
the United States as a whole, with all the information classified
into several hundred industries. The state agencies and the
local employment offices use the data for operational and analytical purposes. The Office of Business Economics uses the
data in the preparation of the national accounts. The Bureau
of Labor Statistics uses the hours information for productivity
indexes. The employment data are useful supplements to the
labor force data from the household survey, and so it goes.
There is probably no other statistical reporting system any-

where that yields such a wealth of information from such a relatively simple report.

Begun by state labor departments about a half-century ago, this employer reporting system provides reasonably representative and accurate data for the approximately 66 million wage and salary workers in our economy. The labor force groups that are missing from this system but included in the Census' Current Population Survey are farmers and farm workers, professional people, small proprietors, the self-employed, and unpaid family workers. The federal Bureau of Labor Statistics has been the agency responsible for coordinating the present federal-state cooperative system. The BLS, together with the Bureau of Employment Security in the Department of Labor, and with the state employment security agencies and labor departments, has developed this statistical system, providing a nation-wide network of figures on employment in several hundred industries, in all fifty states, and in more than 100 metropolitan areas.

Goods and Services Employment

One startling feature of the changing character of American industry since the Korean War has been a marked shift of employment out of industries producing goods and into industries producing services. The former consist of manufacturing industries—those producing durable items such as steel and automobiles and those producing nondurable items such as textiles, chemicals, and paper—and contract construction, mining, and agriculture. The service industries consist of wholesale and retail trade; federal, state, and local government; transportation and public utilities; finance, insurance, and real estate; and other services such as hotels, restaurants, and repair shops.

As Chart III shows, among the goods-producing industries, agricultural employment (farmers plus farm workers) has declined nearly 50 per cent since 1953, while mining employment is down by about one-third.* Employment in the manufacturing industries has increased over 10 per cent, a gain of nearly 2 million jobs, most of them in the heavy industries (durable goods), while contract construction has gained about 700,000 jobs, an increase of well over 25 per cent. But, as a whole, the group has not grown. It is still at the 1953 level of about 27 million workers.

The service industries, quite to the contrary, have grown rapidly and persistently, as evidenced in Chart IV. The fastest-growing of all the service industries is state and local government, which has more than doubled since 1953. This growth has been due partly to the expanding public education system, requiring more teachers and other educational workers, and partly to the increasing public services required for urban and suburban living—water supplies, sanitation, police, fire, recreation, and others. By contrast, federal government employment has scarcely grown at all, amounting to only a few hundred thousand more people than were on the rolls at the end of the Korean War, when it was 2.5 million. In terms of employment, "Big Government" is state and local, not federal.

The miscellaneous-services group has also expanded approximately 50 per cent since 1953. The only service-producing group that has not increased is transportation and the public utilities, in which expansion in airlines and trucking has been offset by decline in railroad employment. All in all, job growth since the Korean War has been primarily in the service industries, which have expanded by nearly 14 million employees, an increase of nearly 50 per cent.

Large as these samples are, in terms of the numbers of total employees in the various industries, they are neither large nor complete enough to continue tabulating year after year without readjustment. As indicated earlier, annual data are avail-

*Agriculture figures are supplied from the household surveys instead of from employer reports.

Chart III

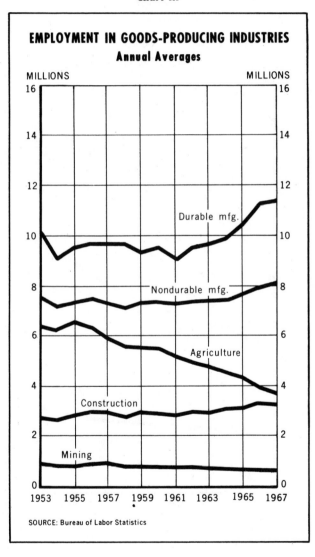

EMPLOYMENT IN GOODS-PRODUCING INDUSTRIES
Annual Averages

SOURCE: Bureau of Labor Statistics

Chart IV

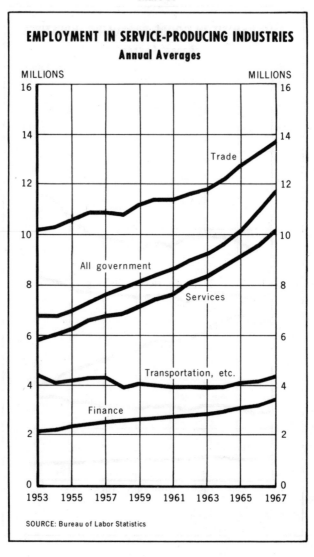

(D. L. 307.)

DEPARTMENT OF LABOR.

...

ORDER.

The reading of newspapers, magazines, books, etc.,

The writing of private correspondence or articles,

Indulgence in conversation not pertaining to the work of the Department,

Visiting from room to room on other than official business, or

Other misemployment of time during office hours by employés

is

STRICTLY PROHIBITED.

...

The hours of service per day which the Government exacts are reasonably brief, and it is expected that during these hours all will attend scrupulously to their official duties and assist the Department, to the limit of their abilities, in putting forward the work.

The attention of clerks and others is called to the fact that this order is continuously in force. Clerks having charge of work will be held accountable for its observance by those under their supervision.

CARROLL D. WRIGHT,
Commissioner.

WASHINGTON, D. C., *July 1, 1893.*

This sign, listing rules for department employees, was posted by Commissioner Carroll D. Wright in 1893.

A BLS field agent prices stoves for the Consumer Price Index.

A housewife (a part-time daily rate agent) prices fresh produce in a local grocery store.

The New York Times

Statistics gathered by field agents are sent to the Office of Prices and Living Conditions, where rows of desks are manned by statistical clerks.

Technicians operate information storage and retrieval systems at the Bureau.

Above, the author, Ewan Clague, as Commissioner, discusses manpower programs with his policy staff.

Below, a U.S. delegation headed by Walsh McDermott (right) and including Commissioner Clague (center) attends an international labor conference in Geneva.

able from the social security reporting system on a very nearly complete count basis for all but farm workers. The BLS, therefore, adjusts its monthly and annual reports to correct any deviation that has occurred. Sometimes this involves readjustments extending back several years.

In order to provide users of the statistics with up-to-date information, the Bureau issued two volumes, each of which is about the size of a large city's telephone book. One is for the United States as a whole—*Employment and Earnings Statistics for the United States, 1909–68*. The other is for states and other regional areas—*Employment and Earnings Statistics for States and Areas, 1939–67*. Subsequent editions of both will come out every year or two.

OCCUPATIONAL OUTLOOK: DOCTOR, LAWYER, INDIAN CHIEF?

Even in the depths of the Great Depression, young people were looking ahead to see what future job prospects might be. In the 1870's, Horace Greeley in New York had said, "Go West, young man," but that didn't seem very useful advice in the 1930's. During the worst of times, some occupations are growing in numbers employed; during the best, some are declining.

In 1938, the President's Advisory Committee on Education devoted much attention to the need for information for young people preparing to choose a career. The Committee recommended that the Bureau of Labor Statistics be designated to conduct studies on the outlook for jobs in various occupations and to make the results available. Two years later, Congress authorized the establishment of the Occupational Outlook Service in the BLS.

During World War II, the staff of the Bureau was assigned more urgent emergency studies, and nothing much was done on the occupational outlook. But, when millions of young ex-servicemen returned to civilian life after the war, the need for such studies was both evident and urgent. By about the middle of 1946, the Bureau had prepared an occupational outlook manual for use by the Veterans Administration in counseling and rehabilitation. Less than a year later, the National Vocational Guidance Association passed a resolution requesting that Congress authorize the BLS to publish a similar volume of occupational information for public sale. Requests also came from other groups and private individuals.

In response, the Bureau issued the first edition of the *Occupational Outlook Handbook* in 1949. It was an immediate success. Within a year, 30,000 copies were sold, and it was revised and enlarged in 1951. (The *Handbook* was popular with congressmen, which may have played a significant part in determining the Bureau's appropriations for manpower studies at that time.)

The Korean War interrupted occupational outlook work for several years, but it was taken up again as soon as the war ended. Increased public recognition of the need for this kind of service to young people induced Congress in 1955 to authorize funds for biennial revisions of the *Handbook,* beginning with the third edition in 1957. The popularity of the *Handbook* is shown by the fact that, in addition to the copies bought by government agencies, the 1966–67 edition sold approximately 80,000 copies to colleges, high schools, and the general public. The 1968–69 edition is now available.*

As successful as the *Handbook* has been, there seems to be a general lack of knowledge of BLS programs and services in occupational fields. One step the BLS took to facilitate wider distribution of its outlook materials was to publish reprints of sketches on specific occupations in the *Handbook*. The advantages of these individual occupation leaflets are that they are inexpensive (5¢ to 15¢) and that a limited selection of them

*The *Occupational Outlook Handbook* can be purchased from the Superintendent of Documents for $4.25. The *Handbook* and all other occupational outlook publications may be purchased with federal funds under Title II of the Elementary and Secondary Act and Title V-A of the National Defense Education Act.

can be useful to young people who already know their major field of interest. Sales of reprints from the 1963–64 *Handbook* exceeded 1 million copies; returns on the 1966–67 edition indicate that those sales have been even higher.

Another step was the publication of the *Occupational Outlook Quarterly,* which the BLS inaugurated in 1957 to provide up-to-date information during the two years between editions of the *Handbook,* as well as to highlight new or unique occupational prospects. This popularly written publication features articles on such problems as skilled jobs for women, school dropouts, and "apprenticeship" opportunities for young students. A recent edition treated such occupations as those of professional athletes, electronic-computer technicians, and social workers. What could be a dry but very important subject is treated in a lively fashion:

> Depending on what papers you read, the computer industry is a fast growing colossus that promises to provide the means to a better life for us all, or threatens to put us all out of work. This giant is a catalyst for change in the traditional ways of computing everything from the month-end bank statement to how to reach the moon; it has a more sophisticated work force than most other industries. A look at a few facts and figures from the Bureau of Labor Statistics continuing research on the changing occupational composition in American industries may alert young people to the kind of manpower it takes to build computers.

A third approach to the problem of distribution was the preparation of a series of charts in the form of slides, with a brief narrative accompanying them and answering many questions on the outlook for job opportunities. The slide in the series that graphically illustrates projected manpower needs, 1965–75, in selected professions is shown as Chart V. It contrasts two important factors—replacement and growth—that determine job opportunities. The narrative that accompanies this chart explains that, in occupations largely made up of

Chart V
TRAINING NEEDS ARE DETERMINED BY REPLACEMENT PLUS GROWTH

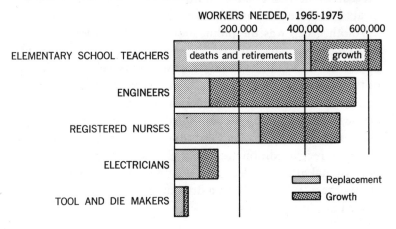

WORKERS NEEDED, 1965-1975

young men who have long working lives ahead of them, job opportunities would generally come from growth. But, in professions that are dominated by older workers, job openings are likely to come from replacement needs. This series can be used by counselors, teachers, parents, and students themselves in analyzing the job prospects in major occupational fields. The advantage of a slide series is its flexibility. The series can be selected and rearranged to fit the particular requirements of a group of students or young workers. The entire series has been reproduced in a pamphlet, *Looking Ahead to a Career.*

In 1955, Secretary of Labor Mitchell, fully aware of, and deeply concerned about, the marked swings in the age composition of the labor force that loomed ahead, set in motion an educational campaign to acquaint labor, management, and the general public with the emerging problems of youth. He arranged for the Department of Labor to publish a chart book— *Our Manpower Future, 1955–65*—that portrayed the key projections of manpower supply and presented brief text sentences interpreting the charts. It was an outstanding success—readable and understandable—and it had an important influence on government programs.

Then, in 1960, looking forward to 1970, the exercise was repeated. This publication was entitled *Manpower—Challenge of the Sixties*. The tone and message were less buoyant, more ominous. The approaching youth explosion into the labor force (1965–70) was emphasized and dramatized. This study, expounded and popularized by the Labor Department staff, had a significant influence upon the manpower legislation of the early 1960's.

Right now the nation is in the midst of a youth problem that had been forecast more than ten years ago. Despite the full employment achieved in an economy geared to Viet-Nam, the structural unemployment problems foreshadowed by the Labor Department studies have not been solved. The industrial and occupational changes have, in general, reflected the following projected patterns sketched by the manpower analysts: Employment in the service industries has surpassed employment in the goods-producing industries; professional and technical occupations have grown rapidly, while common labor has declined; the number of women and teenagers entering the labor force has increased faster than that of men.

But these broad groupings by age, by sex, and by major occupational fields are not sufficiently detailed to meet the needs of young people choosing a career or of businessmen planning future expansion. More precise studies are needed for specific occupations and occupational families. For instance, one class of workers about whom there is increasing national concern for the future—partly because of the long periods of apprenticeship required in many crafts, and partly because of the job opportunities offered to young workers—is that of skilled craft workers.

In April, 1966, the *Monthly Labor Review* published an article that represented several years' work by the Bureau's man-

power staff. This study estimated that employment requirements from 1965 to 1975 for craftsmen, foremen, and kindred
workers would grow from 9.2 million to 11.4 million and provide job openings for 4.0 million workers—2.2 million jobs
representing net growth, plus 1.8 million representing replacements after deaths and retirements. These projections were
then subdivided into eleven building trades, seven classes of
mechanics and repairmen, four grades of machinists, five
printing crafts, and about half a dozen other skilled occupations. These detailed breakdowns of the estimates within the
craft groups are essential for apprenticeship training and manpower planning.

Similar studies have been made of natural science manpower, social science manpower, and teacher projections. During 1966, the President's Committee on Health Manpower was
established to study the future needs in this field. The Secretary
of Labor requested the BLS to "prepare a report on the current and prospective supply and demand for health manpower,
utilizing the research being done in its occupational outlook
program." The results of the study were published in 1967 in
BLS Report No. 323, entitled *Health Manpower, 1966–75.*
This report outlined the prospects for fifteen health occupations, ranging from physicians and dentists to dietitians and
nurses, to therapists and technicians, aides, orderlies, and at-
tendants. Chart VI shows estimated employment needs in
these fields by 1975 in percentages. The breakdown in figures
is physicians, 145,000; dentists, 45,000; professional nurses,
390,000; licensed practical nurses, 290,000; X-ray technicians, 51,000; laboratory assistants, 70,000; medical technol-
ogists, 50,000; pharmacists, 38,000; aides, orderlies, and at-
tendants, 690,000. In all health services, the requirements
total 1.65 million workers for new positions, plus about 1 million as replacements.

Every few years, it is necessary to take an over-all look at the
total manpower picture of the economy. Now it is time to look

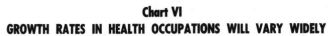

Chart VI
GROWTH RATES IN HEALTH OCCUPATIONS WILL VARY WIDELY

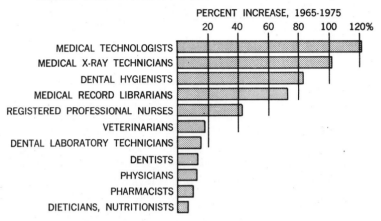

PERCENT INCREASE, 1965-1975

to the 1970's: The youth problem of the 1960's is beginning to take on new dimensions. The problems of city ghettos are becoming more acute. The Equal Pay Act and the Equal Rights Amendment are already producing significant changes in job opportunities for women. The speed of technological innovation is not likely to slacken; more likely, it will accelerate. Marked changes in the industrial and occupational patterns of the American labor force are certain to be one result.

The BLS is preparing a new projection of national manpower requirements, to be published soon under the title *Tomorrow's Manpower Needs*. It will be helpful in planning national programs of education or training and in checking the extent to which these needs are being met. The BLS anticipates that this recently developed feature of manpower research will be a continuing program; so *Tomorrow's Manpower Needs* will be revised and reissued every few years to reflect the most up-to-date information available. Tomorrow's manpower needs must be today's concern.

IV

Prices and Cost of Living

On March 1, 1968, newspapers throughout the country carried a headline "Consumer Prices up Three-Tenths of a Per Cent in Month." Many radio and television stations gave the topic a paragraph in their newscasts. On the previous day, Arnold Chase, Assistant Commissioner for Prices and the Cost of Living, had held a press conference in Washington, D.C., to release to the press and the public the price indexes for January. The Consumer Price Index (CPI) at 118.6 (1957–59 = 100) was up 0.3 per cent from December and 3.4 per cent higher than it had been in January, 1967. The Wholesale Price Index (WPI) had increased 0.4 per cent over the previous month and was 0.9 per cent higher than it had been a year earlier. The assistant commissioner pointed out that price increases were pervading the economy and indicated that the outlook was for more of the same in the months ahead.

The BLS press release also reported on the cost-of-living adjustments in wages, which had been triggered by the January CPI:

> More than 615,000 workers will receive cost-of-living increases as a result of the January Consumer Price Index. About 450,000 employees in the trucking industry, including general freight, automobile hauling, and some tank trucking and cement hauling drivers, will receive 3-cent increases based on the change in the index since July 1967. Three-cent quarterly increases will go to

about 100,000 workers in aerospace, automotive parts and some metalworking firms. Workers in other industries will receive increases of from one to four cents based on quarterly or semiannual changes in the index.

In addition, the release disclosed local indexes for a dozen large cities—monthly figures for New York, Chicago, Detroit, Philadelphia, and Los Angeles, and quarterly for Baltimore, St. Louis, San Francisco, Atlanta, Cincinnati, Kansas City (Missouri), and Honolulu.

Altogether, there are eighteen cities for which indexes appear every three months. Wage escalation contracts are based upon these local indexes, and the local papers carry stories of wage increases affecting their communities.

Is it any wonder that both the national and the local price indexes are good for newspaper headlines, as well as for repeated radio and television news items, in practically every town and city in the country? No single statistic on the U.S. economy is of such immediate and personal interest to the American people, workers and consumers alike. The great majority of housewives and other homemakers have been shopping during the announcement week and have had direct experience with changes in prices and the cost of living. Sometimes their experiences do not seem in accord with the published figures, and some of them write irate letters to the Commissioner asking where he does his pricing. (I can recall one letter from a housewife who explained that she found the clerk marking up the prices on the shelf right there before her eyes, so she dashed around ahead of him and got some cans before he could mark them up. She wondered which prices the Bureau took for the index.)

CONSUMER INDEX PRICING: HOW IT IS DONE

The public can be assured that intensive and continuing efforts are made to maintain and improve the accuracy of the index. Most of the pricing is done by field agents who visit retail outlets and get the prices right from the shelves or from the records. For food prices, the Bureau employs daily rate agents who reside in the community. They are usually housewives, experienced shoppers, who visit the stores during the middle week of the month to price the list of 90–100 foods being checked that month. Certain foods, such as fresh strawberries and watermelons, are priced only during their local season. Others, like meats and potatoes, are priced the year round.

Prices are collected from chain stores and from local neighborhood stores; from department stores and from specialty shops, selling appliances, radios, television sets; from the central city and from the suburbs. Enough prices are collected on each item to insure that the average is reasonably representative of the prevailing price in that community.

Some prices are more difficult to collect accurately and require the services of full-time professional field agents. Dresses and suits are examples of items for which it is necessary to consult with department store buyers and salesmen in order to make sure that the quality is comparable from one season to the next. The price of a new automobile at the dealer's showroom is determined by obtaining the discounts from the list price, coupled with the allowances being made for the old car being turned in.

The telephone can be used to some extent in obtaining slow-moving prices, such as doctor's fees, although office visits are made periodically in order to encourage continuing reporting as well as to make sure that the reported fees are the ones prevailing. Mail reporting can be used for public utility rates and bus fares, since these are regulated and can be changed only by official action.

Not every community can be represented in the index; the cost would be prohibitive. What is needed is to make sure that all sizes of community and all major regions of the country are represented. The largest metropolitan areas (with a population of over 1.4 million in 1960) are automatically included. For populations of 250,000 to 1.4 million, a sample of seventeen areas was selected, while for those between 50,000 and 250,-000 a sample of ten was chosen. A total of seventeen cities represented the smaller communities from 50,000 population down to 2,500. (The cities in the current index are shown in Appendix B.)

What Goes into the "Market Basket"?

The first step in the construction of a price index is to develop what the Bureau of Labor Statistics calls a "market basket," which does not mean a grocery list, but rather a compilation of all the major purchases that a family makes over a period of time. It includes automobiles, household appliances, local transit fares, gas and electricity, drugs, newspapers, movies, doctor's fees, hospital room rates, etc. Formerly, rents alone were used to measure basic housing costs, but now home ownership is included—purchase price of a house, maintenance, repairs, taxes. Obviously, some items are bought again and again during the year, while others may be bought only at long intervals—a new auto perhaps once in five years, a home maybe once in a lifetime. How can a representative list be made up in the face of such diversity?

The answer is that the Bureau must also collect information on the buying habits of thousands of families and single individuals—one-person families, as they are sometimes called. Not every family bought a new auto last year, but with annual sales of over 8 million cars, it is evident that many did. So it is necessary to select a sample of thousands of families, obtain their specific expenditures during a year, and then average these expenditures. If one family in five bought a new car, we can say that the average family bought a fifth of a car. The amount spent by this hypothetical average family on one-fifth of a car would measure the importance of new cars in the market basket.

In selecting families for such an expenditure survey, the Bureau uses the most up-to-date scientific methods of sampling. The selection of cities, neighborhoods within the city, blocks, and houses or apartments—all these are made in advance. The field agent who collects the sampling information follows precise procedures established beforehand. In fact, it is the specific house or apartment that is selected, and the agent interviews whoever lives there.

The primary objective of the BLS Consumer Price Index is to measure the living costs of wage-earners and clerical workers. The index was created primarily to meet the problem of wage negotiations with employers. Thus, the families covered by the index are those primarily dependent on wage or salary income. All blue-collar and white-collar employees who are on employer payrolls are represented in the sample. But professional men, the self-employed, farmers, and farm workers are omitted, as are families without any earners, the retired, the unemployed, and the needy.

It would also be possible to make an over-all index for the total population that would include the classes now left out, but so far there has not been enough demand for this step.

The last consumer-expenditure survey (1960–61) covered a total of 13,728 families (including single individuals)—urban, suburban, rural nonfarm, and rural farm. The expenditures of these households are available in published statistics. But only the urban and suburban dwellers and, of those, only the households of wage-earners and clerical workers were included in the expenditure patterns for the index. These expenditures furnish the weights used for the various goods and services in the index. All important items the surveyed families purchase are automatically included for pricing in the index—house, automobile, radio, TV, refrigerator. But smaller items have to be selected to represent the group in which they belong. Thus, meat must be represented by the full weight of meat expenditures in the average family's budget for the year, although the meats actually priced for the index consist of nine items of beef and veal, six items of pork, and six items of other meats (lamb, frankfurters, cold cuts, etc.). So it is with fruits and vegetables, canned goods, apparel, etc. Altogether, about 400 items are priced for the index, and these are selected to represent the price behavior of the thousands of goods and services that are bought each year.

The conversion into a mathematical index of all these thousands of prices of hundreds of items from nearly three-score cities is a massive job, for which a computer is used. But the calculation process each month requires only simple arithmetic. In order to guard against mistakes, the BLS price staff makes the monthly calculation twice, each time with a different set of statisticians.

The Bureau has printed a leaflet with simple illustrations to show the way the index is constructed. Called *The Consumer Price Index: A Short Description,* it is obtainable free on request from the Bureau of Labor Statistics.

USES OF THE CONSUMER PRICE INDEX

What does the index look like over a period of years? Chart VII shows the behavior of the index for the decade 1957–67. In this chart, we can trace the remarkable stability of 1958–64, and, finally, the latest rise, 1965–67. In addition, the chart shows the fluctuations of the food index as contrasted with the steady and persistent rise in the prices of services. Durable consumer items, such as household appliances and automobiles, are not much higher today than they were ten years ago. One reason is that these items are produced by manufacturing industries, in which automation and other labor-saving devices have been widely adopted and installed. The services require large amounts of personal service (labor) and are not as sus-

Chart VII

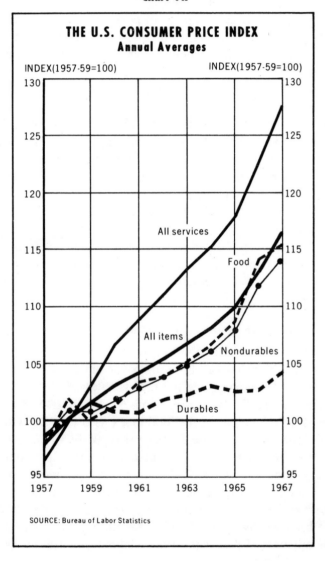

SOURCE: Bureau of Labor Statistics

ceptible to mechanization, although there are exceptions to this general rule.

The Consumer Price Index is one of the most widely used sets of statistics in the world. It enters into practically every collective-bargaining negotiation between employers and unions, which means about 16 million organized employees. It is currently used in wage escalation contracts for as many as 3 million employees. Employers without unions often use it in raising the wages and salaries of their employees. In the federal government, the civil service retirement annuities and military pensions are tied to the index. Many private industry contracts for rents and supplies are based on it. In 1951, the House Committee on Education and Labor called it a "Billion Dollar Index" because so much money changed hands on a movement of one point in the index. In its report, the Committee commented that

> The economic implications are staggering; the load or responsibility carried by that one figure is also staggering. Few factors in labor-management relations or in government policy affecting labor and management today are as important as the Consumer Price Index.

Then, too, the index is used by the government statistical agencies as a deflator in the national accounts; that is, it is used to convert certain output figures for the economy, expressed in current dollars, into real output with price changes eliminated. The index is widely used as a guide to the government's economic policies to maintain stability and economic growth. In the years ahead, it will continue to be one of the most vital statistical measures.

WHOLESALE PRICE INDEX

Although the Wholesale Price Index is not nearly as well known as the Consumer Price Index, it too is of vital importance to the American economy. As indicated earlier, it had its origin in congressional interest in tariffs and international trade in the last quarter of the nineteenth century, and, in the beginning, was confined to raw materials and simpler manufactured goods. The prices are those in primary markets, that is, in the markets where the first selling transaction occurs— cattle at Chicago or Omaha, wheat at Minneapolis, automobiles at Detroit, and so on.

In the days before World War I a number of public and private agencies were collecting and publishing wholesale prices, and there was considerable variation in the results. In 1914, Commissioner of Labor Statistics Royal Meeker obtained the services of Wesley C. Mitchell of Columbia University to survey and evaluate the Bureau's price index in relation to the other indexes. Mitchell's survey has been a classic in the history of index numbers. His preliminary report was published in 1914, and after World War I a revised and more complete analysis was published in 1922 (BLS Bulletin No. 284).

Mitchell made at least two significant findings. The first was that the Bureau's methodology was sound in principle. He endorsed its simple aggregative method, although he recommended some improvements in detail. Second, he emphasized that an index must be evaluated in the light of its purposes and objectives. He found that one of the private indexes was more prompt than the BLS index in detecting shifts in business conditions. However, the more comprehensive BLS index provided a more accurate picture of longer term trends.

The Wholesale Price Index received a lot of attention in the 1920's, particularly with respect to farm prices and raw material prices, which fell to disastrously low levels in the deflation of 1921. In 1926, the BLS revised and improved the index on a then current base, but it was scarcely well established when the 1930's brought another catastrophic deflation, requiring another revision. This was accomplished in the late 1930's at about the same time as the CPI, although the WPI received very little publicity. However, some sector- and industry-group indexes came into favor for escalation purposes, especially in contracts between the government and private firms and in private firms purchasing raw materials from suppliers. In the early 1950's, when the CPI was revised, the WPI was also, and it was widely used for price control in the Korean War.

Revisions of this index are dependent on the dates chosen for the Census of Manufactures and the Census of Business, for these provide the output and sales data necessary to determine the relative weights for the commodities and commodity groups in the index. A comprehensive revision was carried out in 1952 and the index reconstructed back to 1947. Since then, the weights have been changed four times, and the sample of products has been increased, so that by 1967 the index contained over 2,300 products based on data from nearly 7,000 monthly reports.

The chief issue that arose around this index in the 1950's concerned its service, similar to that of the CPI, as a deflator of the national accounts used by the government statistical agencies to show real national output. The output statistics for manufacturing industries were particularly brought into question. Originally, the index had been structured to get prices by stages of production—farm products, raw materials, semifinished products, and finished products. The selection of products to be priced and the weighting system were geared to construct such component indexes. Although this system sometimes yielded prices and weights sufficiently representative to construct a good index for a particular industry, such a result was incidental and occasional. Getting good industry indexes required industry weights and more representative industry products, which in turn meant more resources for collecting industry prices. In the 1960's, the Bureau succeeded in obtaining some funds, enough to publish price indexes for about sixty-seven industries, but its program calls for about 525—a number still far from being reached.

One criticism of the Wholesale Price Index is that the price reports are collected by mail from the sellers and reflect, therefore, mostly list prices rather than actual prices paid by the buyers. The BLS is fully aware of this problem and has tried to deal with it. The Bureau staff tries to establish agreement on the price-reporting requirements with industry and firm representatives. On every report form there is a notation requesting that note be made of any price concessions or price extras that modify the list price up or down. However, the Bureau staff concedes that reporters often do not comply with this request. The result is that the index tends to be more sluggish and less responsive to price changes than it should be. In prosperity, the index and its subindexes lag behind the price increases that are occurring. In business recessions, prices fall sooner and more than the indexes reveal.

Analyses have shown that in comparable years across the business cycle the trends disclosed by the WPI are about right. This long-run accuracy is what Mitchell pointed out half a century ago, and it holds true. But one of the major objectives of the federal government is to maintain stability and to avoid extremes of prosperity and depression. For this purpose, there is need for more sensitive measures of price changes, providing quicker leads on what is happening to the economy in one of its most sensitive areas, namely, prices. In the last few years, the Bureau has proposed that funds be provided to enable it to collect prices from buyers as well as from sellers—the buyer being able to record what he actually paid. A number of the larger manufacturing concerns maintain indexes of the prices they pay for significant supplies and materials.

There is a precedent for this kind of figure in the Consumer Price Index. Before World War II, the BLS used to collect statistics on rents by going to apartment managers. A single visit could yield ten, twenty, fifty, or more rent figures. But when rent controls were imposed in World War II, there was an outcry that landlords were not reporting the extras they were getting for apartments. So, at considerable expense, the Bureau shifted to a system of collecting rent figures from the tenants. That system has been continued in the CPI ever since.

In wholesale price investigation, as in consumer, it would require more personnel and travel funds to get buyers' prices on a scale sufficient to construct indexes. The initial proposal of the Bureau asked only enough money to run a series of checks to see to what extent the sellers' prices in the present index fall short of a reasonable standard of accuracy. But even this appeal for funds was not successful.

In terms of contractual use in the American economy, the WPI is possibly even more potent than the CPI. In the 1950's, when the Bureau was revising the WPI, the staff became keenly aware of the billions of dollars in contracts escalated in accordance with the WPI or one of its constituent indexes. It was estimated at that time that many more billions of dollars in escalations were based on the WPI than on the CPI. For many years, practically all contracts between the Navy and the private shipyards for the construction of ships were escalated in relation to the wholesale price of metal products and the hourly earnings of metal-working employees (another BLS statistic). The Department of Defense continues to employ segments of the WPI in escalating long-term purchase contracts for certain military vehicles. Within private industry itself, some concerns sign escalation contracts on all the supplies they buy.

Unlike the CPI, which includes consumer services, the WPI does not include business services, such as advertising, management, research, legal assistance, and insurance. Nor does it include transportation costs, such as rail, truck, sea, and air shipping rates. Even within the field of commodities (goods), there are no satisfactory indexes of construction costs. Building materials are included, of course, but not the completed commercial buildings (although the CPI does include prices of houses).

GOVERNMENT PRICES ARE NOT INDEXED

Another important set of price data is the purchase of goods by federal, state, and local governments. In 1967, total government purchases of goods plus services amounted to $176 billion—$90 billion, federal; and $86 billion, state and local. Nearly half of that total goes for compensation of employees, military and civilian; another large segment goes for costs of structures such as roads, schools, and office buildings. But there remains perhaps $60 billion for purchases of goods.

Occasionally, especially in wartime, efforts have been made to establish a regular pricing system, so that indexes could be constructed for various classes of government purchases. Such indexes would be useful in rounding out the price picture for the total economy. They would also serve to improve the price deflator used in the national accounts to convert the dollar product of the U.S. economy into real product.

UNPRICED FOREIGN TRADE

Still another important unpriced segment of the economy is foreign trade. The current crisis in the U.S. balance of payments has emphasized once more the crucial importance of the surplus of exports over imports. Criticism is raised that American business is pricing itself out of world markets. However, we do not really know the price trends in our export markets, nor the comparison with the prices we are paying for imports. There are no solidly reliable indexes of export and import prices. For several years, the Bureau has studied this problem. With the National Bureau of Economic Research contributing some staff and other resources to a joint study of the technical difficulties; a method of constructing export and import price indexes has been worked out. But it has not been possible to obtain government funds to carry on the work.

Prices are the key to the successful operation of a free enterprise economy. We have heard in recent years that the Communist nations are waking up to the fact that government price-fixing in a controlled economy is wasteful and inefficient in competition with the flexibility and efficiency of the price system. The United States has perhaps the best price statistics in the world. However, these are still not adequate to the fluctuations and needs of the American economy.

LEVELS AND STANDARDS OF LIVING: EXPENDITURE SURVEYS

The Consumer Price Index is designed to measure the effect of price changes upon the cost of living for the average index family. It does not show the level at which the family is actually living, nor the standard of living that the family sets for itself, nor the level the government may establish for social objectives. When we say that a family is living in poverty, we imply that there is some measure to define the poverty line. When a state minimum-wage board establishes a legal minimum wage for a single working woman it often uses as a guide the budget that would be required to maintain a minimum standard of health and decency, as determined by a study of living requirements.

The levels at which families are actually living can be discovered by making consumer-expenditure surveys of a representative sample of consumer units—families, or single individuals. Such surveys have been conducted in the United States and many foreign countries for the past century. The first expenditure survey in the United States was made in 1875 in Massachusetts by Carroll D. Wright, chief of the state bureau. Wright made a thorough survey of family cost of living, including a full investigation of the sources of income, an analysis of expenditures for the various items bought by the family, and a measurement of the surplus or deficit.

The Massachusetts bureau had been making studies on wage rates and workers' earnings in Massachusetts industries. The 1875 expenditure study was designed to show the living conditions of Massachusetts workers in comparison with those in other states and in foreign countries. Wright concluded that the levels of living were higher for workers in the United States than they were in Western European countries.

When Wright became the U.S. Commissioner of Labor, he undertook in 1888 the first nation-wide survey, which he conducted on the same lines as his 1875 study. In those days, U.S. policy was to maintain high tariff rates in order to protect the high wages of American workers from foreign competition. Wright studied consumption habits and living costs as factors in the cost of production of American manufactured goods. He pointed out that an "essential element in the cost of production and in the efficiency of the labor employed is the cost of living."

The 1917–19 consumer expenditure survey included the objective "of enabling the BLS to compute a cost of living index number." A study of the patterns of family buying was necessary in order to select the items to be priced for the index and to determine the weight, or relative importance, of each item in the average family's budget. That survey also had several other objectives, two of which are significant for our consideration:

> (1) working out, if possible, standards—similar to the recognized dietary standards—for clothing, housing, fuel, house furnishings, education, amusement, medical care, insurance and perhaps some other items, and (2) formulating eventually tentative standard budgets to be used by wage adjustment boards in determining minimum and fair wage awards.

The survey was conducted between August, 1917, and February 1919. About 12,000 families were surveyed in ninety-two cities in forty-two states. The families selected were headed by wage-earners or salaried clerical workers. Information was obtained on family income and expenditures for a period of a year. On the basis of weights derived from these studies, indexes were calculated for thirty-two cities, with an over-all U.S. index derived from the city indexes.

When the Committee on Government Statistics and Information Services reviewed the price index in 1933, it recommended a major revision on the ground that the spending patterns of workers and their families had changed substantially in the fifteen years since the end of World War I. That expenditure survey was conducted during the years 1934–36. At the same time a comparable study of consumer purchases of all segments of the population was conducted by the BLS in cooperation with four other federal agencies wanting to obtain detailed consumption data for analytical and policy-making purposes.

During World War II, the BLS found it necessary to conduct two nation-wide expenditure surveys—one (1941) including rural areas, the other (1944) for urban areas only—in order to obtain data for the consideration of wartime economic policies. Then, in the last year of the war came the Bureau proposal to make a series of consumer-expenditure surveys in several cities each year, thus providing an annual appraisal of changes in family buying patterns. Between 1945 and 1950, surveys of this type were conducted in thirteen metropolitan areas.

STANDARD BUDGETS

In 1945, the House Appropriations Committee, concerned about the wartime controversy over intercity differences in living costs and dissatisfied with the information available to establish a sound program of income tax exemptions, directed the Bureau to prepare a standard budget, measuring in dollars and cents what it cost a family to live in the large cities of the United States.

In taking this step, Congress was not stepping out into no-man's-land. The first budgets of this kind had been developed nearly forty years previously by the Bureau as one phase of an investigation, authorized by Congress in 1907, of the living conditions of women and children working in cotton mills. The Bureau had at that time defined two levels of living— "minimum" and "fair." It is of interest to note that the size of the family selected for the budget was five persons.

As a result of the expenditure surveys of 1917–19, the Bureau was requested by the congressional Joint Commission on Reclassification of Salaries to prepare a budget for government employees in Washington, D.C. At about the same time (1919–20), the National Industrial Conference Board, a private research organization, prepared for a number of cities two levels of budgets for a "minimum" and a "more liberal" standard of living. In 1923, the Heller Committee for Research in Social Economics at the University of California (Berkeley) developed budgets for workers in San Francisco. The Heller budgets were prepared and priced periodically for about forty years for two groups of workers—wage-earners and salaried workers. (These budgets were discontinued in the early 1960's.)

During the Great Depression of the 1930's, public and private welfare agencies were faced with the problem of how to stretch their grossly inadequate funds over the millions of unemployed families seeking relief. They experimented with breadlines, commissaries, and food orders to insure that no one would starve. Next, they found it necessary to pay rents in order to provide housing and, eventually, they had to make provisions for clothing, shoes, and household supplies. These needs finally led to what were called "emergency" budgets— enough for bare subsistence on a strictly temporary basis—developed by the Works Progress Administration and priced by BLS.

When the government relief-work programs were started, WPA Administrator Harry Hopkins decided that the workers should be paid sufficient wages to maintain their families on a continuing basis. For that purpose, the WPA developed a "maintenance" budget, which was above bare subsistence but considerably below a satisfactory standard of living for workers and their families.

Such was the budget history and experience at the disposal of Congress and the BLS when the Bureau was directed to prepare an adequate budget for a decent standard of living in 1946. This was a tough problem. The Bureau was faced with the necessity of discovering or devising objective standards for the consumption of the major items and item groups in the selected family's budget.

The first step was to determine what size and composition of family should be selected for the study. The decline in birth rates during the Depression of the 1930's led to the selection of four persons rather than five as a typical family. The BLS selected a family consisting of a man thirty-eight years of age, a wife somewhat younger, and two children—a boy of thirteen and a girl of eight.

For some consumption items, there were objective standards already recognized. With respect to food, scientific findings by the Food and Nutrition Board of the National Research Council on the quantities of calories and vitamins necessary for adequate nutrition had established a standard. But a problem remained. The prescribed levels of calories and nutrients could be obtained by using many varieties and combinations of foods, with a wide range of costs. Should the standard use steak or hamburger? The Bureau made the decision by arranging the foods eaten by families in a scale, according to the calories and nutrients they provided. The quantities of foods included in the budget were determined at the point in the scale of diets where the consumption of calories and nutrients agreed most closely with the National Research Council's allowances.

Housing standards had been established by the American

Public Health Association and the U.S. Public Housing Administration—one room per person (four or five rooms for a family of four), indoor plumbing, certain standards of equipment, etc. It was then necessary to find the rental costs to families having that standard of housing.

With respect to the remaining items in the family budget, there were no formally adopted standards on which the Bureau could rely. It had to develop its own objective standards. Through analyses of family spending at various levels of living, the Bureau's staff concluded that there was a general principle that could be applied to these items of family spending: When a family has what it considers an insufficient amount of an item, such as clothing, the Bureau found, an increase in income will result in a more than proportionate increase in spending on that item; at some point, however, further additions to income result in less than proportionate clothing expenditures. The Bureau established the standard quantities at the point where the increase in rate of expenditure tipped over into a declining rate of spending in relation to rising income. That was considered to be the point at which a necessity (for that family) moved into the luxury category.

When all items in the budget had been selected and their quantities determined, the next step was to price the budget in retail markets. The budget was priced in the thirty-four cities for which there were consumer price indexes. This choice of cities was based upon the economies that could be achieved by using the prices already collected for the price indexes. Some additional pricing was necessary in each city, but that was a small cost in comparison with the complete pricing required in a city outside the index.

One final step had to be taken in order to determine the income necessary to provide that consumption budget. Income taxes had to be paid (above the $2,400 exemption for a family of four), and those taxes had to be provided for in the total income required for the budget. The Bureau repriced the budget several times in the next few years, but discontinued it in 1951 when the list of goods and services and the quantities became patently out of date.

The 1950 expenditure surveys for price index revision opened up a new opportunity for a revision of the standard budget, but delays of various kinds held up the project. The budget, as of 1959 prices was finally issued in the summer of 1960. In general, the procedures used to construct the revised budget were similar to those for the original budget. For the food component, however, the U.S. Department of Agriculture had translated the National Research Council's allowances into several different food plans based on the choices made by families with different amounts of money to spend for food. BLS used an average of the Department of Agriculture "low-cost" and "moderate-cost" food plans for its revised budget. This budget was priced only once, in twenty large cities.

Following the 1960–61 consumer expenditure surveys, the BLS launched a more comprehensive program of budget studies. The design was for three levels of standard budgets—a medium or moderate standard corresponding to the previous one-level BLS budgets and two other levels, one lower and one higher. The moderate standard budget for the classical four-person family was issued to the public in October, 1967, at autumn, 1966, prices. It provided information on costs for thirty-nine metropolitan areas and four regional averages for families living in nonmetropolitan areas (less than 50,000 population each). These are broad regions—Northeast, South, North Central, and West. The Bureau also published a U.S. urban average family budget ($9,191), a metropolitan average ($9,376), and a nonmetropolitan average ($8,366).

The incomes required to provide this budget standard are higher in the larger cities, generally more moderate in the medium-sized cities, and lowest in the nonmetropolitan areas (small towns). Likewise, the costs of that standard are higher in the North and West than they are in the South.

One other point is vitally important. When these budget costs are compared to those in the same cities in 1959, the increase in general is about 50 per cent. But this increase consists of two factors: One is the rise in the cost of living, that is, in the cost of an identical budget over this period; the other is the rise in the standard itself. As the economic well-being of the American people improves, their standards rise too. The luxury of one generation (television being a good example) becomes the necessity of the next. While the 1959 standard housing budget was based only on rental costs, the 1966 budget introduced home ownership in the degree (75 per cent) that it existed among budget families residing in urban areas. Home ownership makes a big difference—in New York a home owner would require about $1,500 more income than a renter in order to sustain his standard. Further, the progressive character of the U.S. income tax means that, as incomes rise, taxes rise more than proportionately. Also, food costs in the new budget were based on the Department of Agriculture moderate-cost food plan alone, instead of an average of the low- and moderate-cost plans as in the 1959 budget. The higher income requirements recorded in the 1966 study are influenced substantially by these three factors. The Consumer Price Index, which is designed to measure the cost of a fixed market basket of goods and services, rose only about 15 per cent between 1959 and 1966. Thus, it can be seen that rising living standards are primarily responsible for the rise in the cost of the 1966 standard budget as compared to the previous one.

In addition, the Bureau stated:

The budget total should not be compared directly with general levels of industrial wages and wage rates or with average income of all urban families. . . . The level of living represented by the budget is not "minimum" in the sense in which that term is used in relation to standards or goals for public assistance or welfare programs. On the other hand, the standard of living represented by the items and quantities included in the moderate budget is below that enjoyed by a majority of American families of this specific type.

In addition to the moderate budget, the Bureau plans to produce two others, one lower and one higher. The lower will represent minimum adequacy. It will adjust downward some of the quantities and qualities in the moderate budget, while providing for the family's health and self-respect. This minimum budget could be used for establishing goals or evaluating needs in public assistance or income maintenance programs.

The higher standard is somewhat more difficult to define precisely. In the Bureau's own words, it "will reflect a more comfortable level and manner of living sometimes known as the 'American standard of living.' " It could be used to determine the ability of the family to pay for medical and other services or to pay for their children's higher education.

The BLS will also publish in 1968 a retired couple's budget, for a comparable moderate standard, at autumn, 1966, prices. It will include data on home-owner costs, such as taxes, insurance, maintenance, and repair. However, for the retired couple, the home is assumed to be mortgage free, since studies have shown this to be the case for a substantial majority of such couples. This budget will also determine a lower minimum level useful for welfare administration, as well as a higher one based on fully adequate living conditions for a retired couple.

In the spring of 1967, the BLS again priced both the four-person and the retired couple's budgets, to provide a more current set of cost estimates. These budgets will play an important role in helping to determine future U.S. Government policies and practices in the social security, welfare, and poverty fields.

V

Wages and Salaries

The British and American armies, advancing up the Italian peninsula in World War II, finally captured Rome. The Italian civilian workers who had been employed by the German Army were now hired by the Allies. The economic advisers to the Allied Commander-in-Chief, Field Marshal Alexander, had proposed a pay scale for the Italians designed to prevent inflation in a war economy. But one of the labor advisers in the American Army, Colonel Tom Lane, an official in the Department of Labor's Bureau of Employment Security before the war, was so disturbed by the proposal that he fought his way up through the military hierarchy in Italy to the very top with the proposition that "the Allies can't possibly set a wage scale lower than the Germans were paying; we must raise wages." Tom won, and the favorable image of the Allies with the Italian workers was insured for the duration of the war—and long afterward, too.

I cite this as an example of the vital importance of pay scales to all workers in the labor force. The high cost of living may exasperate a worker (or, more likely, his wife), but lowered wages are anathema. To an economist, it is evident that excessively high wages can stimulate inflation or generate a business recession. But it is an article of faith among workers that wage increases are always an unmixed blessing while wage cuts are always an unmitigated evil. In addition, practically every worker believes that he is worth more than he is being paid. (Have you ever met a man who admitted that he was being paid more than he was worth?) Finally, workers watch with an eagle-eye what others are getting. "Why is he getting more money than I am, when we are doing the same work?" they ask. Or the union will argue, "Our skill is just as high as theirs. We are entitled to the same pay."

Thus, the wage or salary that a worker is paid is the dominant factor in his appraisal of his job. And, for this reason, wages constitute the foundation of all labor statistics. Other data, such as the cost of living or productivity, acquire part of their value from their usefulness in comparison with wages.

In the first several decades of the Bureau's existence, the collection and dissemination of wage data was the largest and most important feature of the Bureau's work. In 1888–90 Carroll D. Wright, the U.S. Commissioner of Labor, conducted a series of industry wage surveys designed to determine production costs in industries affected by international trade. These studies were an outgrowth of congressional inquiries into import tariffs. The prevailing doctrine at that time was that high tariffs were necessary to equalize the high labor costs caused by high wages in the United States with the low labor costs derived from low wages in foreign countries. In 1900, the Commissioner issued a comprehensive report, *Wages in Commercial Countries,* which covered nearly all the states and territories in the United States as well as in about 100 foreign countries, colonies, and provinces. But he made no attempt to analyze or interpret the results—"a work of reference," he called it. The data were all derived from secondary sources. Then, in 1901, the Commissioner launched an original fact-finding investigation of his own into wages and prices in American industries. He published statistical tables on wages and hours of work for sixty-seven industries. Since the study took three years to complete, it was chiefly of historical value, although the Commissioner indicated his intention of producing such industry wage statistics at regular intervals in the future.

The first repetitive annual surveys of wage rates were the surveys inaugurated in 1907 of union scales of wages and hours in the construction and printing industries. Since these were collectively bargained scales in individual communities, they generally remained fixed for the bargaining year, and they could be obtained from the local union officials by Bureau agents visiting union headquarters. Data were obtained for journeymen, helpers, and laborers in each craft. Also, since these scales were used for bargaining locally, the published data related to individual communities—sixty-eight in 1967. These union scale surveys cover building construction, printing, local transit, and local trucking.

In 1947, the Bureau of Labor Statistics shifted to a system of statistics-collection by mail instead of by Bureau agents over the country. However, personal visits are still made to question locals that have failed to respond, to make quality checks on the data reported, and to visit each respondent at least once in five years.

The reporting date is July 1, which is in the middle of the year. A majority of the contracts in these industries are negotiated in the first half of the year. However, July 1 makes a good midpoint of the year for trend purposes, and in recent years, the Bureau has collected and published quarterly data on union wage scales in the building trades, so up-to-date information is always readily available for the construction industry.

INDUSTRY SURVEYS

The emphasis on union wage-scale surveys in the wage program of the BLS was due to the character of the labor movement in the first three decades of the twentieth century. Organization of workers proceeded along craft lines, and the strength of the unions was in the locals. The union scale surveys provided a collective-bargaining service to both labor and management. But the large manufacturing industries were largely or wholly unorganized. Their wage structures were primarily of general public and governmental interest. Industrywide wage surveys were made only at longer intervals, sometimes only occasionally.

In World War I, the War Industries Board commissioned the BLS to make more comprehensive surveys of industry wage rates by states and to some extent by major cities. The Board needed these data for its own guidance in making decisions on labor disputes during the war. In the 1920's, the importance of wage data for key industries became more widely recognized. Coal was a major industry, only partially organized, in which each renegotiation became a matter of public concern. Textiles was another example of an industry torn by union versus nonunion competition. Steel, then as now considered a bellwether of the economy, was important as a wage leader. Industry wage studies of these and similar industries were conducted during the 1920's.

But the major push to amass wage data took place in the 1930's. The passage of the National Industrial Recovery Act in the spring of 1933 set the stage. The National Recovery Administration (NRA) attempted to get industries to establish voluntary codes of fair practice limiting hours of work and establishing minimum wages. Since these codes were on an industry basis, the industry became the unit of administration. Wherever unions had a foothold in the industry, they were drawn into the negotiations on the codes.

Eventually the Supreme Court declared the NRA unconstitutional, but in the meantime Congress had passed the Wagner Act (1935), which made collective bargaining a national policy. One result was the successful organization of large industrial unions (as distinct from occupational craft unions), which in turn created a demand for industry wage surveys by these new unions, mostly belonging to what was then called the Committee for Industrial Organization and later became the Congress of Industrial Organizations (CIO).

FEDERAL WAGE LAWS

Another type of legislation that created statistical work for the Bureau of Labor Statistics was the enactment by Congress of federal minimum-wage laws, mentioned in Chapter I. These were of three types. One was the Davis-Bacon Act, which provided that contractors engaged in federally supported public construction must pay their workers the prevailing wages in the locality where the construction was taking place. Since construction wages were then, and are still, highly localized, the U.S. Department of Labor administered this act by holding local public hearings and basing its decisions on them. The second was the Walsh-Healy Act, which provided that contractors supplying goods to the federal government were required to pay minimum wages established by the Secretary of Labor. Since such contractors might be located anywhere in the country, it was thought necessary to develop wage statistics upon which decisions could be based. The Secretary selected the Bureau of Labor Statistics to make the necessary studies. Then, in 1938, Congress passed the Fair Labor Standards Act, which established minimum wages for certain kinds of business engaged in interstate commerce. This act, too, required statistical surveys to assist the Secretary of Labor in making recommendations to Congress for changes in this legislative minimum. Again, the Bureau of Labor Statistics was designated to make the studies.

World War II brought a further expansion of wage work to serve the needs of the War Labor Board in its administration of wage controls. But the disastrous cut in budget that the BLS suffered in the first post–World War II years scuttled the program. The Bureau could make industry wage surveys only when it could scrape up the funds.

However, the outbreak in Korea made extensive industry-wide data on hours and earnings seem very important once again. The BLS was provided with funds to extend its coverage to many more industries. Eventually, the Bureau was able to put the industry program on a recurring basis. In recent years, the Bureau has surveyed about fifty manufacturing industries and about twenty nonmanufacturing industries. The majority of all these are on a cycle of five years, but some of the low-wage industries are surveyed every three years.

COMMUNITY WAGE SURVEYS

During World War II, the BLS had been supported by the War Labor Board in a program of locality, or community wage surveys of occupations in a number of industries. These were cross-industry occupations in both manufacturing and nonmanufacturing industries. For blue-collar workers, they included carpenters, electricians, machinists, sheet-metal workers, tool and diemakers, truck drivers, janitors, guards, and others. Among office employees were clerks, stenographers, bookkeeping-machine operators, tabulating-machine operators, receptionists, and so on. In the postwar period, however, these community wage surveys were cut back from seventy-five cities to twenty.

In 1948, the Bureau of the Budget injected a new idea into this program. For about a quarter of a century (dating back to 1920), the Army and Navy departments had used a system of wage boards for determining the wages to be paid by government establishments—navy yards, arsenals, air fields—based on the principle that the military should pay its civilian craftsmen and laborers the prevailing rates in private industry in that locality. To do this, it was necessary for the boards to make surveys of wages among local employers. The Bureau of the Budget proposed that the BLS become the collecting agency for the wage boards in all localities where BLS was making its own surveys, thereby making it possible for one collection to serve two or more purposes. This step saved the time and patience of employers and insured collection by an experienced research staff. (The BLS had nothing whatever to do with the wage-setting, which was done by the wage boards.)

The success of the federal government's policy of using the BLS as the survey agency for these wage boards attracted the attention of many state and local government agencies with similar responsibilities. State civil service commissions, municipal personnel boards, city school districts, and other agencies with wage-determining functions asked to participate in the BLS cooperative program. In some communities such as San Francisco, as many as a dozen federal, state, and local agencies now use the BLS as the collecting agency for wage and salary data. Of course, they make their own wage determinations.

A further development occurred later in the 1950's. Although the federal government had adopted a clean-cut principle for wage-setting for its blue-collar workers in government establishments, it had no such principle for its white-collar office workers. The salaries in civil service and post office occupations were fixed periodically by congressional legislation without any firmly established policy. The most frequent reference was to increases in the cost of living. But when living costs became more stable, the case for pay increases for government workers became cloudy. In the late 1950's, the Bureau of the Budget proposed that BLS should undertake to enlarge its sample of community wage cities, as well as its list of occupations, in order to provide more data on white-collar salaries throughout the country.

The Budget Bureau's special interest was in finding out whether the wage and salary information collected by BLS in the community surveys could be used in the adjustment of federal civil service pay scales from year to year. When the checks and tests showed that they could be used, the Budget Bureau supported a BLS proposal for a comprehensive program of surveys representing all metropolitan areas in the United States.

For this new and enlarged wage program, the Bureau selected eighty-two metropolitan areas, as defined by the Bureau of the Census, out of a total of 188 that had been designated on the basis of 1960 population. All the largest areas (with more than 1 million population) were selected, together with samples of medium-sized and smaller areas. The selection was made in such a way as to insure that the data for the eighty-two would be equally representative of the 188.

The Bureau's area wage-survey program now regularly comprises eighty-five standard metropolitan statistical areas. Individual reports are issued for each of these areas, and when appropriately weighted, the eighty-five represent all standard metropolitan areas in the conterminous United States—227 in 1967.

In addition, the Bureau conducts similar surveys in an additional eighty-five areas—mostly metropolitan, but including some nonmetropolitan as well. These surveys are made at the request of the Wage and Hour and Public Contracts Divisions of the Department of Labor for use in their administration of the McNamara-O'Hara Service Contract Act of 1965.* Individual reports for each of these areas are published by the BLS, but the results are not incorporated in the Bureau's regular program.

The Bureau's own program serves two functions: First, the long-established local wage reports are used by labor and management for collective-bargaining and wage-setting purposes; second, the enlarged program of private industry wage and salary surveys provides data for use as guides in establishing federal pay scales.

* Public Law 89-286 provides labor standards for certain persons employed by federal contractors furnishing services to federal agencies. The Secretary of Labor is required to establish minimum wage rates based upon prevailing rates in the locality, but not lower than the rates in the federal Fair Labor Standards Act.

This program has worked so well that, in 1962, Congress passed an act establishing the equal pay principle for federal civil service employees and designated the Bureau of Labor Statistics as the agency to make these new wage and salary surveys.

CIVIL SERVICE PAY SCALES

A special salary survey was required to provide information for the higher grade levels in the federal service, which included professional, administrative, and technical occupations —accountant, attorney, auditor, engineer, chemist, and a long list of others. The purpose of this survey was to find salaries in private industry that corresponded to those for the federal civil service grades GS-7 through GS-15. For this salary survey, only firms with 250 or more employees were selected, since smaller establishments might not have comparable positions.

The National Survey of Professional, Administrative, Technical, and Clerical Pay, as it was called, has become the key to the annual congressional review of federal pay scales. The BLS makes the special survey in February and March of each year, while the clerical studies in the local communities are conducted at various times from September through June of each year. Since wages and salaries in these communities are changing all the time, the effect of the Bureau's timing of the clerical studies is to make the national survey approximate the timing of the special salary survey (February and March). The information from both surveys is made available to the Congress by September, so that action can be taken at the next session beginning in January. The Commissioner of Labor Statistics regularly appears to testify before the House Post Office and Civil Service Committee on the Bureau's findings.

Despite the success of the BLS studies and the high popularity of the pay principle among federal employees, the course of this program has not always run smoothly. It has been proposed that the President be delegated authority to make annual salary adjustments by executive order, without congressional review. But the House Post Office and Civil Service Committee have shown no signs of giving up their prerogative of adjusting government pay. Despite the headaches of pressures and persuasion, congressmen prefer to make their own decisions on pay scales.

A second issue of continuing concern in civil service scales is the lag problem. No matter how much the procedures have been speeded up, Congress has invariably been in the position of taking action on data a year or more behind current wage and salary statistics. Federal employees have argued that they can never achieve full comparability because they are always one year behind. On one occasion at a congressional hearing some years ago, the Commissioner was asked whether he could project the results of last year's survey into the current year, which he was reluctant to do. However, in 1967, steps were taken to change the dates of the survey and to speed up the processing. The salary survey was taken over the spring and summer (March to September), and the clerical salaries obtained in the eighty-five community surveys were updated at the same time, so that mid-1967 data could be made available to Congress by January. The 1967 pay increase was made effective on October 1, with provision for a partial catch-up (incorporating the results of the BLS 1967 survey) in April, 1968, and full comparability in 1969.

GOVERNMENT PRINTING OFFICE: A CASE IN POINT

It has been noted earlier in these pages that whenever research and statistics have been needed to solve a critical labor problem, government action has been taken to develop them. But there is another equally observable fact: Whenever good statistical data are available, they will be called into use. For example, in the federal structure, Congress is responsible for the budget and operations of the Government Printing Office (GPO), which prints all government publications. It operates like a public corporation, charging the government agencies for the original printing costs and covering its additional costs from the sale of publications to the public.

In the early 1920's, Congress passed an act specifying that the wages paid to employees in the GPO should be negotiated once a year by the Public Printer with the employee organizations. In general, the bases for such negotiations were the wage scales in the private printing industry in Washington, D.C. In 1948, a quarter of a century later, one of the unions proposed as an alternative a statistical formula derived from BLS data. The Public Printer and the other unions accepted the proposal, which was approved by the congressional Joint Committee on Printing. Since 1948, the procedure has been that the Public Printer shall obtain from the BLS the weighted statistical average of the pay rates of each craft in the twenty-five largest cities in the United States. The average rate in each city is weighted by the number of journeymen on the union rolls in that city.

Every year, the Public Printer writes a letter to the Commissioner of Labor Statistics requesting this information, and a few weeks later the Commissioner replies with the exact national average (to three places, in cents and mills) for each occupation. A corresponding letter is sent by the Commissioner to the head of each union. When the Printer and the unions bargain, they have before them the identical BLS wage rates data. This is one case in which wage rates are determined by a statistical formula, and it is one of the many little-known services of the BLS.

HOURLY AND WEEKLY EARNINGS

Wages and *earnings* are often used interchangeably. In economic literature, *wages* means wage rates, that is, the rate of pay per hour, per week, per month, and even per year. *Earnings* refers to the amounts actually received, which may be more or less than the rates. For example, a worker's rate of pay might be $2 an hour or $80 a week, but his weekly earnings might be $100 because he worked overtime or $48 because he worked only three days.

Nevertheless, industry statistics of hourly or weekly earnings are often used in economic analysis as rough approximations of wage changes over a period of time. The advantage is that earnings data are widely and currently available. Employment and payroll reporting by employers provides continuing monthly statistics on average hourly earnings of production workers in several hundred industries. These data come from the monthly reports of about 150,000 employers, and they represent the earnings of more than 25 million workers. The main limitations of the earnings data are, first, that they are influenced by part-time and overtime work, and, second, that they reflect the structure of the work force—skilled and unskilled, men and women, full-time and part-time. Thus, average hourly earnings could rise because of more overtime at premium pay, or they could rise because some low-paid, unskilled workers were laid off, without any change in wage rates in either case.

But, the sheer volume of the data and the vast amount of detail available for industries, states, and local areas often overshadow the limitations. With caution, analysts can consider the hourly and weekly earnings over a period of years reasonably representative of trends in wages and salaries.

On the average, gross weekly earnings advance to new highs every year, although within the year there are dips mostly due to declines in working hours, with loss of premium pay for overtime. The first bite out of earnings is taken by withholding taxes, which reduce the gross earnings to net spendable earnings. The rise in the cost of living (represented by the Consumer Price Index) makes a further cut in the buying power of the weekly net spendable wage. Up to the end of 1965, a worker's real weekly wage was increasing, but during 1966–67 the wage gains were completely offset by taxes on the higher wages and by increases in prices. In 1968, the wage–price spiral is still working.

FRINGE BENEFITS

A century ago, cash was nearly exclusively used to pay wages. Karl Marx wrote bitterly of "the cash nexus" as the sole bond between men in modern industrial society. Cash was by no means as dominant as Marx said it was, but it was certainly the prevailing method of wage payment. Workers had to organize their own mutual aid programs to counter the risks of a growing, but fluctuating, economy. Many people today are not aware of the fact that our pervasive Social Security System began with the "people's friendly societies" in England. These were organizations of workers who contributed to a common fund used to meet the costs of sickness and death. American fraternal orders later performed similar functions for their members. The early trade unions also built their strength around the provision of various mutual benefits.

As union bargaining power increased during the first three decades of the twentieth century, employers were frequently pressured into contributing to joint funds for various forms of health and welfare. On their own initiative, some business concerns established pension plans for their employees. But many of these advances were snuffed out by the Great Depression of the 1930's. Others, such as the pension systems of the railroad companies, had to be converted into a government system to prevent widespread bankruptcy. At that same time, the Social Security Act established nation-wide government programs for old-age insurance and unemployment compensation, and a beginning was made (in four states) on a system of temporary disability or sickness insurance. In brief, the government stepped in to provide the nonwage benefits people needed.

World War II and its aftermath brought about a shift of emphasis and a change in trends. In the administration of wage controls during World War II (and again during the Korean

War), government policy was to restrict cash wage increases, which would have an immediate inflationary effect in wartime and to accept fringe benefits, which would come due in the more distant future. Contributing to this change was the attitude of Congress, which refused to raise social security contributions on schedule—a move that would have enabled the system to provide health and other benefits out of the trust fund. In consequence, those unions with greatly increased bargaining power were able to negotiate with their employers to provide the health and welfare benefits that otherwise probably would have become a feature of the government's social security program in the early postwar period.

In any case, what happened was that fringe benefits began to expand widely and rapidly. Cash wages became less representative of total pay, and their year-to-year changes were no longer a precise measure of changes in total labor costs to the employer. It became necessary to provide some statistical measure of those fringes.

In 1953, the BLS made an extensive experimental study to find out if employers could and would report their expenditures on these supplementary wage payments (as the BLS calls them). The test was a success, and a few years later the Bureau embarked on a continuing program of measurement on a three-year cycle—manufacturing industries every third year and two nonmanufacturing industries in the intervening years. In 1966, the program was revised to survey the total private nonagricultural economy every other year, with surveys of specific industries in the intervening years.

When the federal government adopted the comparability pay principle for its salaries, the issue of fringes came up in that connection. Many congressmen had the impression that government wage supplements were considerably more generous than those in private industry. The BLS was commissioned to make a special fringe-benefits study, which showed that in sum the costs of fringes were approximately the same, about

25 per cent of payroll, although there were some marked differences in detail. With respect to pensions and annual paid leave, the government was ahead, but in health, welfare, and other fringes, private industry was in the lead. The comparison may in time have the effect of bringing the private and public systems of fringe benefits closer together.

EQUAL PAY FOR MEN AND WOMEN

In many of the BLS surveys, separate data are collected and analyses made of men's wages as compared to women's, at least wherever there has been any significant overlapping of men and women workers. In a number of industries and occupations there is very little overlapping, and even where men and women work together, as in education, textiles, clothing manufacture, there is often a fairly well-established dividing line between men's and women's jobs.

To some degree, the statistical differentiation is due to the protective labor legislation for women that has gradually been adopted in the states over the past half century. At a time when the 12-hour day and the 72-hour week (alternating weeks of sixty and eighty-four hours) was fairly common for men employed in continuous process industries, legislation to protect women workers from such long hours made good economic sense. Protective laws were also applied to night work, weight-lifting, dangerous occupations, and so on. Beneficial legislation providing for lunch periods, rest periods, rest rooms, and other facilities for women was enacted.

While these laws provided much needed protection to women, they also had the effect of limiting women's opportunities for jobs and promotions. The women's departments in the factory shut down at the end of an 8-hour day, while the men stayed on the job to earn overtime pay at premium rates. Women could not be promoted to supervisor's jobs because their daily hours of work were limited by law. Women could not be employed on the second shift because they couldn't work after, say, 10:00 P.M. Some occupations were entirely barred to them, and others were restricted because women were not permitted to work in jobs requiring heavy weight-lifting. A second effect was that, in general, women received lower wage rates and lower earnings than men. Limited job opportunities kept down the wage rates, while limitations on overtime prevented the earning of premium pay.

Two recent pieces of federal legislation have created new problems in this field. Title VII of the Civil Rights Act of 1964 added sex to the prohibited list of discriminations—race, color, religion, and national origin. With this addition, Congress greatly extended the impact of the legislation. Nonwhites constitute only about 10 per cent of the labor force, but women constitute more than one-third. Next, the Equal Pay Act of 1964 intensified the conflict when it prohibited employers from making distinctions in rates of pay on the basis of sex. This opened up a crack in the long-established wage differentials between men and women. Equal opportunity, equal pay, and state protective labor laws formed a new triangle.

The effect of this conflict on research and statistics will be the need for more extensive and intensive surveys of men's and women's wages, salaries, and earnings. The eventual outcome of the conflict could have a significant effect upon the entire wage structure in the American economy.

CURRENT AND HISTORICAL WAGE REPORTS

The Bureau is constantly being called upon to furnish information on the new agreements negotiated each month. Requests come from unions, from employers, from government agencies, and from many others. To save time and money, the Bureau in self-defense has devised a monthly report—*Current Wage Developments*—that summarizes the latest agreements and presents a table of selected wage changes, including the largest and most important ones. The table shows the industry, the employer, the union, the wage increase (if any), and a summary of the qualitative changes in fringe benefits. With such data, the Bureau is able to issue, quarterly and semiannual releases summarizing major wage developments. There is also a summary release on occupational earnings and wage trends derived from the community wage surveys.

One additional, very useful, type of long-run measurement consists of studying the historical record, sometimes for decades into the past, of negotiated wage and supplementary benefits for an individual firm. Recent examples of such wage chronologies are those of the Aluminum Company of America, 1939–67, and General Motors Corporation, 1939–66. These chronologies are intended primarily as a tool for research, analysis, and wage administration.

VI

Productivity and Economic Growth

The Kennedy Administration, coming into office in 1961 after the unsatisfactory performance of the American economy in the preceding four years, plunged actively into business recovery programs. It was the Roosevelt Administration of 1933 in miniature. Then there had been a catastrophic depression; in 1961, there was a minor business recession. But the youth, the zeal, the energy recalled the New Deal.

By good luck and good management, the recession was turned almost immediately into a recovery, which became buoyant by the end of 1961. At that stage, the Council of Economic Advisers, under the chairmanship of Walter Heller, promulgated the economic principle of the guideposts, or guidelines, as they came to be called. The Council's exposition of the policy appeared in the Economic Report of the President, January, 1962:

The general guide for noninflationary wage behavior is that the rate of increase in wage rates (including fringe benefits) in each industry be equal to the trend rate of over-all productivity increase.

It is no accident that productivity is the central guidepost for wage settlements. Ultimately, it is rising output per man-hour which must yield the ingredients of a rising standard of living.

111

Although these guideposts were denounced almost immediately by labor unions and were viewed with skepticism by employers, the economy began to perform as though the principle were working. With continued business recovery, output per man-hour attained good levels (4.6, 3.6, 3.8 per cent a year), while with high unemployment (5.5 to 6 per cent), the wage increases in collective bargaining were moderate (3–3.5 per cent), and unit labor costs of goods and services remained stable. Prices remained unchanged, and real economic growth reached high levels. The United States was able to boast that it had the most stable and balanced economy of all the modern industrial nations.

Focus on Productivity

The temporary success of the policy focused public attention on productivity, a newly popular member of the family of economic indicators. And criticism of the policy directed further professional attention to productivity statistics—their quality, shortcomings, and improvement. Public interest in productivity as a concept and in the statistics that measured it increased.

The concept of productivity as such was not new. Neither was the economic relationship of productivity and wages. What made the Council's statement a landmark in political economy in the United States was its adoption as a government policy for the guidance of labor and management. In addition, the Council's justification of the economic principle was an indirect answer to the false doctrine so prevalent in the early 1960's, namely, that advanced technology and resulting productivity were the primary causes of mass unemployment.

This doctrine had been the major motivation to action in Congress in the 1890's, when it directed the Bureau to make an exhaustive and comprehensive study of hand and machine labor. Congress wanted to know whether mechanization was responsible for the high unemployment rate that had suddenly developed and whether it was resulting in the substitution of child and women workers for men. (See Chapter I.)

In that first survey, the Bureau collected information concerning the time required to produce a product by machine as compared to the time required by hand methods that had been prevalent from a quarter to a half a century earlier. Some of the data had to be reconstructed from old records, but the Bureau was also able to find shops where hand methods were still in use in the 1890's. The number of products surveyed was 27 in agriculture, 2 in mining, 8 in quarrying, 9 in transportation, and 626 in manufacturing. The study took about three years, and the results were not published until 1898, long after the period of depression was over. The key data were the numbers of man-hours of labor required to produce a product under average conditions. Then, by applying wage rates to the labor time, it was possible to estimate the comparative labor costs of the hand and machine methods. There were cases in which the differentials in favor of lower costs for machine methods were relatively small, but in the vast majority of cases the differentials were tremendous. There were many examples of machine costs at one-tenth, one-twentieth, and even one-fiftieth of the hand costs.

The Bureau's conclusion with respect to wages is best stated in the Commissioner's own words:

> The general tendency of wages since the introduction of power machinery and the employment of women and children in its operation has been upward, but it will be difficult to decide positively whether such increase is due absolutely to the use of machinery, or to a higher standard of living, or to the increased productivity of labor supplemented by machinery, or to all these causes combined, or to other causes.

With respect to mechanization and unemployment, the Commissioner came to the sensible conclusion that "There has been a larger increase in the number of persons required for the production of the articles considered, in order to meet present demands, than would have been necessary to meet the limited demands under the hand-labor system." In other words, mechanization may displace labor, but the lower costs raise the demand and so create more jobs.

PRODUCTIVITY INDEXES

The issue of mechanization and productivity did not become acute again until the 1920's. In that decade the emphasis was on the relationship to wages rather than to unemployment, although the Bureau made some studies of spectacular labor-saving developments—one already mentioned, in the glass-bottle blowing industry. After World War I, some of the newer industries like the automobile industry achieved remarkable results in mechanization and productivity. The labor movement had acquired wage increases during World War I on the cost-of-living issue. But during the 1920's the index of the cost of living remained stable and furnished no support for wage increases. However, it was obvious that mechanization was spreading rapidly throughout American industries and that business firms were prosperous. The stock market supplied daily evidence to the public on this point. Unions began pressing for wage increases on the basis of the increase in productivity.

By that time, current yearly statistics of production, employment, and hours of work were becoming available, so it was evident that there was an alternative to the program of making occasional analytical surveys of spectacular developments in productivity in specific industries. The new approach was to devise indexes of output for various industries, based on the prewar year 1914, and then to calculate corresponding indexes of labor man-hours in these industries. The production indexes divided by the man-hours indexes yielded the productivity indexes. Thus, for the year 1925 (with 1914 = 100), the production index for automobiles was nearly 1,000, the man-hours index 320, and the productivity index 310. Stated in reverse sequence, productivity, expressed as output per man-hour of factory labor, had more than tripled, but the output of automobiles had multiplied ten times, which required a tripling of labor requirements. This program of measuring the output per man-hour in individual industries has been continued to the present.

In the depths of the Great Depression of the 1930's, mechanization again attracted attention in Congress, and legislation to levy taxes on machines in order to slow down the mechanization of industry and provide more jobs for workers was introduced. The bill did not pass.

About this time, a new school of economic thought known as technocracy emerged. The technocrats were engineer-economists who enunciated the idea that mechanization could lead to economic abundance and that the major economic problem was to distribute the purchasing power so that people as consumers could reap the benefits. Those thinkers foreshadowed the automation economists of the 1960's, who have advanced the same ideas.

In 1936–39, the Works Progress Administration, naturally concerned with unemployment, chose the subject of productivity developments as one of its research projects. By means of WPA funds, indexes of productivity showing recent trends were developed for more than three dozen industries.

LABOR REQUIREMENTS STUDIES

In 1940, Congress authorized the Bureau to undertake continuing studies of productivity and technological changes, but World War II handicapped and limited this work. Furthermore, World War II changed the products of many industries so radically that continuing indexes could not be made. Instead, the Bureau turned its attention from unemployment to the problem of efficient use of scarce manpower and produced several studies of labor requirements in various defense industries. After the war, production of the annual indexes was resumed, while the new work on labor requirements was extended to a number of important industries.

The labor requirements work became an important factor in the Marshall Plan for Western Europe. Paul Hoffman, the first administrator of the Marshall Plan, requested the Bureau of Labor Statistics to make detailed labor requirements studies for typical production processes in certain American industries that had counterparts in European countries. The BLS American surveys, called "Factory Performance Reports," were made available to European productivity centers, which in turn made comparable studies in the industries in their own countries.

The work on the productivity indexes for individual industries in the United States began to reach a limit. The production indexes were based on physical products, that is, upon tons of coal, barrels of cement, tons of steel, etc. The method worked best when an industry, had a single major product, such as cement, but there were also ways of combining several such products. However, industries such as textiles had a variety and complexity of products that prevented the development of good measures of physical output.

While the Bureau staff was wrestling with this problem, the famous escalation contract between the automobile industry and the United Automobile Workers was negotiated. The provision in the contract for an "annual improvement factor" based on the rise in national living standards pointed in the direction of productivity and was a forerunner of the Council of Economic Advisers' guidepost policy in the 1960's. The escalation was derived from the concept that the largest factor in the improvement of living conditions for the people as a whole is the rate of increase in the nation's productivity. The new type of collective bargaining contract turned the attention of the Bureau staff to the problem of constructing an over-all index of productivity for the economy as a whole and for the major sectors, such as agriculture and manufacturing.

SECTOR AND ECONOMY-WIDE INDEXES

The postwar revision and improvement of the price indexes made it possible to compute production indexes for sectors and industries by a new method, which is to take the total annual output of an industry expressed in dollars and to deflate it by the use of a price index that measures the amount of the dollar output due solely to price changes. By the use of this statistical method, by the mid-1950's the Bureau was producing annual indexes of productivity for the private economy, for agriculture, for manufacturing, and for nonmanufacturing as a whole. These are the productivity indexes the Council of Economic Advisers used in 1962 when they promulgated the economic principle of the guideposts. Thus, productivity statistics have been added to wage and price statistics to make up the trinity guiding the nation's economic policies for industrial relations.

Although the automobile escalation contract brought productivity statistics into collective bargaining, there was at first very little attention to precision. When the contract was first signed in 1948, the Bureau of Labor Statistics had not issued any economy-wide figures on output per man-hour. There was a general impression that productivity was increasing at the rate of about 3 per cent per year, and the annual wage increases in the automobile industry were set at approximately that figure.

But as this type of contract was negotiated in other industries, two distinct issues arose. One concerned the precision and accuracy of the indexes: Exactly what are the right figures? The other concerned the concept of productivity: What productivity are we talking about?

With respect to the first issue, the BLS finally published over-all indexes of productivity for the private economy early in 1956. The year 1947 was chosen as the base, and primary emphasis was put on the postwar period, although figures going back to prewar years were made available. The Bureau figures generally confirmed the 3 per cent annual increase for the private economy as a whole.

The second issue was not resolved so easily. As noted previously, the Bureau had been publishing for years the indexes of output per man-hour for certain industries, one of which was iron and steel. In 1959, a major labor-management dispute arose over the renegotiation of the steel contract. The government made many efforts to avoid a strike, including the appointment of a special board to hear the two sides. In that dispute, the appropriateness of the concept of economy-wide productivity came under review. The productivity increases for the national economy had exceeded 3 per cent per year since 1947, but there was no proof that this applied specifically in the steel industry.

INDUSTRY INDEXES

In order to avoid a trend terminating in the depressed year 1958, the Bureau of Labor Statistics made a productivity estimate for the steel industry for the first half of 1959, which was a high production period, in anticipation of the strike that took place in the second half of the year. The output per man-hour for all employees in steel in the first half of 1959 was at about the same level it had been in 1955, and only about 8 per cent above 1953, posing the question of what should happen to wages in an industry in which productivity was below the national average. Increasing wages to the national average productivity rate clearly implied the risk of a price increase, but holding wages down to the level of the industry productivity rate would carry the implication that wages in high productivity industries should rise more than the national average.

In the steel case, still another issue arose. What was the trend in output per man-hour for all employees in the industry as compared to the trend for production workers only? That a discrepancy existed was highlighted by the fact that from 1947 –57, the number of employees in the steel industry had increased about 10 per cent, but the production workers had increased only 5 per cent, while the nonproduction or office workers had increased nearly 50 per cent. Of course, under those circumstances the output per man-hour for the production workers (measuring the total output against those workers only) showed up much better than the over-all figure. However, labor costs for an industry include all workers in the industry, and the output is the result of the activities of all employees. Separating out production workers would imply differential treatment of white-collar workers. There could hardly be a wage increase for one coupled with a wage decrease for the other.

Nevertheless, the concept of productivity for an industry as against productivity for the economy has continued to be an issue in collective bargaining. In the airlines dispute of 1966, the argument made by the union for a wage increase far in excess of the national productivity rate was based on the argument of a higher industry rate. The argument was that the high productivity insured against an increase in airline travel fares. The difficulty with that argument is that it leaves no place for price decreases to occur. If all high productivity is absorbed by wages, while wage increases in low-production industries equal or exceed the productivity gains, where are price decreases to come from? The steel strike was settled in 1959 without basically resolving any of these questions, but the settlement turned out to be fairly close to the national average productivity rate. However, when the guidelines were promulgated by the Council of Economic Advisers in 1962, these problems of productivity measurement became much more acute. The Council made it perfectly clear that the guideposts were based upon economy-wide productivity rates for the private economy.

GOVERNMENT PRODUCTIVITY

A curious problem exists in attempting to study government output and employment. No satisfactory way of measuring output has yet been devised. Since most government operations consist of services that are available to the community without charge, government activity is usually reflected in the national accounts only by the wages and salaries of the employees. Hence, by definition, their productivity record is zero. In actual fact, this is not the case. Studies made on the subject of productivity of federal government agencies have proved conclusively that most agencies for which the output can be measured on some reasonable basis compare quite favorably with private industry. But until some new method of national accounting brings government into the equations, it is necessary for the Bureau of Labor Statistics to measure productivity for the private economy only. It should be pointed out that this does no violence to the wage and salary policies of the federal government, *if* the productivity rate of increase for government as a whole is about equal to that of private industry.

PRODUCTIVITY AND WAGES

To return to the basic issue, the problem of how to relate productivity to wages and unemployment is one of the most difficult unsolved problems of the domestic economy in the United States and in every large industrial nation. The nature of the problem can be very simply portrayed by a table for the period 1960–67 in the United States. The table shows the relationship among output per man-hour for the private economy; compensation—which includes wages, salaries, and other compensation for personal service—per man-hour; and unit labor costs. The behavior of the two price indexes is also shown.

	Percentage Change	
	1960–64	1965–67
Output per man-hour	16.6	7.8
Compensation per man-hour	18.3	17.8
Labor costs per unit of output	1.5	9.4
Wholesale Price Index	− 0.2	5.6
Consumer Price Index	4.9	7.6

It is evident that for the period 1960–64, the annual gains in personal compensation remained within reasonable range for the annual increases in productivity, while the Wholesale Price Index remained stable and the Consumer Price Index rose slowly at a little more than 1 per cent a year. However, as the nation approached full employment in 1965–67, the annual gains in compensation rose faster, while productivity increases slackened. Over the three years, compensation rose twice as much as productivity. Both price indexes responded by rising sharply.

Chart VIII shows the typical pattern of the business cycle. As economists have often pointed out, in a business recession some firms go out of business, others shut down their less efficient plants and lay off workers. Many employers take advantage of the opportunity to install new machinery and to reduce their labor costs. When business recovery takes place, output can be increased significantly without a corresponding rise in the number of employees. Productivity rises sharply to its best levels. Then if full prosperity is attained, less efficient factories and workers are brought into production, and the average productivity increase each year begins to slow down. By this time, some scarcities of labor bring about higher wages and salaries. These are made possible by higher prices. There is much argument among economists as to whether the higher prices cause the higher wages or whether the higher wages produce the higher prices. The former is called demand-pull inflation, the latter cost-push inflation.

At the peak of prosperity, unemployment is comparatively

Chart VIII

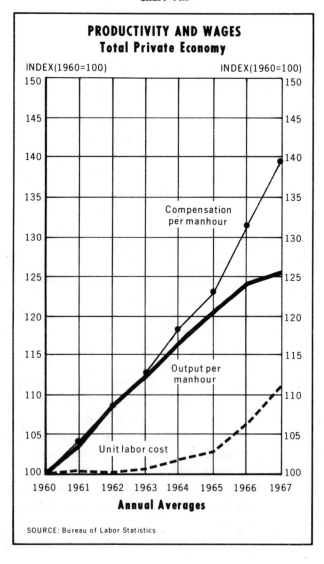

PRODUCTIVITY AND WAGES
Total Private Economy

SOURCE: Bureau of Labor Statistics

low. It can't go down to zero, because there is always some turnover in a growing economy (in prosperous times, more workers voluntarily quit their jobs on their own initiative than are laid off by employers). In addition, there are structural unemployment problems, such as lack of skill, lack of education, and geographic location. But labor scarcity can exist with such unemployment. This situation is shown by the overtime worked by employees on the job, as well as by the moonlighting of workers who hold two or more jobs at the same time.

LABOR-MANAGEMENT ADJUSTMENTS TO PRODUCTIVITY

When the productivity rate in a firm or an industry advances more rapidly than output, workers are less likely to raise the issue of automation and unemployment. Of course, in any advancing technology, some individual jobs and occupations may be eliminated, but when expanding output creates the need for more jobs, neither management nor the union is subjected to the pressure of workers displaced through changed technology or automation. In such cases, management has many new jobs into which the workers can be placed, or at least trained for placement.

But when the productivity rate is greater than actual output, some displaced workers will lose their jobs and labor-management relations are likely to heat up. The problem is: How can the firm or the industry adjust to declining employment that is directly attributed to automation?

In this dilemma, some unions accept the economic logic of the case and leave the adjustment decisions to management. The United Mine Workers, under the leadership of John L. Lewis, is the outstanding example of the use of this policy. Employment in coal mining fell from about 425,000 in 1947 to about 140,000 in 1968. Many coal miners had to leave the industry, and the poverty in Appalachia today is in part the result of the cutbacks in mining employment. However, from the start the Mine Workers accepted management's responsibility for productivity and made no effort to resist or to slow down the automation process. What the union did was to require management to put a charge on every ton of coal mined, in order to create a fund for the protection of the workers. Miners were entitled to retire on pensions at age sixty, although the Social Security System and most private industries had set the minimum retirement age at sixty-five.

Other unions take the opposite tack and resist the introduction of new methods and machines and insist on maintaining the work force by spreading the work. This method usually results in high labor costs and high prices for the product, which in turn produce a further slackening in demand. In any competitive industry, this policy is eventually self-defeating for both management and labor: The more productive firms and industries get the business.

In some cases, joint labor-management agreements have been successful in easing the problems caused by automation. One of the most highly publicized (and successful) of these was the agreement negotiated in July, 1959, between the Pacific Maritime Association (employers) and the Longshoremen's and Warehousemen's Union. The employers agreed to set aside $5 million a year for five years as a fund for the protection of dock workers who might lose their jobs. In exchange, the union agreed to forego certain work rules and restrictive practices that had kept down productivity and raised the costs of shipping.

The $5 million fund was to be used, when needed, to provide early retirement to certain workers, to supplement the unemployment benefits of those laid off, and to guarantee pay for thirty-five hours a week for all Class A workers kept on the payroll. Productivity was sharply increased, but the interesting result was that so many older men retired voluntarily that the fund was never fully used. Eventually, it became necessary to recruit additional Class A workers for the industry.

Another interesting example was the contract negotiated in

1962 after three years of study by a committee of economic experts by the Kaiser Steel Corporation and the United Steel Workers of America. This plan was developed and administered by a tripartite committee consisting of outstanding industrial relations economists in the United States and was in fact, a guarantee against loss of jobs and income by technological change in the Kaiser company. Under it, no workers could be laid off because of technological change, except insofar as normal attrition occurred. Workers displaced from one job could be assigned to an employment pool that would conduct work that otherwise would not have been done. The most significant feature of the Kaiser plan was a sharing of the benefits of the increased productivity resulting from the introduction of improved methods. Workers were to receive 32.5 per cent of any savings in materials or labor costs made as a result of the improved technology, and during the early years of the plan, Kaiser employees received quite substantial amounts of extra pay because productivity increased at an exceptional rate due to worker interest.

In still another agreement, negotiated in 1959 by Armour & Company with two meat-packing unions, the company agreed to set up a fund to finance research on methods of cushioning the effects of automation. The fund was also used for a program of counseling, training, and placing employees who had been laid off in the shutdown of six meat-packing plants. Provision was made for "technological adjustment pay" to hire workers with seniority permanently separated from their jobs by a plant or department closing. The fund was also used to provide for early retirement at fifty-five years of age.

PRODUCTIVITY AND INFLATION

The above examples, interesting as they are, cannot be considered representative of labor-management relations in connection with productivity. When unemployment is low and labor is scarce, wages tend to rise faster than productivity.

"World's champion" wage increases are obtained in collective bargaining. But nonunion wages and salaries follow along, and government employees join in the procession. It is pointless to debate whether high wages cause high prices or whether high prices create demand for higher wages. The fact is that wages and prices rise together.

The problem is how to achieve a balance between the increases in wages and salaries and the increases in productivity so that prices can remain stable and unemployment can be kept low. This is more than just an American problem. It is a problem of the Free World. Americans cannot look abroad for successful solutions. Every major industrial nation in Western Europe has had the same experience, namely, that with full employment it has not been possible to hold wages and salary increases within the limits of productivity. The outcome everywhere has been rising prices, with mild inflation in some countries and much more serious inflation in others. The United States has now joined the procession. The problem for economists, for governments, and for people everywhere is how to achieve the balance that will yield full employment prosperity without inflation.

ECONOMIC GROWTH

In 1758, a Frenchman named François Quesnay published his *Tableau Economique,* a table that attempted to express in quantitative terms the operations of the economic system of his time. The *Tableau* portrayed the flow of the production process in much the manner that we do today, through the national accounts—Gross National Product (GNP), National Income, and so on. However, Quesnay was far ahead of his time. Statistics were not adequate for his intellectual concept, although even as Quesnay was writing, an Italian named Giovanni Rinaldo Carli was, by strange coincidence, constructing the first index number that history records. Adam Smith's *Wealth of Nations* captured the attention of economic thinkers, and

Quesnay's *Tableau* became merely a footnote to the history of economic thought.

During the statistical explosion that took place in the United States during the 1930's, a young Harvard economist named Wassily Leontief conceived the idea of developing a table of the operations of the economy and filling that table with numbers from the statistical series then becoming available. The leaders of the Bureau of Labor Statistics recognized the potential of Leontief's idea and made arrangements for him to come to Washington in a cooperative program of what came to be called "input-output studies," more recently termed "interindustry relations."

In its simplest form, an interindustry, or input-output, table is a set of numbers showing in dollars what each industry sells to various other industries, or, to look at the figures in the other direction, what each industry buys from others. Looking forward in the production process, the data are sales; looking backward, they are purchases.

FULL EMPLOYMENT PATTERNS

Using the 1939 Census as a foundation, the BLS developed an input-output table, which was published in 1944. Then, with that table as a base, the Bureau converted the sales figures into estimated employment for each transaction, thus creating an interindustry employment table, based upon the technology of the various industrial processes. Since one of the Bureau's assignments, at the specific authorization of Congress, was to study the post-World War II readjustment problems of converting a war economy back to a peacetime economy, BLS, using the input-output table and the manpower translations of it into employment, next made a five-year projection (1945–50) for the U.S. economy. Since the Labor Department's primary interest was employment, the resulting report was titled *Full Employment Patterns, 1950*. Full employment was not a prediction; it was an assumption of what the economy would look like in five years under conditions of full employment. The study marked a new step in employment projections, because it estimated both the supply of labor and the demand for labor. The demand involved estimates of total production in the economy as a whole, as well as by sectors and industries, and an appraisal of the rate and character of technological developments, since the productivity ratio determines the labor requirements for a certain volume of production.

The publication of the BLS report attracted considerable attention among labor and management groups, but two years passed before the Commissioner had an opportunity to present the results to Congress. In the spring of 1947, the Senate Special Committee to Study Problems of Small Business held hearings on the postwar prospects of the steel industry in which widely divergent views were expressed by experts on the likely long-range demand for steel. The BLS presented two estimates for steel production in 1950: in a high-consumption economy, 100 million tons; in a high-investment economy, 120 million tons. Both figures indicated that the steel-producing capacity of the industry would have to be increased, not reduced, in order to match the need for steel in the postwar economy.

The Air Force was the branch of the armed services most concerned with this BLS work. The Air Force had supported the postwar study and, now that it had proven its value, increased financial support of it. An interdepartmental committee was established under the chairmanship of the Office of Statistical Standards of the Bureau of the Budget, with the Bureau of Labor Statistics playing a leading role. A new project was begun on a postwar input-output table based on the 1947 Census of Manufactures. Instead of the limited cross-classification of the original table, the new, revised table was constructed for 400 sectors and industries (although these were compressed to 200 sectors for publication). Of course, with so much detail, there were many statistical gaps, and much time was spent collecting and estimating statistics to fill out the table. Nevertheless, the work was accomplished, and the table was ready during the Korean War.

Then an unfortunate decision that set back the work for the remainder of the 1950's was made. During the Korean War, the War Production Board was responsible for allocating scarce raw materials. The Board decided to make use of the input-output table. They made a public announcement of their intention—without consulting or notifying the BLS. So, as with the Price Index in World War II, the BLS found itself pushed into the center of a major controversy. The response of some segments of American industry was immediately and vigorously adverse. To businessmen, this move seemed like the first steps toward a planned economy. The business economists on the BLS Business Research Advisory Council were aware of the new table but there were few of them in comparison to the masses of businessmen who had never heard of the input-output table and were suspicious of the government's ultimate purposes. The storm blew over in a short time, but suspicion remained, and business doubt again found expression when the Eisenhower Administration took office in 1953.

With the ending of the Korean War, the new Administration was intent on cutting the government budget—and especially the Defense Department budget. The under secretary of Defense—and the Secretary, too—had come from the automobile industry. Both men were aware of the flurry input-output had caused in the preceding year. In casting about for ways to reduce the Department's budget, the under secretary came across the Air Force grant, which had been supplying the bulk of the funds for the input-output study. He conducted a hearing at which the BLS Commissioner and members of his staff, supported by Air Force personnel, appealed for the work to be continued. But the under secretary took the position that input-output was a civilian, not a military, project and that it should be supported by the civilian budget. He permitted the orderly closing down of the enterprise so as to preserve the records. It was quite impossible at that time to finance the work from the regular budget of the BLS, so the project lapsed.

The shutdown revealed the fact that there was a good deal of private-industry interest in input-output work. The BLS thought there might be enough interest to warrant setting up a modest project to be supported by private funds. (The BLS has authority to contract for work done for private firms.) Accordingly, a leave of absence was given to Duane Evans, one of the assistant commissioners, to enable him to cooperate with interested businessmen in devising a proposal. Unfortunately, the timing was bad. The economy started sinking into the business recession of 1957–58, and private research funds were hard to get. The project failed.

In 1959, the Bureau of the Budget financed a special study by a survey committee of the national accounts produced by the Office of Business Economics in the Department of Commerce. The findings of the committee included a recommendation that it would be helpful to the national accounts to have an up-to-date input-output table in order to improve the accuracy and consistency of the accounts. In the next fiscal year, a modest amount was put in the budget of the Office of Business Economics to enable it to start constructing a table from the 1958 Census of Manufactures. An 82-place table was developed and published at the end of 1964, with a revision in the survey of current business, September, 1965.

In 1959, the BLS proposed to the Secretary of Labor that an effort be made to get money to enable the Bureau to devise an employment version of the input-output table and thus improve the manpower projections the Bureau was making. The Secretary was interested and made an effort to enlist Budget Bureau support, but the time was not propitious. No funds were obtained.

Such was the situation when the Kennedy Administration took office in January, 1961. The BLS budget had already been set for the coming fiscal year, 1961–62. But word soon came to the Commissioner that Wassily Leontief and John Kenneth Galbraith had conferred with the President at the White House and that, if the new Secretary of Labor Arthur J. Goldberg would request an appropriation for a program of manpower studies in relation to economic growth, it would receive thoughtful consideration. The BLS presented a budget request for $500,000, which was approved and became an item in the BLS budget for 1961–62.

The program, as now set up, is interdepartmental, with more than half the funds going to the Office of Business Economics and other agencies outside the Labor Department, as well as to universities and other private research organizations. An interdepartmental committee on economic growth was established under the chairmanship of a member of the Council of Economic Advisers. The BLS established a branch under an expert in productivity and input-output statistics.

One of the first products of the reconstituted program in the early 1960's was a study by the BLS of the effect of exports upon employment in the United States. The study, entitled *Domestic Employment Attributable to U.S. Exports, 1960,* was updated to 1965 and published in the *Monthly Labor Review* for December, 1967. It showed that almost 3 million jobs in the American economy, or about 4 per cent, were derived from exports.

In late 1966, the Bureau, under the auspices of the Interagency Growth Project, issued BLS Bulletin No. 1536, *Projections, 1970 Interindustry Relationships, Potential Demand, Employment.* The report provided detailed projections of final demand, input-output relationships, and employment on an industry-by-industry basis. This study showed that in order to achieve levels of high employment in 1970, the growth rate of real GNP would have to be between 4.3 and 4.5 per cent a year for the 1965–70 period.

Here, it is necessary to distinguish a projection from a prediction. In its simplest meaning, a prediction is an unqualified assertion that something will happen. The sportswriter predicts the home team will win the game next Saturday. Sometimes a forecaster hedges by saying, "The outcome will be either (a) or (b)."

A projection is a much more carefully circumscribed description of things to come. It is based on a specified set of assumptions, which in themselves contain strong elements of probability. An economist making a projection of the shape of the economy in 1970 might begin by assuming that the war in Vietnam will be ended by that time. He may have no basis for such a guess, but if his purpose is to analyze the pattern of employment in a free economy (no war demand and no controls), this is the only assumption on which it is possible for him to proceed. If he wants to characterize a war economy, he would make another assumption.

Secondly, if he is trying to sketch the characteristics of a full employment economy, he necessarily assumes high employment and low unemployment. In its projection of 1970, the BLS made two alternate assumptions—a 3 per cent unemployment rate and a 4 per cent unemployment rate. For a useful projection, these should be both possible and probable, but they cannot be considered as definitive for any one year. The year 1970 must be interpreted loosely to mean any high-employment year near the beginning of the 1970's.

Sometimes a detailed and integrated projection will disclose gaps or surpluses (lack of fit among the parts), which could result in remedial action. Thus, an educational projection that showed more college students in prospect than teachers and equipment could trigger government action for more training and building—falsifying the projection, but solving the problem.

One significant contribution of input-output and economic growth studies at present is their capacity to provide evidence

of imbalances in the economy. The projections we developed
in the growth studies are intended to provide a more systematic and integrated framework for the Occupational Outlook
reports of the BLS, as described in Chapter III.

VII

Industrial Relations Research and Statistics

The primary objective of an established American labor union is negotiation of a collective bargaining agreement with an employer. If the negotiation does not result in an agreement, there may be a labor dispute in which the union calls a strike or the employer shuts down the plant. Of course, a disagreement or a dispute may not at first result in any action so drastic. Government mediators may be called in, work may continue for a time without a contract, or emergency arbitration boards may be created, particularly in a crucial industry in which the government may not want any stoppages of work.

Hence, there are two broad kinds of research and statistics on the subject of industrial relations. One consists of studies of agreements, union-management cooperation, and arbitration awards. The other consists of analyses of labor-management disputes—strikes, lockouts, lost time, and the like.

STUDIES OF WORK STOPPAGES

In the early days of the labor movement, when unions were not recognized by most employers and when contractual agreements often did not exist, labor disputes dominated the industrial-relations picture. Strikes occurred when a union attempted to organize employees in a plant or when unorganized employees struck for a wage increase or against a decrease. It is, therefore, not surprising that in those days a study of industrial relations consisted primarily of analyses of strikes and lockouts.

The first statistical record of strikes in the United States was contained in a report issued by the Bureau of Labor Statistics of Massachusetts in 1880, accounting for strikes in that state since 1825. A year later, the Pennsylvania Bureau of Industrial Statistics issued an account of strikes in that state since 1835. The first federal agency to compile statistics on strikes was the Bureau of the Census. In 1880, the Census sent questionnaires to employers and workers involved in disputes during the year and received information on 762 disputes. In 1886, the U.S. Commissioner of Labor made a study of the "industrial disturbances which have been so frequent in this country since 1877." However, he linked his study with the Census report for 1880. The staff of the Bureau of Labor examined the files of newspapers, trade journals, and commercial periodicals to obtain references to strikes during the years 1881–86. Agents of the Bureau visited the areas where the strikes were reported and obtained information from employers and workers about each strike. The results were published in the Third Annual Report of the Commissioner of Labor. In 1894, the U.S. Commissioner of Labor published a comprehensive report entitled "Strikes and Lockouts," which accounted for stoppages between 1887 and 1894. That report (the Tenth Annual Report of the Commissioner of Labor) was published in two volumes, with 1,900 pages of tables.

In 1901 and 1906, similar, intensive surveys of strikes during the intervening years were made by the U.S. Bureau of Labor. As a result of these studies, the Bureau was able to publish data for the years 1881–1905 on the number of strikes each year and the number of workers and establishments involved. There was also a figure on the percentage of strikes involving labor organizations.

Nothing more was done until 1914, when the Bureau of

Labor Statistics began to compile an annual report of all strikes and lockouts during the year. It relied exclusively on references to strikes and lockouts in newspapers and periodicals, with mail questionnaires going to both unions and employers. This system was much less costly than the earlier method of using field agents to collect the information. These annual statistics have been continued to the present. In 1927, improvements in the program resulted in data on the number of workers involved in all work stoppages and the computation of the number of man-days lost. The modern series on monthly and annual strike data dates from 1927.

In the early days, the Bureau attempted to distinguish between strikes and lockouts, strikes being an action initiated by the workers; lockouts, by the employer. However, it became evident that this distinction was often meaningless. In a dispute where no agreement was in prospect, the union might issue a strike call for a future date, but the employer in the meantime simply closed down the plant. In either case, there would have been a shutdown; which party initiated it was unimportant. The Bureau adopted the term "work stoppage" to include both strikes and lockouts. In popular usage, the term "strike" was and still is used, and it is generally quite appropriate, since in the great majority of cases the stoppage is initiated by the workers.

As in all statistical measurement, work-stoppage statistics require definitions that insure comparability in figures over a period of time. The Bureau of Labor Statistics defines a work stoppage as one that continues at least one full day, or one shift, and involves six or more workers. This definition has served quite well in American industrial relations, but of course it leaves out certain kinds of stoppages that in some countries would loom quite large in the statistics. For example, a demonstration strike of thousands of workers for a couple of hours would not be counted in BLS statistics. In many countries, where contractual collective bargaining is not a major objective of the unions, such strikes occur from time to time and would need to be taken into account in measuring strike activity. However, in the United States, such demonstrations have been infrequent and have generally not involved enough workers to make any significant difference in the statistics.

Within this definition, the Bureau of Labor Statistics attempts to compile a record of all strikes in the United States, regardless of their causes or legality. For instance, a jurisdictional strike is one in which two or more unions are engaged in a dispute over work, with the employer on the sidelines. Such strikes, recorded in BLS statistics, are most frequent in the building trades, but they can occur in any occupation or industry in which different unions claim jurisdiction. A wildcat strike is one in which members of a union working under a contract go out on strike in defiance of the union leadership. These usually occur over local or craft grievances.

The federal government operates under a law passed by Congress forbidding strikes of government employees. The penalty is discharge of the striking employees. A number of states have laws prohibiting striking by government employees, but enforcement of the law has not always been successful. New York State had such a law on the books in January, 1966, when the Transit Authority employees of the New York City subways and bus lines went out on strike. Under that law, penalties were assessed against the striking employees as individuals and not against the union or its officers. In practice, it was difficult to obtain convictions in the courts because juries were sympathetic to the individual employees, torn between their loyalty to their union and their duty to their government. Accordingly, the legislature in 1966 amended the law to provide that the union and its officers should be subject to substantial fines in the event of a strike. This law was tested in September, 1967, when New York City school teachers went out on strike in disregard of an award made by a mediation board appointed by the mayor. The American Federation of Teachers argued that technically it was not striking because the teachers were simply resigning their positions en masse. The Bureau of Labor Statistics recorded both these New York cases as work stoppages.

The basic statistics on stoppages consist of three items: the number of stoppages beginning in the year; the number of workers involved in the stoppages, that is, the number of striking employees; the total number of idle man-days during the month or the year. For the monthly statistics, the Bureau produces two supplementary figures: the number of stoppages in effect during the month, and the number of workers involved during the month. Most strikes do not last more than a few weeks, but in many instances this would carry them over from one month to the next, so the number of strikes begun in a month gives only a partial picture of the strike situation. Of course, a strike could also carry over from one year to the other, but those that do are so few (in relation to the total during the year) that their data appear only in the statistics of man-days idle.

There is a fourth statistic that the Bureau calculates on work stoppages, namely, the estimated percentage of working time lost. That figure is obtained by dividing the man-days idle by the total number of man-days worked by all employed workers (as shown by the Bureau's figures for nonagricultural employment in the United States, excluding government workers). Thus, that figure relates loss of time in work stoppages to the total working time of all employees, blue-collar and white-collar, in all industries except agriculture and government. Under that definition, all self-employed persons, including business proprietors, would also be excluded from the calculation. In no year since 1959 has the time lost through work stoppages amounted to as much as 0.2 per cent, which means that the lost time of striking employees in each of these years amounted to less than two days in one thousand. Even in the postwar strike year of 1946, the percentage was only 1.43. That percentage reflected the strike activity of 4.6 million workers in 4,985 stoppages, aggregating 116 million man-days idle. By contrast, in the year 1963, there were 3,362 stoppages involving 941,000 workers and 16.1 million days idle, a loss of 0.13 per cent.

The amount of work time lost in industrial disputes is a reasonably good measure of industrial conflict, but it is a wholly inadequate measure of the effect of strikes upon the nation's economy. Although occasionally a strike in one industry may cause a temporary increase in employment in another, much more often a strike in one industry, one firm, or even one plant may cause the unemployment of thousands of workers elsewhere. Sometimes the connection is quite evident, as when a strike by a building-trades union idles all other construction crafts in the community. But as the effect spreads further in time and in distance, the resulting unemployment is concealed, because the connection cannot always be traced.

From time to time, the BLS has been requested to develop some figures on this indirect unemployment. In fact, whenever the government is faced with the prospect of declaring a national emergency in a strike situation, the effect of the dispute upon employment in the economy is one criterion. But precise and continuing statistics of this kind are not available.

Occasional statistical studies have provided good data in specific situations—as in the aforementioned New York City transit strike, when the Transit Authority contracted for the Barrington Associates' study, "Effects of the 1966 New York City Transit Strike on the Travel Behavior of Regular Transit Users." The study was conducted by a random-sample survey of the transit riders. That strike lasted almost thirteen days, including two Saturdays and two Sundays. Counting Saturdays and Sundays as half days, about eleven workdays were lost by the striking transit workers. Since they numbered about 40,-

000, the total man-days lost amounted to about 440,000 days. (This is the figure—calculated more precisely, of course—that the BLS would report as the time lost due to the strike.)

Barrington Associates developed another table showing the extent to which other New York City workers failed to get to their jobs due to the transportation failure. In brief, about 31 per cent failed to get to work in the first two days (Monday and Tuesday), about 25 per cent missed the next four days (Wednesday through Saturday), and about 20 per cent missed the last three days (Monday through Wednesday). Applying these percentages to the New York City labor force produces an estimated total of about 4.25 million days lost, not counting Sundays and counting only the second Saturday (and that as half a day). In crude round numbers, the lost work time in New York City was about ten times the loss of the strikers. Nor is this all. Large numbers of suburban workers were unable to get to work. Had they been counted, the total loss would have been boosted to well over 5 million man-days.

Of course, not every strike creates this amount of unemployment. The sanitation workers in New York struck for nine days in February, 1968, and the streets filled with garbage. The secondary unemployment in that strike was undoubtedly very small, although certainly the sanitation men created other problems—some of serious economic consequence. The problem for the statisticians is that in most strikes there is no satisfactory way of arriving at the resulting indirect unemployment. In the case of the New York transit strike, it was possible to collect some sample figures and to make some fairly close estimates. But a nation-wide steel strike, to take a hypothetical example, of indefinite duration, would produce all kinds of indirect economic consequences that might not even seem to be due to the strike itself. For example, a user of steel who found himself in short supply might cancel an order for some new equipment. The equipment manufacturer might then lay off some workers, who would scarcely be aware of the fact that their unemployment was due indirectly to the steel strike. Stated more simply, the effect of a work stoppage rippling out through the economy produces losses at times far distant from the source of the stoppage.

Despite the fact that no firm and accurate statistics can be developed to measure this economic impact precisely, there is evidence to show that certain industries at certain times would slow down the economy so much and cause so much unemployment that the government feels impelled to take special measures to prevent, or to end work stoppages in those industries. In these cases, doctrine of the public interest enters. Theoretically, the public-interest principle is brought to bear when the losses borne by the innocent public exceed the combined losses suffered by the workers and employers.

In the United States, there has been great hesitation on the part of the government to intervene in industrial disputes until the public interest is overwhelmingly evident. The federal government and a number of state governments have established mediation and conciliation services whose functions are to assist the parties in arriving at a free collective agreement. When mediation fails, the government has at times appointed fact-finding and arbitration boards to develop solutions that both parties might accept. But in wartime, and even occasionally in peacetime, the situation becomes so critical that the President and the Congress find it necessary to impose a settlement.

Measured by the amount of working time lost in industrial disputes, the United States ranks near the top among the world's major industrial nations. In absolute terms, this is not surprising, since the United States is the largest in population and labor force. But even when the data are adjusted for size, the United States is exceeded in strike activity only by Italy, which seems to have the most strike-prone labor force in the world. France, Great Britain, and Belgium fall in the intermediate range (based on statistics for a recent ten-year period). Canada's rate is somewhat higher than the above three countries and amounts to about one-half the rate of the United States.

Conversely, Switzerland is almost immune from strikes, and Denmark, Norway, Sweden, and West Germany have few strikes and little lost time. Australia and New Zealand are interesting in that they have established judicial systems for the compulsory settlement of labor disputes by law. In the event that the parties cannot agree, there are established labor courts to which the dispute must be referred, and the court decision is final. New Zealand has one of the lowest strike rates in the world, rivaling Switzerland. But Australia's rate ranks higher up the scale—lower than Great Britain's, about half the rate of Canada, and about one-fourth the U.S. rate. There are some significant differences in the compulsory settlement systems in Australia and New Zealand, and these differences may be a factor in their respective strike statistics.

Strike statistics differ from all other major statistical series produced by the Bureau of Labor Statistics in that they are designed to yield a total count, or census, of all work stoppages. In other fields, the BLS works with representative samples that can be adjusted to portray the total situation in the economy. Sampling can be used when over-all data for the nation or the economy are available periodically from other sources, such as the Census of Population, the Census of Manufactures, the employment reports received by state employment security agencies, and many others. In the field of strike statistics, the BLS has to operate as a census taker, so to speak.

In view of this situation, a major problem of the BLS is getting a record of the strikes that take place. A strike in the steel industry speedily becomes known throughout the country, but a small strike in the building trades in a small town does not get into the metropolitan newspapers. However, most strikes, no matter how small, do get into the local papers, so the Bureau has found that the major source of information on strikes can be obtained from newspaper clippings. At the present time, the clipping service uses approximately 400 newspapers and periodicals. The clippings are obtained from a commercial service, manned by housewives clipping from a list of papers all references to strikes.

In addition, the Bureau obtains from the federal and state mediation services notices concerning cases referred to them. Also, the local employment offices of the state employment security agencies come across notices of strikes because they do not refer workers to a struck plant. Employers, unions, and other federal agencies are also tapped for information.

Of course, the newspaper clippings do not supply the information the Bureau needs to compile its statistics. On one occasion, when the Bureau was justifying its appropriation for the clipping service before the Senate Appropriations Committee, one of the senators remarked: "I go along with the appropriation, but sometime I wish you would explain to me just how you can possibly get strike statistics from the newspapers." The Commissioner had to explain that the statistics come from questionnaires sent to the employers and the unions; the clippings are only to get information on where to send them.

COLLECTIVE-BARGAINING AGREEMENTS

Work-stoppage statistics measure labor-management conflict, while the collective agreement spells out the terms under which labor and management will cooperate in production. The negotiation of an agreement marks the beginning of a new period of industrial peace.

As far back as the turn of the century, the Commissioner of Labor began a program of analyzing collective agreements. Copies of important agreements were published from time to time in the bimonthly bulletin. In 1912, the Bureau began the systematic assembling of collective-bargaining agreements. A special bulletin on the subject first appeared in 1925. Studies and reports appeared more frequently as unions expanded and agreements multiplied during the 1930's. The Bureau's re-

sponsibility in the collection and analysis of agreements was
formally established by the Taft-Hartley Act in 1947:

> *Sec. 211.* (a) For the guidance and information of interested
> representatives of employers, employees, and the general public,
> the Bureau of Labor Statistics of the Department of Labor shall
> maintain a file of copies of all available collective bargaining
> agreements and other available agreements and actions thereun-
> der settling or adjusting labor disputes. Such file shall be open
> to inspection under appropriate conditions prescribed by the Sec-
> retary of Labor, except that no specific information submitted
> in confidence shall be disclosed.

In response to this assignment, the Bureau established a collection system and maintained a file of such agreements. At
present the file consists of approximately 5,000 current agreements, covering about 10 million workers. All industries are
represented except railroads and airlines, which are required
by law to submit copies to the National Mediation Board. The
Bureau's files are open to inspection by interested parties.

The maintenance of a current file is, in itself, a major operating task. The typical agreement has a fixed duration, which
means that it eventually expires and a new agreement has to be
negotiated. The Bureau must constantly revise its files to keep
them up to date.

The submission of copies of agreements by either the union
or the employer is strictly voluntary; the Bureau has no compulsory powers. However, voluntarism has seldom caused any
problems for the Bureau. Generally speaking, employers and
unions are quite willing to send in their agreements.

In analyzing these agreements, the Bureau has several
major objectives. One is the presentation of data for major sectors or industries in the economy. Such a study is designed to
present to the public the major characteristics of the agreements.

In addition, data are sometimes presented for the major regions of the country, or by union affiliation. A further step consists of the analysis of important subjects, such as insurance, health and welfare plans, paid vacations, hours of work, overtime payments, etc. Finally, an effort is made to select new or uncommon practices that may foreshadow a trend in collective bargaining.

The Bureau publishes the results of its studies in a bulletin series entitled *Major Collective Bargaining Agreements.* Some of its recent studies have been: "Severance Pay and Layoff Benefit Plans," "Supplemental Unemployment Benefit Plans and Wage-Employment Guarantees," "Deferred Wage Increase and Escalator Clauses," "Management Rights and Union-Management Cooperation," and "Arbitration Procedures."

In 1962, President Kennedy officially established the principle of collective bargaining for federal employees. Prior to that time, there were many employee unions that had established limited collective bargaining relationships with federal agencies. Among these were the metal-trades unions, which were active in navy yards, army arsenals, and air depots. Another example was the printing-trades unions in the Government Printing Office. In addition, there were postal unions in the Post Office and white-collar unions of clerical and administrative employees. The President's action in 1962 consisted in requiring government agencies to sign formal agreements with the unions of their employees. Two years later, the Bureau of Labor Statistics made a survey and published a study *Collective Bargaining Agreements in the Federal Service.*

The rapid growth of unions in state and local government agencies has opened up another field for Bureau study and analysis. The Bureau has begun a collection of representative agreements, not only from regular users, but also from professional associations that negotiate agreements with government agencies.

The Bureau also produces several periodic publications that

are of general public interest. One is the *Directory of National and International Unions in the United States,* which is revised and reissued every two years. On the same schedule, the Bureau also issues statistics of union membership in the United States and in Canada.

VIII

Industrial Hazards Statistics and Studies

Accidents occur in every walk of life. Whether we travel by train or plane, drive a car, work in a factory, operate a farm, or remain quietly at home, we run the risk of accidents, ranging from the inconsequential to the fatal. Even the bathtub can be lethal—if not used with care.

Throughout the centuries, the major causes of death have been disease and famine. The advent of modern science and the growth of a complex industrial system have completely changed the picture. Only in the less-developed countries of the world today are the major causes of death the classic ones of disease and famine.

Today, the leading cause of teenage deaths in the United States is accidents, whereas in Southeast Asian countries, the major causes are infections and endemic diseases, such as typhoid fever and dysentery. In a mechanized society, the tools, machines, and gadgets that we use at home and at work multiply the risks of most of our daily activities.

Life has always been hazardous, but when work accidents began to multiply as a result of the increasing industrialization in the nineteenth century, some private groups began to urge correction of the working conditions that contributed to work injuries. Enlightened employers, employee organizations, and public-spirited individuals joined forces in urging measures to provide greater safety in factories.

147

State governments were slow to act but were eventually induced to adopt accident prevention legislation. In 1867, the first factory inspection law was adopted by the state of Massachusetts. Ten years later, Massachusetts passed another act, requiring employers to guard hazardous machinery.

Another problem was the legislation governing responsibility for accidents. Under English Common Law, an employer could be held legally responsible for an injury to one of his employees only if it could be proved that he was solely responsible. Thus, if the employee was neglectful in some respect and so "contributed" to the resulting accident, the employer was not liable. Nor was he liable if an employee made some mistake that brought on the accident. Under these circumstances, few employees could win lawsuits and collect damages for their injuries. In 1885, the state of Alabama adopted an employer's liability law, which substantially increased the employer's responsibility for injuries suffered by his workers. The effect was to subject the employer to lawsuits that sometimes resulted in expensive damages.

Some employers responded by adopting safety programs in their own plants. Steel, for instance, was an especially high-accident industry. The first in-plant safety program was established in the Joliet Works of the Illinois Steel Company in 1892.

Some Americans responded by looking at the experience of several Western European countries that had established systems of workmen's compensation providing financial assistance to injured workers without regard to responsibility for the accident. In 1893, U.S. Commissioner of Labor Wright initiated a continuing series of reports on work injuries, beginning with a study of European workmen's compensation procedures. Compensation payments were made through administrative procedures rather than through lawsuits. Employers paid the bill, but they were also protected financially in that the compensation payments were specified in the law.

This idea eventually spread to the United States. The federal government took the lead by enacting in 1908 a workmen's compensation law for some of its own employees—those engaged in manufacturing and construction work and in certain services designated as especially hazardous. In 1916, the law was extended to cover all federal employees. In 1911, the state of Wisconsin adopted a law applying workmen's compensation to private industry. From then on, the compensation method, supplemented by state factory inspection and accident prevention, spread throughout the nation.

STATISTICAL SERVICE TO SAFETY

In 1910, the Bureau of Labor Statistics inaugurated a program of annual injury-rate compilations for the iron and steel industry. This work was undertaken by the Bureau at the specific request of the steel companies, which promised full cooperation. Their objective was to obtain industry-wide statistics with which individual company data could be compared and by which the progress of the safety programs could be measured.

For a number of years, the iron and steel injury-rate data were not published by the BLS; they were simply compiled and made available to the industry itself. However, in 1918, the BLS published a bulletin entitled *The Safety Movement in the Iron and Steel Industry.* In 1922, the Bureau issued another bulletin, *Causes and Prevention of Accidents in the Iron and Steel Industry,* which reported that the injury-frequency rate for that industry had declined from 80.8 (number of injuries per million man-hours worked) in 1907 to 41.6 in 1920.

Meantime, the BLS had extended its accident-statistics program to additional industries, so that by the mid-1920's, injury rates were being published for about two dozen industries. Summarizing the statistics of industrial accidents up to the end of 1927, the Bureau made this comment in an official publication:

That accidents can be prevented by intelligent study of the situation, which is possible by the publication of statistics of this kind, is well illustrated by the record of the iron and steel industry. . . . A definite safety policy has been consistently maintained and rigorously enforced throughout the years, . . . until in 1927 the injury frequency rate had declined to 19.6.

Similar spectacular improvements were reported in other industries, such as cement, paper mills, and chemicals. The utilization of statistics as. a tool in the safety program was firmly established.

In 1912, the Association of Iron and Steel Electrical Engineers, fortified perhaps by the injury-rate statistics that the BLS was gathering for them, sponsored a national conference on safety. At a second meeting in 1913, the National Council for Industrial Safety was organized, and in 1915 became the National Safety Council. The Council is a private organization, and a majority of major employers in the United States are members. The National Safety Council has taken the lead in the development of industrial safety standards and has stimulated competition among its members to achieve low accident rates. The results are evident in the statistics published by the Council in comparison with those published by the Bureau of Labor Statistics. The Bureau collects information from a representative sample of firms in the various industries. The list includes firms that are not members of the National Safety Council. That these firms have higher accident rates is shown in the higher rates reported by the BLS than those recorded by the National Safety Council.

In 1914, the International Association of Government Labor Officials (IAGLO) was organized as the result of a merger of the Association of Chiefs and Officials of Bureaus of Labor and the International Association of Factory Inspectors. The Bureau of Labor Statistics became a member and, for about thirty years, the Commissioner of Labor Statistics served as secretary-treasurer of the organization. In 1946, this position was taken over by the assistant director of the Bureau of Labor Standards. The IAGLO has been through the years an active supporter of accident statistics and safety programs.

Early in 1915 a conference of state safety officers was held in Chicago. Commissioner Meeker of the BLS was an active participant in that conference. He served as a member of the Statistics Committee and prepared the committee report. Toward the end of 1915, this organization of state officers became the International Association of Industrial Accident Boards and Commissions. Commissioner Meeker became the Secretary to the Association and provided office services through his Bureau. Succeeding commissioners of Labor Statistics served in this capacity until 1934, when the Office of Labor Standards (now the Bureau of Labor Standards), established by Secretary of Labor Frances Perkins, took over secretarial responsibility for the organization. Secretary Perkins had an intense interest in occupational safety and worked vigorously to stimulate nation-wide interest in the movement. Her interest stemmed from her experiences in the famous Triangle fire in New York City in 1911, when about 300 workers, mostly women, died in a factory fire.

"E" FOR EXCELLENCE

When World War II began, the Maritime Commission required companies engaged in shipbuilding to make accident reports. The Commission furnished funds to the Bureau of Labor Statistics to tabulate and analyze the data. The Bureau received statistical summaries from the shipyards, as well as individual reports of accidents, which enabled the Bureau to make special studies of the types of injuries being experienced.

The War Department soon picked up the same idea and arranged for the Bureau of Labor Statistics to collect accident data from every industrial concern supplying ordnance or other materiel to the Department. In terms of employment, a substantial part of American industry was brought into this reporting system. The War Department obtained over-all injury rates for each industry and individual rates for each plant, which was then ranked within each industry. War Department inspectors brought pressure on the establishments with high rates. In fact, no plant could be awarded an "E" for excellence of performance if it had a comparatively high accident rate.

The Navy Department (at that time separate from the War Department) adopted the Army program, which was then conducted by the BLS for both departments.

At the end of the war, both the Maritime and the Army-Navy surveys came to an end when those agencies ceased supplying the BLS with funds. However, the Bureau invested some of its own funds in converting the Army-Navy survey into a voluntary reporting system, on a quarterly instead of monthly basis. The Bureau was also limited to a sample of 15,000 establishments, but careful selection enabled the Bureau to cover over 100 industries. These surveys proved the seasonal pattern of work injuries—high in midsummer and low in January.

Then the Bureau shifted the resources it had been using in the Maritime Commission survey into a detailed and comprehensive study of the productivity of handicapped workers in American industry. For many years this study constituted a landmark in the history of the program for the employment of the handicapped. A by-product of this study was the demonstrated effect of long hours in lowering individual worker productivity. Subsequently, the Bureau developed the accident-cause studies, which it has conducted for the past twenty years.

The Bureau of Labor Standards has from time to time suggested to the BLS certain industries in which such studies could be useful. The Business Research Advisory Council developed a set of criteria for the BLS to use in selecting industries: an adverse accident record for a period of years, an industry with plants widely distributed among regions and states, and an industry willing and interested enough to put the reports to immediate use. Unfortunately, the Bureau has never had enough funds to do anywhere near the volume of studies that have been requested.

Some years ago the Bureau of the Budget requested the BLS to report on the effect of these studies upon subsequent accident rates. The Bureau was able to make a convincing analysis showing that a beneficial effect was felt as soon as the study was launched and that this continued for periods of three to five years. After that, some backsliding would begin to show up; however, in most industries the accident rates never returned to their previous high levels.

Chart IX shows the progress of the safety movement in manufacturing industries over nearly three decades. The injury-frequency rate is the number of disabling injuries per million man-hours worked. In round numbers, 1 million hours is equivalent to about 500 full-time man-years. So a rate of 15 in 1938 meant about one accident a year for every thirty-three men.

The rate rose to record levels during World War II, partly as a result of the employment of many inexperienced new workers hired to replace the men called into the armed forces. Another peak was set in 1946 when there was a reverse shift with the ex-servicemen returning to their jobs. The federal government, through the Department of Labor, launched a nationwide safety campaign, capped by an annual President's Conference on Occupational Safety, in which several thousand people participated. These included federal and state officials, management representatives, union leaders, safety experts, and interested citizens, including such organizations as the National Safety Council. The chart indicates that the special effort may have aided in bringing the rate down to about 12 in the middle 1950's.

The record of the last ten years re-emphasizes an earlier point, namely, that the rate declines when employment goes

Chart IX

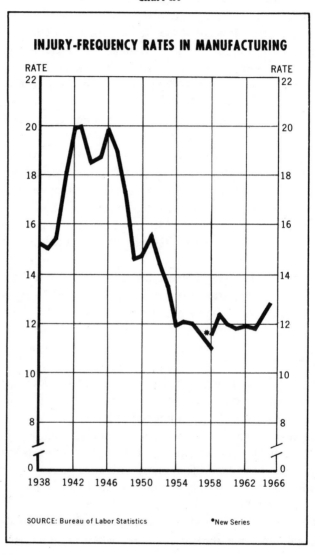

INJURY-FREQUENCY RATES IN MANUFACTURING

SOURCE: Bureau of Labor Statistics   *New Series

down. Note 1958 (despite the break in the series) and 1965–66, when peak employment brought in many young inexperienced workers.

In the shipping industry, accident rates have been exceedingly high—just about the highest in any industry. The Longshore and Harbor Workers Compensation Act, administered by the Bureau of Employees' Compensation in the Department of Labor, provides benefits to injured workers who come under federal jurisdiction. Because of the high injury rate, the Bureau of Labor Standards inaugurated a voluntary safety campaign among the stevedoring companies. This program achieved relatively little success. The Secretary of Labor then delegated authority to the Bureau of Labor Standards to establish safety regulations that would have the effect of law, and the Bureau was provided with a field staff to make inspections and obtain compliance. Under these regulations, the Bureau of Labor Standards required every firm to file with the Bureau of Labor Statistics a quarterly accident report. The BLS tabulates the results and transmits the statistics to the Bureau of Labor Standards, which then publishes general summaries. This combination of safety regulations and statistical reporting has produced a significant decline in accident rates in that industry.

OTHER HAZARDS

As far back as World War I, the problem of occupationally induced diseases attracted public attention. During the war, many young women who were engaged in painting watch dials began suffering the effects of radium poisoning; workers in the printing industry suffered from lead poisoning. The BLS studies of working conditions often called attention to problems of this kind.

The most recent example of this occupational hazard has been with uranium miners who may be exposed to radioactive materials. Although the Atomic Energy Commission has been well aware of the risks involved in its own installations, uranium mining has developed outside federal control. As the peaceful uses of atomic energy become widespread, there is the likelihood that serious occupational diseases may develop. This responsibility is the province of the states, which have not all shown sufficient interest. Accordingly, in 1968, Secretary of Labor W. Willard Wirtz proposed new health and safety legislation, designed to coordinate the activities of federal agencies in this field, and to establish federal-state cooperation for those functions and areas that are now subject to state jurisdiction.

The public interest in safety has been aroused recently by the growing death rate on the highways. In the United States, more accidents are caused by automobiles on the road than machines in the factory. Automobile accidents, however, have never been subjected to the carefully defined statistical standards that have been applied for years in work injury statistics. Consequently, statistics from different local jurisdictions are not yet sufficiently comparable, and there are wide differences of opinion as to the causes of highway accidents. Now, some of the public interest in highway safety is spreading to injuries on the job. As part of its proposed program for health and safety at work, the Department of Labor had requested funds for the development and improvement of work injury-rate statistics.

NEED FOR MORE PROGRAMS

Despite the successes that research and statistics have achieved in the promotion of occupational safety, there is still a wide gap between the achievements and the possibilities. In 1915, when Commissioner Meeker set in motion a statistical reporting system for the International Association of Industrial Accident Boards and Commissions, that organization had made a magnificent start toward creating an authoritative body of operating information on which the Workmen's Compensation system could build and grow. Yet, forty-three years later, at the convention in Seattle, Washington, in September,

1958, when speaking as the Commissioner of Labor Statistics, I addressed the convention on the need for workmen's compensation statistics and regretfully reported that nothing resembling the original goals had been achieved. The 1949 report of the Administration and Procedure Committee of the Association had contained this statement: "Only a few of the (state) statistical programs are comprehensive; in many States such programs are rudimentary, while in other States there are virtually no such programs." If the Commissioner of Labor Statistics in 1968 should be called upon to report, he would have little to add to what was said ten, or even twenty, years ago. Statistics have not yet been marshaled to render the service that they could to improve occupational safety.

IX

International Comparisons

World War II ended. Peace came. But the world economy was a shambles. Bombing had destroyed docks, railroads, factories, and machinery. Food was scarce. The American people were asked not to eat bread with their meals, so that wheat could be shipped to the starving millions overseas. Economic misery posed the threat of political disaster in many nations.

In June, 1947, General George C. Marshall, serving as Secretary of State in President Truman's Cabinet, made his famous speech calling for a massive program of international assistance by the United States—the program that came to be known as the Marshall Plan. In brief, Marshall proposed that the United States furnish financial aid, tools and equipment, and technical assistance to those nations willing to join the Plan. Most Western European nations participated (the Iron Curtain countries refused) and the program was launched within a year by a newly created agency—the Economic Cooperation Administration (ECA).

Early in 1949, Paul Hoffman, former President of the Studebaker Company, who had been persuaded to head ECA, received in his office a delegation from the Department of Labor, including Secretary Tobin, myself as Commissioner, and several members of our staffs. The meeting resulted in an agreement that the Department of Labor would devote some of its resources to assist in the recovery of Western Europe's industry. The Bureau of Labor Statistics accepted responsibility for making statistical surveys of technology and labor productivity in American industries to provide guides for stimulating the productivity of Western European industry. The European nations were encouraged to establish productivity centers of their own, with the objective of improving the productivity of their work forces as well as making parallel productivity studies for comparison with the American experience. The BLS dispatched one of its productivity experts on a tour of European capitals in order to speed the plans for the studies, and arrangements were made for teams of European statisticians and economists to come to the United States for experience and training with the BLS staff, which was making the companion studies in this country. It would be a gross exaggeration to say that statistics did the trick, but it is fair to say that these studies played a significant role in the spectacular economic recovery of Western Europe.

EARLY INTERNATIONALISM

The interest of the Bureau in international statistics goes back further than World War II and the subsequent economic recovery of Europe. The Bureau has been deep in international activities since its earliest years. Its creation in 1884 was a by-product of the business recession of that year, which had international implications. The first study undertaken by Commissioner Carroll D. Wright was a survey of business depression over the preceding fifty years. In his first annual report, Wright observed that "the great producing nations of the world, Great Britain, France, Belgium, Germany, and the United States, have been so closely allied in industrial conditions that they really constitute a group of nations which should be considered, integrally and as a whole, in any logical study of panics and depressions."

Even before that, as director of the Massachusetts Bureau of Statistics of Labor, Carroll Wright had been active in promoting the development of similar statistics-gathering bureaus in foreign countries. He was also instrumental in founding the International Statistical Institute (1886), an association of government and academic statisticians, which is still active. The initial conference of the Institute passed a resolution citing the need for "bureaus of labor on the plan of those of the United States" and calling for widespread collection of industrial statistics. Since 1886, the federal Bureau has regularly been represented in international conferences on labor statistics.

In 1888, when the Bureau was designated as the Department of Labor, although without Cabinet status, the Commissioner was assigned the responsibility of making studies of "the cost of producing articles, at the time dutiable in the United States, in leading countries where such articles are produced." It was in response to that assignment that the Bureau of Labor first began conducting various studies of prices and wages in foreign countries, and in 1899, began publishing in its bimonthly *Bulletin* domestic labor statistics as well as compilations of labor laws being adopted in various European countries. The Bureau was serving as a channel for communicating to the American public the significant developments in protective labor laws at home and abroad.

During the decade of the 1890's, about a half-dozen European countries had formed voluntary associations of citizens and government officials interested in promoting legislation for the protection of working people. At the Paris Exposition in 1900, delegates from a number of nations, including the United States, formed the International Association for Labor Legislation (IALL), which was to be a federation of autonomous national units, headed by a Swiss president and vice-president, and based in Berne. Among its objectives were the following: to organize an international labor office comissioned to publish in French, German, and English, a periodical collection of labor laws; to facilitate the study of labor legislation in different countries; and to study how agreements on labor codes and on international labor statistics could be obtained. As stated in 1907 at the first annual meeting of the Association, by Richard T. Ely, then president of the organization:

> The International Association . . . has as its special function the impartial scientific examination of labor measures and investigation of actual conditions underlying labor legislation. It is semiprivate, also quasi-official in character. . . . It is a voluntary organization, largely of experts and officials, but it receives subventions from most civilized governments, including a small one from our own federal government.

Commissioner Wright was an active participant in this new venture, and the subvention mentioned by Ely was an annual $200 contribution, which Wright persuaded Congress to make to the new organization through the U.S. Bureau of Labor. At the first convention of the Association in 1901, Wright proposed that each of the state labor bureaus in the United States be permitted to send a delegate to the conferences. (Apparently, the decision had been that each country should form a section of its own and would then be entitled to send delegates.) In 1906, the American Association for Labor Legislation was formed, and although Wright was no longer Commissioner, a representative of the U.S. Bureau became an officer in the American association and is recorded as the official government delegate to the international conference in Lucerne in 1908. Four private American citizens also attended, including such prominent people as Florence Kelley, long-time president of the Consumer's League, and Josephine Goldmark.

THE INTERNATIONAL LABOR OFFICE

The present-day significance of the International Association is that it was the forerunner of the International Labor Office, (ILO), which was sponsored in 1919 by the League of

Nations and exists today. Although the United States declined to join the League, in 1934 it became a member of ILO, which today is a very important organization.

The ILO works through international agreements to improve labor laws and working conditions in member countries and periodically sets up conferences on labor statistics. These conferences have been devoted to the establishment of international standards for statistics on employment, the cost of living, industrial injuries, and working hours; the measurement of underemployment; and methods of making international comparisons of real wages. (It is noteworthy that Commissioner Royal Meeker resigned in 1920 from the Bureau of Labor Statistics to become chief of the ILO Scientific Division.)

In 1930, the Ford Motor Company asked the International Labor Office what minimum wages the company would have to pay employees in various European cities to assure the workers a level of living equivalent to that of the company's Detroit employees. The Bureau of Labor Statistics was called upon and responded by making a survey of a sample of Detroit auto workers, who at the time were earning about $7 a day, to find out how they spent their money and what they obtained for it in food, housing, and other goods and services.

When the United Nations was established in 1945, an agreement was negotiated between the United Nations and ILO in which the United Nations recognized the ILO as a specialized agency responsible for the international activities appropriate under its basic constitution. Thus, ILO is one of the U.N. organizations. However, it continues to be an independent agency with its own membership and its own operating budget, which is supplied by its member states. The representation of a state in ILO consists of four representatives, of whom two are government delegates, one a representative of employers, and one a representative of the workers. Most, though not all, of the U.N. members are also members of ILO. Nonmembers of the United Nations may be admitted to ILO. In actual practice, there is close collaboration between the two agencies; for example, ILO serves as a technical assistance agency for the United Nations.

OFFICE OF FOREIGN LABOR AND TRADE

Prior to 1945, BLS studies of foreign labor conditions were made by individual researchers assigned to this particular work. But in that year, the Bureau established the Foreign Labor Problems Branch to conduct studies and research of this nature. The function of the branch was to make studies of labor-related subjects in foreign countries and to cooperate with governments seeking to improve their labor statistics. This unit later became known as the Division of Foreign Labor Conditions, and its responsibilities were broadened to include training of statisticians from the countries of Western Europe and later from developing nations throughout the world.

By the late 1950's, the postwar pattern of economic growth and development had changed. The industrial nations of Western Europe and the industrial giant of Asia (Japan) had achieved business recovery. Their rates of economic growth exceeded that of the United States, even though their output and productivity levels were low. American policy was directed toward lowering tariff barriers, which put increased emphasis on imports and exports, international comparisons of wages and prices, productivity, and labor costs. The Bureau was called upon for service. At first, studies were conducted by the offices and divisions of the Bureau most directly concerned with the subject matter.

In 1967, the Bureau was reorganized again, and the functions formerly assigned to the Division of Foreign Labor Conditions were given to the newly created Office of Foreign Labor and Trade, headed by an assistant commissioner. This office consists of three divisions: Foreign Labor Conditions, International Technical Cooperation, and Foreign Labor Statistics. In each of these areas, the office acts as the research arm of the Department of Labor. Policy matters, such as the formulation of the U.S. position on matters of foreign labor and trade, are the responsibility of the Labor Department's Bureau of International Affairs, headed by an assistant secretary. The research-and-statistics work on all matters germane to the functions of BLS is delegated to the Office of Foreign Labor and Trade.

The Division of Foreign Labor Conditions maintains comprehensive information on foreign labor, and conducts research on manpower, labor conditions, laws, and practices in foreign countries. It continues the program started during the 1950's of publishing booklets helpful to American businessmen and government officials abroad. Early in the decade, the BLS published a booklet, *The Gift of Freedom,* which outlined and documented for other nations the achievements of a free economy. Later, the Bureau began publication of *Labor Developments Abroad,* which, in 1956, became a regular monthly publication, serving American concerns doing business abroad. In 1968 it was distributed on a paid subscription basis. Another publication that had great popularity was a pamphlet entitled *Economic Forces in the United States,* which summarized in statistical terms, the growth and expansion of the American economy with minimal interpretation. The seventh edition of this report reached a circulation of more than 100,000 copies. In addition to the preparation of the monthly publication *Labor Developments Abroad,* the division publishes several series of monographs on individual countries. One series consists of general labor studies, which include such subjects as manpower and employment, wages, cost of living, labor organizations, labor-management relations. Some of these have been done in cooperation with the Agency for International Development. Supplementing these more comprehensive studies are brief labor digests on individual countries, which are combined in larger reports on each continent.

Another series consists of studies on foreign labor laws and practices, which contain information useful to American business concerns that are considering doing business in the countries covered in the studies. Labor unions engaged in international activities also make use of these reports. According to a recent listing, nearly forty countries have been covered in this series.

Occasionally, special reports are made, such as "Recent Changes in Labor Controls in the Soviet Union," published in *New Directions in the Soviet Economy,* issued by the Joint Economic Committee of Congress.

The Division of International Technical Cooperation is responsible for the training of foreign statisticians, which the Bureau has been doing for the past two decades. By 1967, more than 400 statisticians from more than a score of countries had visited the BLS for intensive and comprehensive training in statistical methods suitable for the development of sound labor statistics in those countries. Many participants in these BLS programs occupy highly responsible positions in their own national governments.

Members of the division staff periodically make trips abroad to render service to foreign countries as well as to keep up to date on what is happening there. This division also prepares technical manuals on labor-statistics methods designed to enable the user to apply the methods in his own country. Some of these manuals (and their BLS Report numbers) are: *The Forecasting of Manpower Requirements* (No. 248), *Conducting a Labor Force Survey in Developing Countries* (No. 263), *Computation of Cost-of-Living Indexes in Developing Countries* (No. 283), *How To Establish Current Reporting of Employment, Hours, and Earnings in Developing Countries* (No. 302), and *How To Make an Inventory of High-Level Manpower in Developing Countries* (in preparation).

In the Division of Foreign Labor Statistics is centered all the work, to which many parts of the Bureau contribute, of making economic and statistical analyses of the impact of international trade upon labor and of preparing international comparisons of labor factors, both over-all and specifically, for individual countries and products.

The factors that govern the competitive status of American industry in international trade are the interrelationship of wages, prices, productivity, and labor costs. Wage comparisons are the most readily available, but their value is limited because although cash wages are not too difficult to obtain, the nature and amount of the fringe benefits differ widely from country to country. For instance, France has a system of family-wage payments in which deductions of about 14 per cent (in the early 1960's) are made from the basic wage of all workers and then are redistributed proportionately to married men with more than one child. In Great Britain, the health insurance system is supported to a considerable extent by income tax. Although it is difficult to compare wages for similar occupations or industries with dissimilar payment systems, comparison can be made. Several years ago, a joint team from the Bureau of Labor Statistics and the Japanese Ministry of Labor conducted a comparative survey of U.S. and Japanese wages.

Despite shortcomings, international wage comparisons are useful, and the Bureau will continue to publish them. Price trends are readily available in the form of consumer and wholesale price indexes for individual countries. A nine-year comparison of these two sets of indexes in twelve countries was published in the June, 1967, issue of *Labor Developments Abroad*. The figures showed that the United States had the most stable prices among the twelve. Chart X shows the twelve consumer price indexes. Even these well-developed indexes generate comparability problems, the most important of which is the rate of exchange of a nation's currency. Although the recent devaluation of the British pound (and of several related currencies) will have very little effect on the indexes in the short run, it is clear that British prices are now lower in terms of American dollars. (In fact, the devaluation enables Great Britain to compete in international markets.)

Just as increasing productivity is the basic source of a nation's internal standard of living, so too is comparative productivity the key to a nation's position in international trade. But, it is not productivity alone that determines position; it is productivity in relation to wages, that is, to the labor cost per unit of product. The great emphasis on productivity since World War II has stimulated efforts to obtain better measures in many countries, but productivity still ranks below wages and prices in the quantity and quality of measurement because productivity data (output per man-hour) are difficult to obtain in detail.

Over the years, the BLS has made persistent efforts to obtain some indirect trend comparisons of labor costs. In 1966, the Office of Foreign Labor and Trade published Bulletin No. 1518, *Unit Labor Cost in Manufacturing Trends in Nine Countries, 1950–65*. The indexes of unit labor costs were obtained by dividing the total manufacturing output in each country by the aggregate labor compensation in manufacturing. The results showed that unit labor cost in the United States in the second half of the period had declined slightly, while in all other countries, costs increased—in one case, as much as 5.5 per cent a year. However significant these comparative trends may be, the value is seriously affected by fluctuations in the worth of currencies. France and Canada, for instance, devalued during that period, while Germany and the Netherlands revalued.

What is most needed is an occasional direct country-to-country comparison of labor costs in specific industries, so that the trends will have some anchors from time to time. The BLS has done this for the iron and steel industry, on which a great deal of data are available in major industrial nations. The study covered four major steel-producing nations—the United

Chart X-a

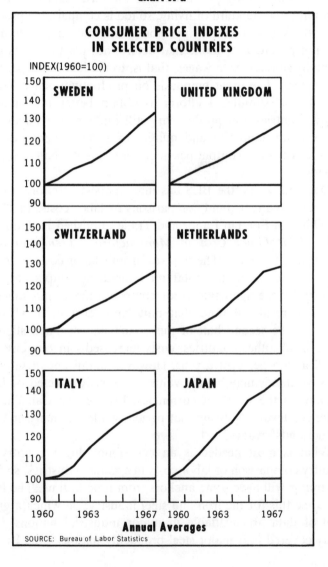

CONSUMER PRICE INDEXES
IN SELECTED COUNTRIES

INDEX(1960=100)

SWEDEN

UNITED KINGDOM

SWITZERLAND

NETHERLANDS

ITALY

JAPAN

Annual Averages

SOURCE: Bureau of Labor Statistics

Chart X-b

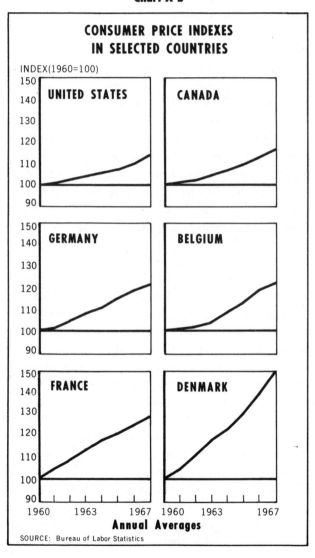

CONSUMER PRICE INDEXES
IN SELECTED COUNTRIES

INDEX(1960=100)

UNITED STATES

CANADA

GERMANY

BELGIUM

FRANCE

DENMARK

Annual Averages

SOURCE: Bureau of Labor Statistics

States, Great Britain, France, and Germany. It will be published in 1968 as a report entitled *International Comparison of Unit Labor Cost in Iron and Steel, 1964*. The study showed that although U.S. productivity averaged about twice as high as that of European countries in 1964, American wages were roughly three times as high, so that the labor cost per ton of steel was higher in the United States. This divergence may have been narrowed in the last few years, as unit labor costs of manufacturing industries generally have risen more in European countries than in the United States.

Another subject on which a great deal has been written is the comparative levels of unemployment in the United States and in foreign countries. In the United States, it has been difficult to get the unemployment rate much below 4 per cent. Yet, various European countries have for years reported rates of 3 per cent, 2 per cent, and 1 per cent. How can these countries achieve full employment at a higher level than we can? Again, the BLS has made several studies of this subject, analyzing both the figures and the national patterns of employment. A special study of the problem was made for the President's Committee to Appraise Employment and Unemployment Statistics, and articles were published by BLS staff members in the *Monthly Labor Review*. In summary, the facts are that the American statistical system (used also by Canada) more fully measures the number of unemployed than most European systems but even though allowances are made for statistical differences, the United States simply has less stable employment than European countries. A number of institutional factors help to explain the reasons. One is that most European countries have had widespread labor shortages, for which they have imported hundreds of thousands of laborers from neighboring countries. For example, in Switzerland, about 30 per cent of the labor force consists of foreign workmen brought into the country to do a particular job, but when the job is done, they are returned to their countries of origin. The unemployment problem is exported, so to speak. But, in 1967–68, some indications of higher levels of unemployment began to appear in most European countries. In France, the drift from the farms to the cities is beginning to exhibit characteristics similar to those in the United States since the end of World War II.

In the United States, the institutional factors that have caused relatively high unemployment, such as lack of education, lack of training, and a surplus of the unskilled, are being tackled by government and private programs designed to find jobs for the disadvantaged groups in the labor force.

X

The BLS and the Public

There are government agencies in Washington that actually shun publicity. The Central Intelligence Agency is a good example. CIA officials dare not highlight their successes, for that would give away their secrets. They have no need to publicize their failures—their critics do that for them. From the agency's point of view, any publicity is bad publicity, so it publishes no journals, issues no reports, and its employees make no speeches. But for every agency like the CIA, there are a score or more that seek to attract public attention in one way or another. Even agencies that have a high level of secrecy in their operations—the military services, the National Aeronautics and Space Administration, the Atomic Energy Commission—must impress upon the public from time to time the value of their performances. If they don't, it won't be long until their appropriations fall off. Think of the early, spectacular demonstrations of the astronauts, with a hundred million Americans (and countless others throughout the world) keeping all-day vigils before their television sets. But public memories are short. In a few years, with a war on and taxes going up, querulous voices began to be heard in the land. "What do we want to go to the moon for?"

Then there are agencies that must try to reach the public with news about their services, if they are to do their jobs at all. In the early days of the Social Security Board, it was urgently necessary to inform people of their rights and obligations. Employers had to be told that they were covered by the law; workers had to be told why they were required to contribute; eligible beneficiaries had to be apprised of their rights. Such processes are never-ending. Whenever the original legislation is amended, new instructions have to be issued.

The Bureau of Labor Statistics has no such nation-wide clientele. Its services reach a more limited audience—those who use labor statistics in one way or another. The BLS has to provide easy and adequate access to its facts and figures and provide answers to inquiries about its work. It must supply explanations of its results that are understandable to the average citizen.

PUBLICATIONS

In the first decade of its existence, the chief outlet for the Bureau's products was the annual report of the Commissioner. But as the work expanded, a few special reports became necessary. Then in 1895, it was decided to issue a continuing publication called the *Bimonthly Bulletin of the Bureau of Labor*. The primary function of the *Bulletin* was to serve as an outlet for the Bureau's research and statistics reports, although there were certain special features, such as summaries of changes in state labor laws, and occasionally articles by outside authors who made special studies of interest to the Bureau.

In 1915, after the Bureau had become part of the newly constituted Labor Department, Commissioner Royal Meeker converted the bimonthly bulletin into a monthly review, which later was named the *Monthly Labor Review*. For over half a century, the *Review* has been the basic publication of the Bureau. Throughout the years, it has established a solid reputation for accuracy, objectivity, and timeliness. As a friendly reader once said: "If you see it in the *Review,* it's so."

A major factor in the prestige achieved by the *Review* with labor, management, social scientists, and the general public was the high quality and long service of its editors. Two men have dominated the *Review* for nearly half a century. The first great editor was Hugh Hanna, a sound research statistician, who took over in the early 1920's and served for more than two decades. During that period, he was not only editor of the *Review;* he was also a member of the top policy team of the Bureau. When he retired in 1945, his successor was a young labor statistician, Lawrence R. Klein, who guided the *Review* from 1945 until his retirement in 1968. Those two men furnish proof that good editors make great publications.

One change introduced by Klein early in his service was a major revision in the format, appearance, and content of the *Review*. Due to its origin as a bulletin, it had previously been published in book size. It was hard to read and not well adapted to the reproduction of tables and charts. In the revised version, there were more feature articles, more charts, more tables, and an extensive book review section. There was a new sense of awareness and sophistication in the contents.

Another of Klein's innovations was the introduction of occasional "reader surveys" in order to obtain from *Review* readers their preferences on content and their suggestions for improvements. On a recent survey, there was a response rate of 83 per cent, which is considered phenomenal in magazine circles. Each survey demonstrated anew the extremely high quality of the readership and the informed character of their suggestions.

The *Monthly Labor Review* was awarded certificates of excellence in the National Institute of Graphic Arts magazine shows of 1950 and 1951. It was the only government magazine ever invited to compete. The *Review* format had been designed by Charles Pollock (brother of the late Jackson Pollock), Professor of Art at Michigan State University.

Another feature introduced by Klein was the publication of special issues of the *Review,* such as the July, 1950, issue celebrating the publication's thirty-fifth anniversary. It contained a special section of a dozen articles under the general title "Fifty Years' Progress of American Labor." Equally successful was the issue honoring the fiftieth anniversary of the Department of Labor in 1963. Scores of editors of national publications wrote letters of commendation and appreciation on that issue. From time to time, special issues have been devoted to various regions of the United States, as well as to particular subjects. In October, 1946, the first planned effort in the history of the publication to concentrate on a single subject in a single number of the magazine examined "Labor in the South." Subsequent special issues, on California and the Northwest, New England, and several other regions have recently been followed by a repeat of "Labor in the South" (March, 1968), in which seventeen authors, inside and outside the BLS, discussed industries and occupations, training and retraining manpower, the worker and the man. This issue, capped with its "Review Essay on the Growing South," by Ralph McGill, was another landmark in the history of the *Monthly Labor Review*.

The *Review* has been edited with such probity and painstaking care that it has acquired a national and international reputation as a research journal. Although it functions primarily as an outlet for BLS statistics and research, it does publish materials from other bureaus and offices of the Department of Labor and occasionally contains articles by outside contributors. In general, the *Review* adheres strictly to its fact-finding and research character although in the special issues, it often contains articles by outsiders on controversial subjects and policy problems.

The Department of Labor has never had a Department journal, and on several occasions proposals have been made to convert the *Review* into a Department publication with widened representation on its editorial board and an enlargement of the content to cover a greater range of subject matter. During Secretary Mitchell's administration of the Department, a proposal was made to give the Department's director of information supervision and direction of the *Review* editor and his staff, while leaving the personnel and budget within the BLS. On behalf of a unanimous BLS executive staff, I opposed the move on two grounds: The Office of Information was not an appropriate location for a research journal; it was unsound administration to make such a complete separation of responsibility and authority. Under-Secretary James O'Connell, whatever he may have thought about the first point, was keenly aware of the second, and he quietly buried the proposal.

About five years later, another proposal recommended the direct transfer of staff and funds of the *Review* to the Office of the Assistant Secretary for Research in the Department. For that proposal, there was some support within the BLS staff on the ground that such a move would enhance the status and prestige of the *Review* without changing its research character. However, most of my colleagues were opposed, some of them strongly; and I was moved by my previous experience in the Social Security Board, where a flourishing *Social Security Bulletin* housed in the Bureau of Research and Statistics became a wraith after it was transferred to the administrator's office. As an alternative, there was established a Department-wide planning advisory committee to the *Monthly Labor Review,* a high-level professional committee responsible for giving the BLS Commissioner and the editor advice on policy and program.

Today, the Department, through its office of information, exercises a final review function over all publications of the Department. At times, this practice has given rise to sharp differences of opinion. The Department staff is much more sensitive to political and public opinion than is the BLS. In addition, the Department represents the interests of other bureaus and offices, which may object to a BLS publication. The *Review* editor has to be a man of strength and competence, one who can stand firm or engineer the concessions that can safely be made. I recall only one instance when a scheduled *Review* article was temporarily withdrawn in deference to the needs of another bureau—and then it was only postponed for a month.

In addition to the *Monthly Labor Review,* the Bureau publishes these periodicals: *Employment and Earnings and Monthly Report on the Labor Force, Occupational Outlook Quarterly, Labor Developments Abroad,* and *Current Wage Developments.* There are also some significant periodic book-size bulletins of general interest: *Occupational Outlook Handbook, Handbook of Labor Statistics,* and *Directory of Labor Unions.* Then there are the periodic bulletins in the major fields of Bureau activity—manpower, prices, wages, etc. Every six months the Bureau issues a *Catalog of Publications,* which contains a complete list of all recent periodicals, bulletins, reports, and releases, including those for sale and those that are free. The latter can be obtained by applying to the Bureau or to one of its regional offices. The paid publications are for sale through the Superintendent of Documents, Government Printing Office, Washington, D.C. 20402, or at BLS regional offices, which act as sales agents for the GPO.

The Bureau has recently begun the publication of two new series—*Labor Issues in Perspective* and *BLS Staff Papers.* The Bureau has kept adding to its bulletin series and special reports, numbered consecutively since publication began. The bulletin series has now reached the 1,600 mark.

OTHER WAYS OF REACHING THE PUBLIC

The Bureau reaches the general public by a variety of other methods of communication. Every month, when the Consumer Price Index is released, the Commissioner or one of his subordinates conducts a press conference, which is open to all members of the press who care to attend. The index numbers, together with the Bureau's interpretation of the figures, are published in newspapers throughout the country. Several millions of workers and their families read these newspaper stories with special personal interest since their wages are increased or decreased from time to time depending on what is happening to the index.

Similarly, when the employment and unemployment picture is presented to the public each month, a press conference is held in order to answer the questions of the newsmen and to explain the economic factors behind the figures. Occasional press conferences are held whenever a research or statistical report of special significance is being published.

Despite all its publications—and partly because of them— the Bureau's staff receives citizen inquiries by letter, telephone, or personal visit. Answering these requests has required the Bureau to maintain small information units in Washington and in each of the regional offices.

Finally, there are public appearances of the Commissioner and members of the Bureau staff at conferences, forums, and meetings of all kinds. At meetings of national organizations, members of BLS headquarters staff usually attend and participate. There are many more regional and local meetings, at which the BLS regional director and members of his staff are represented.

In June, 1962, an incident occurred that illustrates the public-relations problem of the government official in a highly sensitive position. At the Interstate Conference on Labor Statistics held at Atlantic City, New Jersey, I interpreted the current economic situation for the audience, which consisted of federal and state government statisticians, state labor commissioners, university professors, and a few business and labor statisticians. After the address, a small group gathered around for further discussion. A young newspaper reporter, noting the four recessions since 1945, asked me whether a recession could develop in 1963. I incautiously replied that one might. Within a few hours, there were headlines in the press: "BLS Predicts Recession Next Year." Telephones began ringing, and for the next twenty-four hours an embarrassed Commissioner

was busy explaining that he had no intention of flatly predict-
ing a recession for 1963 but had only agreed that after several
years of business recovery a readjustment is always possible.
The stock market dropped some ten points the next day. Thus
I learned, once again, the hazards of careless or incautious
statements by a government official.

THE BLS AND THE LABOR MOVEMENT

The Bureau has always had close relationships with the
labor movement, even though at times relationships were
strained and stormy. In the 1880's, both the Knights of Labor
and the American Federation of Labor supported the Bureau.
Commissioner Wright must have had a perceptive insight into
the future, because at the Sixth Annual Convention of the
American Federation of Labor he invited Samuel Gompers to
visit the Bureau and become acquainted with its work. As it
turned out, Gompers dominated the American labor movement for the next forty years. Some years later, Terence V.
Powderly, the head of the Knights of Labor, became an employee of the Bureau.

Commissioner Wright acted as chairman of the commission
investigating the great Pullman strike of 1894, and the *American Federationist,* the official organ of the American Federation of Labor, praised Wright and his fellow commissioners for
their "lucid and conscientious report on the strike." Wright
also served as recorder of the Anthracite Commission investigating the coal strike of 1902. Neither side accepted the suggestions of the commission for the settlement of the strike, but
Wright continued as one of President Theodore Roosevelt's
trusted advisers on labor matters.

In 1901, when President Theodore Roosevelt first proposed
the establishment of a new department of commerce and labor,
the *American Federationist* strongly affirmed its stand for a
separate department of labor and its opposition to the inclu-

sion of the Bureau of Labor in the new department. It is some-what surprising that the Knights of Labor, by that time almost moribund, favored the bill and directly attacked Commissioner Wright for opposing it.

When the Department of Labor was finally established in 1913, the interest of the labor unions in statistics and research became secondary to their more pressing interest in various kinds of labor legislation; thus, the Department rather than the Bureau of Labor Statistics became the focus of their attention. Of course, the unions continued to make use of the Bureau's statistics on wages and prices in their collective-bargaining negotiations.

Following the passage of the Wagner Act in 1935, there was intensive union reorganization, leading to the creation of many new unions and a rapid expansion of union membership. A number of unions found it necessary to appoint research statisticians to assist in collective bargaining and contract negotiation. Such statisticians were especially useful in establishing contacts with government agencies important to labor, such as the Social Security Board, the Labor Department, and the National Labor Relations Board. The Bureau of Labor Statistics was a key agency for union activity since it supplied many of the statistics needed for those purposes. As a result, there developed close but informal working relationships between the union research group and the Bureau of Labor Statistics. This relationship led to an annual group meeting of the union statisticians and the Bureau staff. This was the situation that existed when the World War II controversy over the Consumer Price Index erupted. When certain members of the union research group took an active part in attempting to discredit the Bureau's Cost of Living Index, they acted as individuals rather than as representatives of the group. Other members refrained from joining in the attack. Nevertheless, Secretary of Labor Perkins, affronted by the activity of the attacking members, instructed Acting Commissioner Hinrichs to put a stop to the annual conferences. No additional group meetings were held.

When I became Commissioner in August, 1946, I took counsel almost immediately with certain members of the union research group whom I knew personally. During my ten years with the Social Security Board, I had had occasional meetings with union statisticians on social security matters. The Bureau of Labor Statistics staff was in agreement that it would be desirable to establish good working relationships with the union group, while at the same time avoiding some of the risks of the former system. It was finally decided to establish a formal Labor Research Advisory Committee consisting of twenty members—eight nominated by the AFL, eight by the CIO, and four by the Railway Labor Executives—all to be formally appointed by the Commissioner. The first meeting of this group occurred in February, 1947 (see Appendix C).

THE BLS AND BUSINESS

At the same time, I sounded out some of my friends among the business economists about the possibility of a business advisory group. At first, their reaction was in favor of an informal working relationship on an individual basis. However, when the announcement was made to the public about the appointment of the Labor Research Committee, there was a reaction from the business community. The executive director of the National Association of Manufacturers wrote to Secretary of Labor Schwellenbach, pointing out that business as well as labor made constant use of BLS statistics and therefore had a legitimate interest in establishing an advisory relationship. Secretary Schwellenbach was ill at the time, but Under-Secretary Keen Johnson gave me clearance to negotiate with the business community for the appointment of the Business Research Advisory Committee. The U.S. Chamber of Commerce joined with the National Association of Manufacturers in providing lists of names from which the Commissioner could appoint the members of the committee. It was decided to begin with a formal membership of twenty-four. The first meeting was held in October, 1947 (see Appendix D).

FUNCTIONING OF THE ADVISORY COUNCILS

Shortly after these two advisory committees began functioning, an agreement was reached to change their names. The two top advisory groups were designated as advisory councils, and the working subcommittees were designated as committees of the councils.

Throughout the twenty years of their existence, the councils have nearly always met separately with the BLS staff. At times, informal suggestions have been made on both sides that some joint committee or council meetings might be held, but the prevailing opinion has been against such a move. The advantage of separation is that the differences of opinion and judgment within each group can find freer expression in the council and committee meetings. A joint meeting might lead to a polarization of labor versus management and a shift of the discussion into policies instead of technical and professional issues.

There was one occasion when subcommittees of the two councils met in joint sessions—in the early 1960's when the revision of the Consumer Price Index was proceeding. The Price Committee of each council appointed a special subcommittee on the revision program, and these two subcommittees met jointly with the Bureau staff engaged in the revision. In effect, these meetings were seminars by Bureau staff members to insure that both groups would have mutual understanding of the Bureau's policies and procedures in the revision.

The principle on which the council members were—and still are—appointed is that they should serve as individuals and as technical experts in statistics, not as policy-makers. Congress expressed its judgment on this subject through the House Education and Labor Committee in its report on hearings on the Consumer Price Index in 1951:

> The subcommittee heartily approves the present system of advisory committees. We believe, however, that the advisory committees should remain just that: in an advisory capacity. In the final analysis it is up to the Commissioner of the Bureau of Labor Statistics to make the technical policy decisions.

Because I served as Commissioner with these advisory councils over such a long period of time, I have often been asked whether pressure has ever been brought to bear on the Commissioner and his staff. If pressure means the presentation of technical arguments with forcefulness and vigor, there certainly was plenty of that kind of pressure. On a couple occasions, the labor group, disappointed with a Bureau decision, retired to consult as to whether they should attempt to carry the issue to a higher level. But they always decided not to do so. There was also an occasion when members of the Business Council proposed that the salaried secretary to the Council be a person outside the government and responsible directly to the Council. The Bureau of Labor Statistics had always furnished from its own staff two secretaries, one for each council, and each secretary was responsible for a multitude of administrative details involved in several council meetings a year, in addition to numerous committee meetings. When the full Business Council took up the proposal, it firmly and categorically rejected it, without ever formally presenting it to the Commissioner.

As far as I am aware, at no time did either of these councils make a formal appeal to the Secretary of Labor to reverse a decision of the Bureau. If any individuals did so, it was without effect. Indeed, no Secretary of Labor ever approached me on any of the technical decisions made by the Bureau in the construction of its indexes or the development of its statistical series.

THE BLS AND THE PROFESSIONS

The Bureau has always maintained close working relationships with the professions directly concerned with its work. When Carroll D. Wright was director of the Bureau of the Statistics of Labor in the state of Massachusetts, he became acquainted with Francis A. Walker, who was at that time the dean of American economists. It was from Walker that Wright took the advice that moved him in the direction of nonpartisan objective research.

When Wright became the Commissioner of Labor in the federal government, there were even more occasions for professional consultation and collaboration. In 1880, Walker was the director of the Census and called upon Wright to be his adviser and assistant. In 1891, Walker and Wright collaborated in an effort to obtain legislation making the Census office a permanent instead of a temporary agency. In the Senate Finance Committee investigation of prices in 1891, Walker was one of the economists consulted by the Committee. Roland P. Faulkner became the Committee's statistician, while Wright with his Bureau of Labor staff performed service in the collection and tabulation of statistics.

In 1914, Commissioner Royal Meeker, who had been an economics professor at Princeton, turned immediately to his professional colleagues for advice and assistance. Wesley C. Mitchell of Columbia University was persuaded to undertake a thoroughgoing examination of indexes of prices in the United States and foreign countries. Later, during World War I, when the President directed the Commissioner to develop a cost-of-living index, Mitchell was again called in. He served as an adviser on the family-expenditure surveys of 1918–19, which were necessary for the construction of the price index.

In 1933, as noted in an earlier chapter, Secretary of Labor Perkins had barely taken over the reins of office when she made a formal request to the American Statistical Association for the appointment of an advisory committee to assist her in reviewing and improving the statistics of the Labor Department—which meant primarily the Bureau of Labor Statistics. The statistical association accepted the assignment, and an advisory committee to the Secretary of Labor was appointed. Due to the subsequent creation of the larger Committee on Government Statistics and Information Services, with government-wide scope, the labor committee was absorbed into the larger one and assigned responsibility for the review of Labor Department statistics. Thus, from two sources Secretary Perkins got the advice she wanted. The achievements of these committees have been set forth in previous chapters.

In World War II, when the cost-of-living controversy broke out into the open, the Bureau again asked the American Statistical Association to appoint a committee to review and evaluate the Cost of Living Index. A committee was appointed under the chairmanship of Fred Mills of Columbia University, one of the most respected statisticians in the country. The Mills Report was a strong reaffirmation of the soundness of the Bureau's statistical methods, but the controversy did not respond to professional treatment. It boiled into a policy battle, which led to the creation of another committee, appointed by the National Labor Relations Board and headed by Wesley C. Mitchell.

Still later, when the House Appropriations Committee in 1944 (perhaps in response to labor's criticism of the Cost of Living Index) authorized the Bureau to make a study of what it costs a family to live expressed in current dollars, the Bureau found it advisable, once more, to set up a statistical advisory committee on the development of standard family budgets. Its five members were all recognized statisticians, but on this occasion two came from the labor movement, two from academic circles, and one from an employer organization. They endorsed the work of the Bureau when the four-person family budgets were issued to the public in late 1947.

Finally, in the revision program for the Consumer Price Index, 1949–53, and again in 1959–64, the Bureau thought it necessary and desirable to appoint advisory committees from the statistical profession. Likewise, a committee was appointed to assist in the development of the standard family budgets, 1965–67. Throughout its history, the BLS has sought and welcomed (and acted upon) advice from professional economists and statisticians.

XI

Interrelationships with Other Agencies

When the Department of Labor was established in March, 1913, the Bureau of Labor Statistics was the largest and best known in the Labor Department's family of agencies. The stature of the Bureau and its Commissioner was further enhanced during World War I, when the Bureau took on new responsibilities—the creation of the Cost of Living Index, for example. New bureaus were added to the Department—the Women's Bureau, Children's Bureau, and the Conciliation Service—but subsequently others were taken away. The Bureau of Immigration and the Bureau of Naturalization were first combined within the Department and then later transferred to the Department of Justice. In 1935, the original proposal submitted to Congress for social security legislation assigned responsibility for unemployment insurance to the Department of Labor. However, Congress took exception to the Administration's organizational proposals and set up a new agency—the Social Security Board—to administer the social security program.

In the midst of all these changes, the Bureau of Labor Statistics continued to perform the growing research and statistics responsibilities of the Department. Symbolic of the importance of the Bureau and its Commissioner was President Roosevelt's decision in 1941 to move Commissioner Lubin into the White House, where he served as adviser to the President on labor matters and as a direct channel to the Bureau of Labor Statistics for guidance in its activities.

GOOD RELATIONSHIPS WITH THE DEPARTMENT

In general, during these first decades of the Department's existence, relationships between the Department and the Bureau were very good, despite the fact that the Bureau continued to maintain a semi-independent status with respect to certain functions. The Commissioner had authority to issue his own annual report to the Congress. Certain other responsibilities were assigned specifically by the Congress to the Bureau. Each succeeding Secretary of Labor apparently recognized this and accepted it. The Bureau was in the Department but not wholly under the control of the Department.

As far as the record shows, there was only one occasion, in 1931, when there was a serious break (described in Chapter III). That occurred when William M. Doak was Secretary of Labor and Ethelbert Stewart was Commissioner. The Bureau of Labor Statistics' employment reports were contradicting the Employment Service employment forecasts. Reports from witnesses indicate that on one occasion, when the Secretary of Labor was holding a press conference, newspaper reporters directed a question to Commissioner Stewart, who was present. The Commissioner gave an answer that, in effect, contradicted the interpretation the Secretary had been giving to the press. Nothing happened at the time, but when Commissioner Stewart's term expired in 1932, he was not reappointed. However, since he was well over seventy years of age, it is questionable whether the episode had greatly influenced the Secretary of Labor.

Relationships between the Bureau and the Department came to a head again in 1950, when the President's Reorganization Plan No. 6 was presented for congressional approval. The intent of the plan was to give the Secretary of Labor more authority over his constituent bureaus and offices. The Plan was not aimed primarily at the Bureau of Labor Statistics, but rather at a general problem that had developed throughout the history of the Department of Labor—and, indeed, has characterized much of the history of congressional action relating to all departments. Whatever may have been the reason on the part of the executive branch, certainly there had been a general tendency on the part of the Congress, in legislating new functions and agencies for the Department, to assign specific, semi-independent responsibilities to the subordinate agencies. The administrator of the Wage and Hour and the Public Contracts Divisions was specifically designated by law to make minimum-wage decisions. The transfer of the unemployment insurance program from the Social Security Board in 1949 left uncertain what responsibilities of the board itself had been transferred to the Secretary of Labor and to the director of the Bureau of Employment Security. Certain long-time responsibilities of the Commissioner of Labor Statistics had remained unchanged and unchallenged over the years.

The Reorganization Plan of 1950 was designed to assign to the Secretary of Labor full administrative responsibility over all the agencies under his command. This plan was discussed with me as Commissioner before it was sent down to the Congress. I discussed it with the staff of the Bureau. We in BLS were in agreement that there was no occasion for the Bureau to do other than support the proposal. In a number of instances, such as the authority of the Commissioner to issue independent reports to the Congress, the responsibility had lapsed through lack of exercise. Furthermore, as a matter of sound administration, I believed that the Secretary should have administrative authority over the agencies for which he was responsible. The independence of the Bureau and its Commissioner in technical and professional matters should rest upon firmness of purpose and mutual consent rather than upon legislative authorization. Therefore, I not only assented to the reorganization plan but I also appeared before the congressional committee to testify in its favor.

EMPLOYMENT SECURITY AND BLS

There have been difficult organizational problems between units within the Department. When the Social Security Board began operations in 1936, the Bureau of Unemployment Compensation (now the Bureau of Employment Security) had a strong interest in developing monthly employment and payroll reports in its constituent state agencies. However, the Bureau of Labor Statistics at the federal level and a dozen or more state labor departments at state and local levels had for a long time been operating their own reporting programs of employment and payroll statistics. Furthermore, the Bureau of Labor Statistics and the state labor departments had worked out a cooperative system. The effort of the Social Security Board to set up a monthly reporting system in every state engendered duplication problems at both the state and the federal level, because the Bureau of Labor Statistics was collecting reports from samples of employers in states where state labor departments were not active.

The problem came to the attention of Congress during World War II. In December, 1941, a few weeks after Pearl Harbor, President Roosevelt federalized the state employment services, while leaving the unemployment insurance functions of the state employment security agencies in the jurisdiction of the states. The federalized U.S. Employment Service later became a branch of the War Manpower Administration. The House Appropriations Subcommittee, which was responsible for both the Department of Labor and the War Manpower Administration appropriations, became convinced that there was duplication in employment statistics and reacted by ordering the elimination of the Research and Statistics Branch of the

Employment Service. The War Manpower Administration had to readjust its organization and its functions.

However, the problem could not be resolved simply by legislative fiat. There were legitimate reasons for the employment security agencies to obtain monthly employment and payroll reports from covered employers, while at the same time the BLS needed the complete employer coverage of the unemployment compensation laws to serve as annual bench marks for its sample employment series. Since every employer covered by state law had to report, quarterly and annually, his employment and payroll data, the state agency obtained a total count of all employees by firm and by industry. The Bureau of Labor Statistics' sample of employers served admirably to measure each month the changes in employment in the nation as a whole, in each state, and in a hundred or more cities, but a sample has to be checked back against the total or universe.

Thus, the problem of statistics arose again in the postwar period and became especially acute when the Bureau of Employment Security was transferred to the Department of Labor in 1949. The full responsibility for employment statistics was then located in the one department, and after the Reorganization Plan of 1950, the Secretary of Labor had authority to resolve the problem.

There are potential administrative difficulties in having two federal agencies dealing with a single state agency. In the early days of the Social Security Board (1936–39), it proved to be impossible to develop an effective working relationship between the Bureau of Unemployment Compensation in the Social Security Board and the U.S. Employment Service in the Department of Labor. A presidential reorganization plan was necessary in order to combine them into the Board's Bureau of Employment Security, which then operated as a unit in dealing with the state agencies. When the program was transferred from the Board to the Labor Department in 1949, the Bureau of Employment Security, including its unemployment compensation program, was transferred as a unit. The administrative problem then became the inclusion of the BLS in the partnership.

The arrangement finally worked out provided that the Bureau of Labor Statistics pay half the costs of the employment statistics functions in the state agencies, while the other half was financed by the Bureau of Employment Security in those states where the state Employment Security Agency was the cooperating agency. In about half a dozen states, the state department of labor was the cooperating agency that financed the state share of the costs.

On the administrative side, the BLS deferred to the operating bureau on all contacts with the state agencies. Whenever the Bureau of Employment Security was having difficult negotiations with one of its state agencies—on budgets or conformity with federal standards—the BLS stayed away from the state until the issue was settled. In this way, a combined federal-state employment statistics program has been made operational during the past decade and a half.

War Agencies

During World War I, adequate labor statistics did not exist. It was necessary to create them. The most significant feature of the Bureau's participation in the war effort was the development of the Cost of Living Index (see Chapter IV).

During World War II, the story was quite different. When the war broke out, the Bureau had just completed a major revision of the Cost of Living Index, which was immediately put to use in the government's program of price control. In addition, the Bureau became the special fact-finding agency for the Office of Price Administration, and the Bureau's activities in this phase of war activity gave rise to the wartime controversy over the Price Index.

An equally important activity was the BLS service to the

National War Labor Board, which had the responsibility for resolving wage disputes and for establishing modified wage controls. The activities of this labor board resulted in the price controversy noted above.

For the Selective Service System, the Bureau in World War II, made an analysis of the war production program to determine how large an armed force could be supported with the available resources. The Bureau concluded that conscription of labor would not be necessary in order to obtain sufficient workers for the civilian labor force. The Bureau's studies were used by the Senate Military Affairs Committee and by Bernard M. Baruch in advising against the drafting of workers.

For the Office of Production Management, the Bureau made studies of the relative labor cost of using premium pay for overtime versus second- and third-shift operations. Its conclusion was that premium pay at time and one-half was more efficient than manning additional shifts.

For the Senate Subcommittee on War Contract Termination, the Bureau made an intensive survey of contract termination experience after World War I and submitted a report entitled "Problems of Contract Termination." The Contract Settlement Act of 1944 incorporated the major objectives urged by the Bureau and the Department of Labor.

Among the more fruitful long-range achievements of the Bureau in World War II was the translation of the war production program into labor requirements and the compilation of estimates of essential civilian requirements for the War Manpower Commission.

One outcome of these services to war agencies was the establishment of BLS regional offices, which eventually became a permanent feature of Bureau organization (see Chapter II). In December, 1941, the Bureau initiated eight regional offices to cooperate with the Office of Price Administration. Later, in 1942, the Bureau established a total of twelve offices in order to provide wage service to the War Labor Board. In the postwar budget cuts of 1947–48, the Bureau lost all but five of these offices, but it was eventually able to establish a sixth, and in 1968 two more were added to make eight, all of which are listed in Chapter II.

THE BLS AND THE CENSUS BUREAU

The relationship of the Bureau of Labor Statistics with the Census Bureau has been sketched earlier in this book. When the Commerce-Labor agreement was worked out in 1959, the BLS became responsible for obtaining the appropriations for the program of collecting labor force statistics through household surveys. The Bureau then negotiated an agreement with the Census Bureau for the collection of the data in the field through the continuing Census organization, as well as the tabulation of the results on the Census computers. The BLS assumed responsibility for the analysis and publication of the data. This cooperative arrangement has proven to be both efficient and economical.

AGRICULTURAL RESEARCH SERVICE FARM SURVEYS

In 1960–61, when the Bureau of Labor Statistics was conducting its surveys of family expenditures for the purpose of revising the Consumer Price Index, a decision was made to enlarge the scope of the surveys to include farm, rural, and nonfarm families. For that expansion, the Bureau of Labor Statistics negotiated an agreement with the Agricultural Research Service for the collection and tabulation of the data from the farm families. The farm family-expenditure data were published by Agriculture, with a cross-referencing of the publications in the two agencies.

BUREAU OF THE BUDGET

With the Bureau of the Budget, the Bureau of Labor Statistics has a direct professional connection through the Office of Statistical Standards. Under the leadership of that office, Bureau staff members serve on many interdepartmental statistical committees. When the first input-output studies were made (see Chapter VI), the Office of Statistical Standards supplied the chairman of the Interdepartmental Committee, which reviewed the work of the Bureau and the other cooperating statistical agencies. When the economic growth project was set up in 1961, the chairmanship of the Interdepartmental Committee was assigned to the Council of Economic Advisers, while the Bureau of the Budget continued to supervise the allocation of funds among the cooperating agencies.

Council of Economic Advisers

With the Council of Economic Advisers, the relationships have been close and cooperative. The Bureau of Labor Statistics is custodian for a number of the most critical and controversial of the economic indicators that the Council uses as guides to its economic policies—such indicators as employment, unemployment, wholesale and consumer prices, wages and earnings, productivity. The Council's policy of the guideposts for collective bargaining, first formally set forth in 1962, related the wage increases in collective-bargaining agreements to the productivity increases of the private economy.

The Council from time to time has taken an active interest in the Bureau's statistics, both in supporting their extension and improvement as well as in suggesting analytical refinements. For example, during the early Eisenhower years, Council Chairman Arthur Burns was a vigorous proponent of extensive seasonal adjustments of statistical data. In some series, the seasonally adjusted data have practically superseded the original data in the Council's publications.

White House

Reference has already been made in several places to the contacts of the commissioners with the White House. President Cleveland and President Theodore Roosevelt both had occasions to make effective use of Commissioner Wright's knowledge of labor problems. President Wilson was well acquainted with Commissioner Royal Meeker, who, like Wilson, had been a professor at Princeton. In 1941, President Franklin Roosevelt brought Commissioner Lubin on to the White House staff to serve as labor and statistical adviser. In 1953, when labor-management problems arose over the revision of the Consumer Price Index, I had extended discussions in White House offices with Budget Director Dodge and Gabriel Hauge of President Eisenhower's staff.

Finally, even though there is now less direct contact between the Commissioner and the President, there is no doubt that the White House is keenly aware of the importance of the Bureau's activities. Every month, before critical statistics, such as the unemployment rate and the Consumer Price Index, are released to the public, advance copies and explanations of the figures are forwarded to the White House to insure that the President is fully informed.

State and Local Agencies

Reference has already been made to the activities of the federal Bureau of Labor during its first three decades in encouraging the creation of state bureaus of labor statistics. Commissioner Wright was a leader in the creation of the International Association of Governmental Labor Officials (of the United States and Canada).

An operating partnership with the state labor departments began about the time of World War I, when the BLS started the collection of employment and earnings statistics from employers and negotiated cooperative arrangements with the state statistics bureaus so as to avoid duplication. This cooperation became nation-wide (involving all states) when the employment-security statistical program went into full operation after World War II, as noted above. The BLS then had a cooperative employment statistics program with every state.

Meantime, other BLS programs began to take on state co-operation. One of the earliest was statistics of industrial haz-ards—work accidents and other hazards. In this case, the Bu-reau had no funds for grants-in-aid nor for contracts, but it did grant franking privileges for mail. A total of sixteen states now cooperate with BLS in this field.

In 1949, the BLS inaugurated a program of federal-state labor statistics conferences, which have become a significant factor in the promotion of federal-state cooperation as well as in the expansion and improvement of state and local statistics.

The original idea of these conferences was developed at a meeting of the Department of Labor Conference on Labor Legislation (in the states) in North Carolina in 1948. The BLS Commissioner Ewan Clague, the supervisor of BLS regional offices Walter Keim, and the North Carolina Labor Commis-sioner, the late Forrest Shuford, worked out a plan that culmi-nated in a conference held in North Carolina in 1949, at-tended by a dozen or more persons from perhaps half a dozen states. At first, the conferences were largely regional, so that nearby states could readily send representatives. But as the groups grew in number and size, they were converted into the annual Interstate Conference on Labor Statistics, composed of representatives of the Department of Labor, other federal agencies, state departments of labor and other state agencies, the Dominion Government of Canada, and the Canadian pro-vincial governments.

Over the years since 1949, a total of twenty-five conferences have been held in eighteen states and Toronto, Canada. At-tendance in recent years has averaged more than 250 persons. The increasing attendance and participation of representatives of the Dominion of Canada and the Canadian provinces, as well as of the Commonwealth of Puerto Rico, persuaded the delegates in 1967 to change the name to the North American Conference on Labor Statistics.

The International Association of Governmental Labor Officials, in its original resolution sponsoring the Conference, recommended that each state should establish a statistical program according to its own needs. At this writing, thirty-three state departments of labor have statistical units, either separately or in combination with the state employment security agency. At least twenty-seven states have initiated new programs or revised old ones in the past five years.

The Interstate Conference programs emphasized statistics of various types needed in the administration of legislation—to define areas of coverage, to measure progress, and to evaluate effectiveness of labor standards. Subject matter has included injury statistics for safety programs, minimum wages, labor-management relations, mediation, conciliation, employment-unemployment and manpower data on training, skill development, education, automation, productivity, labor-force characteristics, and data needed in studying local socio-economic problems, such as state economic indicators modeled on the national economic indicators of the U.S. Council of Economic Advisers.

In addition to the conferences, the BLS provides a variety of other services to the state labor departments: advice and consultation in establishing new statistical programs and improving regular work; training and orientation to state statistical personnel; technical procedures, statistical forms, and guidance on standard programs; and, cooperative programs for joint collection of data.

The emerging "crisis of the cities" has spotlighted the need for state and local statistics of many kinds. The employment and poverty programs initiated in the last few years require detailed data not now available through national series. Congressional interest in the development of social indicators, or welfare indexes, may stimulate state and local governments to seek more effective cooperation with federal statistical agencies such as the Bureau of Labor Statistics.

XII

The Commissioner and the Congress

Between a government career executive and a congressman there is a gulf far wider than the distance from the White House to Capitol Hill. There are public officials who can say truthfully that congressmen are among their best friends, and there are congressmen who admire and respect the public officials with whom they come in contact. Furthermore, there are times and circumstances in which they both find it advantageous to work in close collaboration in pursuit of common objectives. But, as a general rule, their viewpoints and purposes are likely to be so divergent that they are frequently in indirect, or even open, conflict. In over thirty years of experience as a senior public official, I have had a wide variety of contacts with congressmen in many different circumstances, yet the words that best describe my attitude in official contact with congressmen are "alert" and "cautious."

The difference in viewpoint is solidly based upon the differences in those men's respective functions in government. A high-level public official is directing an agency or promoting a program. His outlook is national; his immediate interest is bureaucratic and programmatic, using those words in a literal sense without any stigma attached to them. Conversely, the congressman's interest is geographic and diversified. His outlook is local (state-wide in the case of senators). He must never forget to serve his local constituency, or else he will not be in office beyond the next election. Furthermore, his years of service in the Congress provide him with no assurance of a public career other than through winning the next election. In this respect, a public official has a continuity and a security that congressmen usually cannot achieve. The official can look hopefully for promotion to division chief, office chief, bureau director, or commissioner.

As I reflect on my own friends who have followed these wholly different careers, I am struck by the differential treatment. For example, Paul Douglas and I have been personal and professional friends since 1919, when he was teaching economics at the University of Washington and I was a graduate student in political science. We both have taught economics at various universities. I entered the federal civil service, while he entered government through the political route, first in the Chicago City Council and then in the U.S. Senate. He became one of the most respected senators of his time, yet at the climax of his career he went out of office by being defeated in an election, while I in the executive branch retired with honors. I cannot imagine that Senator Douglas would have exchanged his public experience for mine, but I can understand that many congressmen may resent the contrast.

The contacts of a government official with members of Congress can be divided into four main classes: appropriations, programs, personal relationships, and conflicts on issues. For the head of a bureau, the dominant one is appropriations.

APPROPRIATIONS

The one feature of my work as Commissioner of Labor Statistics that I heartily disliked was the task of obtaining appropriations. This task is basic and all-important, for without appropriations, neither the agency nor the program would exist. But this is one field of executive-congressional relationships in which the two parties are on opposite sides of the table. At best it is a difficult relationship; at its worst it is almost unbearable (for the executive). On one side is the executive with his staff of assistants, each with briefcases loaded with exhibits. On the other side is a chairman with some members of his subcommittee, who drop in and out of the hearing. The subcommittee has a clerk who obtains such information as he can and assists the subcommittee in developing its line of questioning. From the congressmen's point of view, the problem is whether they are getting full answers to their questions, or even the right answers. Sometimes a congressman feels frustrated, and even infuriated, because he thinks he is not getting the whole truth. In this situation, we in the Bureau of Labor Statistics hew to the axiom that honesty is the best policy.

For example, a Republican member of the House subcommittee was questioning me about the relationship of wages and prices. He asked why we didn't publish in the *Monthly Labor Review* the average weekly earnings of workers, with the rise in the cost of living and income taxes deducted. I explained that we did issue such figures regularly and that we could put them in the *Monthly Labor Review*. Later, we did just that. When a congressman has an idea like this you can expect him to return to it. So, the next year at the hearing, I brought along a copy of the *Review*. Sure enough, the first question he asked was a reminder of what he had suggested last year, with a query as to what had happened to his idea. I simply handed across the table to him the *Review*, opened at the page where the table appeared. He said, "Well, I have always heard that you were an honest man, and now I see that you are." We had no trouble that year with our appropriation.

The Bureau of Labor Statistics is a general-purpose statistical agency, which has no great glamor for a congressman. As mentioned above, a congressman's primary interest is in his own district. Membership on the Appropriations Committee insures him access to the flow of federal funds. His decisions will be in the direction of agencies and programs that can provide grants or contracts to his district. There have been occasions (and not infrequently) on which the Congress has appropriated more money to an agency than the Bureau of the Budget permitted the agency to request. I can recall several occasions when the attempt of the Bureau of the Budget, on behalf of the President, to impound some of the appropriated funds was blocked by congressional insistence that the funds be spent as appropriated.

At the Bureau of Labor Statistics, we considered ourselves lucky if we came through the hearings with nothing more than small cuts. Furthermore, our requests were usually quite modest. When I first took charge of the Bureau in 1946, we had about 1,700 employees, supported by regular appropriations and other funds. When I retired in the autumn of 1965, the Bureau averaged about 1,550 employees. Of course, our dollar appropriations nearly tripled—from about $7 million to $20 million—but most of these funds were absorbed in rising salaries and other costs.

After our initial run of bad luck in 1947–48 (see Chapter I), the Bureau had some luck. It was a stroke of good fortune to have Congressman John Fogarty of Rhode Island as chairman of the House Subcommittee and Senator Lister Hill of Alabama in the Senate. Congressman Fogarty had been a trade union man before he entered the Congress, and he was deeply interested in the Department of Labor. Senator Hill was primarily interested in public health matters, but he was a good friend of the Bureau of Labor Statistics. On one occasion, when the Bureau was requesting a vitally important appropriation for our wage program, the request was in the form of a deficiency appropriation, which came before another subcommittee in the Senate. I asked Senator Hill if he could find time to attend the hearing, so that our regular committee would be fully informed of our action. Senator Hill not only attended the hearing; he also arranged to conduct the questioning on my presentation. We obtained the whole amount. It is possible that the history of the Bureau of Labor Statistics would have been quite different had it not been for the assistance of friendly legislators like Fogarty and Hill.

In approximately thirty years of service as a bureau director in the federal service, I never missed an appropriation hearing. The importance of this was borne upon me through an episode that occurred in the early years of the Social Security Administration. Federal Social Security Administrator Paul McNutt was away somewhere on a speaking trip when the Senate committee called a hearing on the agency appropriation. His deputy and staff appeared in the hearing room. The first question by the chairman was, "Where is Mr. McNutt?" It was explained that he was out of the city and could not get back in time for the hearing. The chairman then said (in substance): "In that case we'll adjourn the hearing. When Mr. McNutt is available to testify, we'll schedule another hearing." The committee was miffed that Mr. McNutt did not think it important enough to arrange to be there.

In general, there are two sources of strength in getting appropriations in Congress. One is to have substantial and vocal public support, such as is enjoyed by agencies dealing with war veterans. When I was director of the Bureau of Employment Security, one of my units was the Veterans' Employment Service, which was associated with the U.S. Employment Service. The Veterans' Service was a small unit—one man in each state, with a few regional supervisors. The purpose was to assist state employment services in finding jobs for veterans. On one occasion (after I had left that Bureau) the director of the Veterans' Service made such a careless and ineffective justification of his appropriation that the House Subcommittee made a drastic cut. The public response was electrifying. The veterans' organizations had put on heat. One House member, who had voted for the cut, actually appeared before the Senate committee to urge that it be restored. Later, this director was eased out of his position, because congressmen do not like to be humiliated.

The Bureau of Labor Statistics has no such aggressive clientele. It has been well supported by labor unions, businessmen, and veterans' organizations. But nobody ever threatened a march on Washington on behalf of the Bureau of Labor Statistics. Therefore, it has always had to fall back on the second method, namely, making the most effective and persuasive presentation possible. In the beginning, and for a good many years, I was not very good at this job. I was always a program man rather than an administrator, and I had little skill or interest in budget matters. But, by dint of hard work and constant rehearsals with the staff, plus prolonged experience in such hearings, I finally got to the point where one congressman, having listened to an enthusiastic exposition of mine on the value of statistics in preventing business recessions, said, "You're too eloquent; I'm trying to save some money."

There is one significant difference between the Senate and the House in the appropriations procedure. In the Senate, the hearings of the appropriations subcommittees are usually open to the public. When testimony is presented there on behalf of departments and agencies, newsmen and visitors are frequently in the audience. On the other hand, the House has always kept its hearings private, which has the effect of enabling congressmen to haze the witnesses without the risk of publicity. It is true that the hearings are eventually published, but then no one reads them except possibly the agency executives who explore them in preparation for the next year's hearing.

The United States differs from most other modern industrial nations in its budgetary processes. I often envied my counterparts in Great Britain, France, and other European nations who obtained their appropriations within the framework of the executive branch of their governments. In those countries, the full budget has to be submitted to the parliament for scrutiny and approval, but individual executives never appear before the parliamentarians.

The American system subjects the executive to individualis-

tic and localized pressures, which may be quite inconsistent
with national policy. Even the Bureau of the Budget, in pass-
ing upon agency budget requests, has to take into account the
temper of the House subcommittee that will eventually pass
upon it. On one or two occasions, the Bureau of Labor Statistics was the beneficiary of a decision about which agency
should request funds for a certain program, because it was felt
that its chances would be better than others. But I can recall
many more instances in which a coordinated interagency program went down the drain because one or another of the agencies failed to get its appropriation.

There is one advantage of the American system: it produces
a forceful, public-minded official. My counterpart in Great
Britain, for example, would never dream of issuing a public
statement in his own name. Labor statistics there are published
with a minimum of interpretation, and there is not a single
name in the official *Labour Gazette*. In the United States, the
Monthly Labor Review and other publications are strewn with
the names of the officials and most of the interpretative articles
are signed. There is certainly far more freedom in public relations in the American Government. In this sense, our federal
government is highly decentralized.

PROGRAMS

The feature of the Commissioner's job that I enjoyed most
was testifying before congressional committees on programs
and legislation. From the day of its origin, the Bureau has always enjoyed excellent relationships with congressional committees on program matters. These appearances of the Commissioner, or members of his staff, represented an opportunity
to display the Bureau's statistical wares. Although the Commissioner usually took the lead in such hearings, there was
often ample opportunity for assistant commissioners and division chiefs to testify along with the Commissioner, or on their
own responsibility. One of the qualifications considered essen-

tial for a good division chief was the capacity to handle himself (or herself) before congressional committees.

Reference has already been made to the House Education and Labor Committee, which is the program committee for the Department of Labor. It was this committee that took up the challenge to the Consumer Price Index during the Korean War (see Chapter XIII). That committee has less contact with the Bureau of Labor Statistics than it does with other agencies in the Department of Labor that are more directly concerned with labor legislation.

In the Senate, the Committee on Labor and Public Welfare is the program committee on labor matters. Like its House counterpart, it also is usually much more concerned with the legislative program of the Labor Department than it is with the Bureau of Labor Statistics as such. However, that committee has a vital significance for the Commissioner because it passes upon his nomination for the office. When I was first nominated in 1946, Senator Joseph Guffey of Pennsylvania was the senior Democrat, and it was through him that Secretary of Labor Schwellenbach negotiated the special hearing that was called. At that hearing, Senator Robert Taft was the Republican member who asked a few questions concerning Bureau statistics. He must have been satisfied, because he was a good friend to the Bureau on a number of occasions afterward. In fact, once he went in person before the Senate Appropriations Subcommittee to testify on behalf of a Bureau appropriation.

When my renomination was submitted to the Senate in 1950, Senator Francis Myers, Democrat, of Pennsylvania endorsed me, so there was no problem. But when Secretary Mitchell proposed my name again in 1954 a snag developed. Senator Edward Martin, Republican, objected. Senator James M. Duff, the junior Republican senator, endorsed me, but that was not sufficient. The senior senator from a state can block an appointment by declaring the nominee unacceptable to him personally. Secretary Mitchell assigned me to Labor Department work in my civil service capacity, while Deputy Commissioner Wickens became acting commissioner.

I took no part in the campaign for my renomination, and I do not know all the steps that were taken. What I do know is that my friends and supporters never gave up. My labor friends could not do much; they had no influence where it counted. But my business friends were able to reach into the top levels of the Republican party in Pennsylvania. Their zeal was not simply a matter of friendship for me. They were deeply concerned that the Commissionership of Labor Statistics should not become a political appointment. Eventually, they were able to persuade Senator Martin to withdraw his objection. When that occurred, President Eisenhower submitted my nomination.

When the hearing was held in the summer of 1955, Senator Lister Hill was in the chair. There was a good representation in the committee meeting. Senator Barry M. Goldwater was among the Republicans. Many letters from individuals and organizations were read into the record. Senator Alexander Smith of New Jersey asked me a friendly question about a 1933 clipping from a Philadelphia paper that had received some publicity (1955 was the era of McCarthyism). When the questioning was over, Senator Hill said: "Now, Mr. Clague, if you will retire from the room the Committee will discuss your nomination." I gathered up my papers and walked toward the door. I had barely reached it when Senator Hill called out, "Come on back. We have just approved you unanimously." It was a heart-warming experience.

In 1959, the journey to the Capitol was a pleasure trip. Again, President Eisenhower submitted the nomination and at that hearing Senator Joseph Clark, Democrat, endorsed me. One of my treasured mementos is a copy of the five-minute hearing that took place.

A much more active and continuing relationship has been maintained by the Bureau with the House Post Office and Civil

Service Committee, which is responsible for legislation on government wages and salaries. Nearly every year the Commissioner and Bureau experts on wages and salaries testify in hearings on federal pay bills. The community wage surveys, which the Bureau conducts in eighty-five cities throughout the country, and the special salary survey of higher level positions in private industry, constitute the data that the Congress reviews in arriving at its decisions. In the early postwar years, attention was centered on the Consumer Price Index, since the cost of living loomed large in people's minds as the foundation for wage increases. Once, when a Bureau expert, answering questions on the composition of the index, disclosed that whiskey was one item listed under "other goods and services," a congressman on the committee demanded to know why the Bureau put whiskey in and left church contributions out. The expert explained that the Bureau did not "put items in" on its own responsibility but merely recorded what people actually bought and that church contributions were a gift and not a price paid for the minister's sermons. This logic was accepted by the committee.

In the later 1950's, it became evident that wages and salaries in private industry were responding to productivity increases as well as to the cost of living. It was then that the President and the Congress began to look more closely at wages and salaries in private industry as guides to government policy on federal pay. And it was then that the Bureau's wage and salary surveys became the foundation for government action.

On occasion, a congressional committee devoted to subjects quite remote from labor problems considers it desirable to obtain tesimony from the Bureau. The Senate Banking and Currency Committee is an example. One day in the mid-1950's, the Bureau presented testimony on wage increases over a period of time. The next day, President George Meany of the AFL-CIO was testifying on the same subject. Almost immediately, I got a telephone call from Senator A. Willis Robertson of Virginia requesting me to come down at once to explain to the committee a discrepancy between some figures presented by President Meany and those supplied by the Bureau. The answer turned out to be simple. Meany had measured the wage increase from a different, earlier, year; he had used exactly the same table of data the Bureau had. The suspicion that had begun smoldering among committee members was immediately dissipated. Ever after that, Senator Robertson was a friend to the Bureau and to me.

The program committee with which the Bureau has most frequent relations is the Joint Economic Committee. Since its formation in 1946, working relations, both formal and informal, with that committee and its staff have been close. This is not surprising in view of the committee's responsibility. The Joint Economic Committee operates differently than do most congressional committees. On most, the chairman is permanent until he is retired from Congress or unless he moves on to what he regards as a higher chairmanship. But with the economic committee, the chairmanship shifts between the House and the Senate every two years. Of course, a previous chairman may serve a second or third time if he continues to hold his seniority in his own branch.

The Bureau's relationships with the Joint Economic Committee have been mentioned in a number of places in this narrative, and there is no point in repeating them here. It is sufficient to note that, from the program point of view, this is the congressional committee that most closely represents the professional interests of the Bureau of Labor Statistics.

PERSONAL RELATIONSHIPS

Contacts with individual congressmen can occur on a variety of matters—requests for information, a job for a constituent, action on a grant or a contract, etc. I was often amazed at the extent to which congressmen took an active interest on behalf of some constituent whose case seemed positively inconsequential. In general, the congressmen in these situations fall into two groups. On the one hand, there are those like the late Senator Kenneth McKellar of Tennessee. In the years of controversy with Chairman David E. Lilienthal of the TVA, Senator McKellar announced categorically that every federal job in the state of Tennessee was a matter of direct interest to him. Chairman Lilienthal was trying to establish a merit system and succeeded in doing so in the face of McKellar's bitter opposition.

Fortunately for us, the Bureau of Labor Statistics was not subjected to very much of this kind of pressure. We had several advantages: We were small; we were highly specialized; and we were national and regional rather than local. But even we once came in contact with Senator McKellar. Whenever the Consumer Price Index is revised, it is necessary to hire temporary local agents for a period of a few months. The task requires educated and personable individuals who can visit families in the community and fill out a detailed questionnaire. Since there are no civil service lists for such jobs, it is always necessary to obtain a proviso in the appropriation that the jobs can be filled without regard to civil service. To assist in obtaining qualified personnel, the BLS arranges with the U.S. Employment Service to conduct an examination in each community in order to screen out the best applicants. In one community in Tennessee, a young woman who wanted a job appealed to McKellar's office, and we in the Bureau were asked about giving her a job. She had not taken the examination, which was already over. This was a very minor matter, but it could have affected our appropriation materially. We compromised by reopening the examination so that she could take it. She came to the local employment office, took one look at the questions, and walked out. On another occasion, when we were testifying before the Senate subcommittee, a small appropriation of ours involved a couple of dozen jobs of this exempt kind. As I was leaving the hearing, the administrative assistant to one of the senators followed me out in the hall and asked if any of those jobs were available to citizens of his state; the senator had requests from several persons who seemed to be right for them. Upon examination, it turned out that these candidates could not possibly be interested in our temporary positions. But the senator's office could not afford to overlook a possibility.

On the other hand, among those congressmen concerned with every detail affecting their constituents, there is the kind represented by Senator Leverett Saltonstall of Massachusetts. When the Bureau of Labor Statistics was being urged by both labor and management to conduct a special wage survey in the textile industry, with a view to obtaining data for a forthcoming collective-bargaining session, the New England textile employers had notified their congressional delegations. Senator Saltonstall called me personally on the phone and spoke somewhat as follows: "If it is appropriate for me to do so, I would like to urge that you make this special study; it would be of great service to us in Massachusetts." I assured him that it was quite appropriate and that the BLS was working out plans about how it could be done.

Employees within the government sometimes appeal to congressmen when they get into trouble with their superiors. In 1950, when we were conducting the Consumer Expenditure Survey for the revision of the Consumer Price Index, we had a considerable number of temporary employees exempt from civil service employed in our statistical pool here in Washington. The Korean War had broken out, and the task was complicated by the rapid changes taking place within the government. The pool was lodged in wooden temporary buildings remaining from World War II. Our BLS supervisors worked heroically to maintain discipline and productivity. One young man from Boston became enamoured of one of the young women and spent much of his time talking to her at her desk. Repeated warnings had no effect, so we finally dismissed him. He went down to the Hill and enlisted the support of members of the House Post Office and Civil Service Committee, who conducted an investigation. Several disgruntled employees testified that the work was disorganized and inefficient. The staff of the committee came to see me and my chief subordinates but would not show us the details of the testimony nor give us the names of the complaining employees (the latter point being that we might punish them for testifying). We opened up our records, permitted them to explore as fully as they wished among our employees. Our general impression was that their findings were completely favorable to the Bureau. It is impossible to exaggerate our dismay when a headline story appeared in the Washington newspapers to the effect that the BLS was wasting its $850,000 appropriation for the survey. When we obtained a copy of the subcommittee report we were even more astonished at the contrast between fact-finding and the conclusions in the document. The committee staff had made a simple statistical survey of BLS employees, asking such questions as whether they received good supervision, whether they were properly instructed in the work. This survey showed that the vast majority of the employees were completely satisfied. On the strength of this statistical table, which was published, the Bureau wanted to carry on a dialogue with the staff of the subcommittee, but the Secretary of Labor felt that he could handle it much better from his level. He made an arrangement by which we would write a letter promising to tighten up our administration and correct any deficiencies that were found. In exchange, the committee agreed to drop the matter.

In this case, we never did find out exactly what happened. We had the distinct impression that the committee staff was convinced of our probity but that one or two congressmen had some gripe against the Department of Labor. The fact that the Secretary was able to snuff out the blaze would indicate that he had some bargaining power. In any event, the incident was closed, and our appropriation for the revision of the index did not suffer in any way.

Here is another incident that illustrates the way in which an agency may be caught up in a political storm. During the Korean War, the Bureau of Labor Statistics was engaged in providing research and statistics service on certain subjects for the War Production Board. In an emergency situation involving copper, the Board requested the Bureau to conduct a statistical survey of the copper industry, with the results to be available in a week or so. In order to elicit a response, I as Commissioner sent a telegram to the presidents of the companies requesting their cooperation in answering the few key questions being asked. In some way or other, a congressman learned of this inquiry. He got up on the floor of the House and denounced the Bureau of Labor Statistics for spending thousands of dollars in telegrams when they could just as well have sent an air-mail letter. It was 1952, an election year. Furthermore, it was in the spring, and the Bureau's regular appropriation was up for congressional consideration. In this crisis, I requested help from Henry Fowler, then chief of the War Production Board, more recently Secretary of the Treasury. He came promptly to our rescue. He sent down a letter indicating that he had authorized the survey and had paid for it and that we were acting under his instructions. The subject was dropped immediately; the critic did not want to take on the War Production Board. Fowler was—and is—an example of the type of executive who accepts responsibility readily and forcefully.

CONFLICTS ON POLICIES

One of the most difficult of all situations for an executive arises when the agency is committed to a policy opposed by Congress or by an influential congressman. Anyone who has ever lived in the District of Columbia is keenly aware of the extent to which the District committees of the Congress exercise control over the policies of the D.C. government. District executives have on more than one occasion been called down to the Hill by a chairman of a District committee and told that the policy must be changed. The District of Columbia does not have a responsible city government in the ordinary meaning of that term.

This same situation can arise in federal agencies, also. It is not a matter of conflict over legislation. The Executive Branch may propose legislation, which the Congress has the power and responsibility to reject, if it opposes. What I am talking about here is the exercise of control by the executive branch over the administration of a law that is already on the books or over the operations of an agency within its own sphere of responsibility. Among several experiences of this kind that I had during my years in government service, the following, which occurred when I was director of the Bureau of Employment Security, is an extreme example and a curious footnote to history.

Today in Washington, D.C., we have a Negro mayor and an integrated city council. The situation was different in the spring of 1941. The House Subcommittee was holding hearings on the social security budget. The Bureau of Employment Security and the U.S. Employment Service had recently been combined. The USES was responsible for the supervision of the D.C. Employment Center, in which there were three separate offices—two for whites and one for Negroes. This situation confronted every prospective employer with the decision of whether he wanted a white or a Negro worker, and handicapped the white employment offices in referring Negroes to skilled and commercial jobs, because files for Negroes were in another building.

Martin Carpenter, the director of the USES, had just completed an administrative survey of the center and had recommended to me and to the Social Security Board that the offices be combined in the same building. It was a very modest proposal—a central room where files for both Negro and white applicants could be kept, with a waiting section for whites on one side and a section for Negroes on the other. Employment interviewers could then consult both files.

Carpenter had discussed the proposal with the District Center Director and his staff and had encountered some resistance from some of the whites (not all). Taking advantage of the fact that appropriation hearings were coming up, the dissident group got out an anonymous circular, which was sent to the members of the Appropriations Subcommittee. The circular was an exaggerated and untruthful distortion of the plan, which had not yet been approved by the Social Security Board. But the issue exploded in the appropriation hearings.

On the first day of the hearings, the issue was raised with Chairman Arthur J. Altmeyer of the Board, but he knew very little about it, except in the most general terms. On the second day, I was questioned and was under a disadvantage because I did not have all the details. The plan was still only a proposal for discussion with the Board. Many of the questions were of the "answer yes or no" variety by congressmen who had distorted pictures in their minds. However, it became clear that we were proposing a consolidation of the offices.

The Subcommittee's chairman, who came from Georgia, closed the subject for that day with the following admonition:

> Well, I am very much disappointed that a man of your type is in charge of this service. I don't know where you hail from or what your training may have been. But let me say to you and to everyone else who may entertain the unfortunate ideas that seem to afflict you, that whenever you try to do away with the distinctions which God Almighty made between people you are attempting the impossible.

For the next day, the Subcommittee requested the appearance of Martin Carpenter plus the top officials of the D.C. Center. I stayed away so that Carpenter would not be affected by the prejudice against me, but it did not help. For hours, Carpenter was questioned and finally was dismissed with these words by the chairman: "Of course, I regret very much that a man of your type is in a position of authority in the government, Mr. Carpenter."

One interesting and significant sidelight came out in the questioning by a Wisconsin congressman, who asked the D.C. director if all the applicants who came to his office were white. The answer was: "With one exception. We have, connected with the D.C. Employment Center, but not on the payroll of the Center, a veterans' placement adviser whose function it is to advise veterans. And he sees both white and colored applicants."

Even in those days, the military was ahead!

The outcome in that year was that the Subcommittee required that the plan be set aside for the time being. But after Pearl Harbor, when the United States was in the war, the plan was put into operation, and the D.C. Employment Office has been integrated ever since.

XIII

Conflicts and Controversies

It might be assumed that a bureau of research and statistics would be practically immune from conflicts and controversies. The BLS enforces no laws or regulations; it obtains its reports from respondents by purely voluntary methods; it issues statistics and reports that are strictly factual; and it assumes no responsibility for the decisions on the government's economic policies. However, the Bureau has discovered through bitter experience that statistics that serve as the foundation for government policies can subject the statistical agency to attack by those who object to the policies.

It is possible that during the first half-century of the Bureau's experience (up to the middle 1930's), there were a number of occasions on which the Commissioner or the Bureau came under attack, but none seems to have attracted nation-wide attention. Most likely, the conflicts were confined to the Executive Branch and to the Congress. It is only during the last thirty years, when statistics have begun to play such an important part in the nation's economic and social policies, that major controversies of public importance have focused upon the statistical agencies and their data.

THE PRICE INDEX IN WORLD WAR II

It was noted in Chapter I that as a result of the recommendation of the Committee on Government Statistics and Information Services, the Consumer Price Index was revised and brought up to date during the period 1935–39. The revision was completed soon after World War II broke out in Europe. As the U.S. defense effort expanded in 1940–41, the index began to be used by the government agencies concerned with the developing problems of wartime.

The sequence of economic events in a war economy is inevitable:

1. Government demand expands rapidly and persistently.

2. Labor becomes scarce, thus making the bargaining position of unions very strong and the resistance of employers very weak.

3. High wages are established in the war industries, partly in order to attract labor from other industries and partly because war industries usually require higher skills.

4. Overtime becomes widespread, which means that weekly earnings expand much faster than straight time hourly wage rates; hence, the purchasing power of the workers expands more rapidly than their wage rates.

5. The pressure of excess demand sends consumer prices upward, and the government turns to price control in order to halt the wage-price spiral.

6. To facilitate price control and to assure an adequate distribution of necessities among the population, a system of rationing is introduced; money alone will not buy beefsteaks—that requires "red points."

7. An inflationary gap develops, because there is more purchasing power in circulation than there are goods and services available for the civilian population.

8. The government raises taxes, but these tend to lag behind the expansion in purchasing power, both in time and in amount.

9. To mop up the excess purchasing power, the government sells savings bonds to induce people voluntarily to convert

their wartime earnings into government funds for the prosecution of the war.

This sequence will occur in every war that is of any significant size in relation to the civilian economy. It took place in the Korean War, and the early stages were evident again in 1966–68.

During World War II the Bureau was drawn into a major controversy about the price index. The controversy arose over prices, but the initiating factor was wages. It was not price control, but wage control, that triggered the battle. Furthermore, it was not the activities of the Bureau that initiated the issue; it was the War Labor Board, which administered wage control, that generated the problem. Only in the end did the Bureau of Labor Statistics become the victim. It was like a Greek tragedy in which government, labor, management, and the general public were all drawn, step by step, into a conflict that eventually focused on the statisticians. This episode was described in detail by Kathryn Smul Arnow for the Inter-University Case Program (see Bibliography). What I propose to do here is to summarize the highlights of the drama in three acts.

During Act I, the defense period, 1940–41, the Roosevelt Administration established a seven-man council (the National Defense Advisory Commission), which guided the government's expanding defense effort. There were no serious economic problems, since unemployment was at high levels (about 14 per cent in January and February of 1941) and plenty of workers were available for the expansion. However, by the end of the year, unemployment had fallen to about 6 per cent, and the economy was beginning to heat up.

The shock of Pearl Harbor produced immediate and forceful responses by the Roosevelt Administration. For example, within two weeks, the President obtained the consent of the state governors to federalize the state employment services. In January, 1942, the President appointed the twelve-man War

Labor Board, consisting of representatives of labor, management, and the public. This board was to have jurisdiction and final determination of all labor disputes. By Executive Order, price ceilings were established on many commodities at wholesale, and it was hoped that these would force employers to resist wage increases. Shortly thereafter, a general price freeze was established on commodities at retail.

Three months later, in April, the Administration announced a seven-point plan, one point of which was that wages were to be "stabilized." It was at this time that the Little Steel Case came up for consideration by the War Labor Board. "Little Steel" included the steel companies other than the U.S. Steel Corporation. The Steelworkers Union was asking for a 13 per cent increase in wages due to the rise in the Consumer Price Index since April, 1941, when they had obtained their last increase of 11.8 per cent.

In considering this demand, the Board was faced with a policy problem: From what date do we begin to measure? The Board was especially concerned that the strong (union workers) did not get wage increases far beyond the small and the weak (unorganized workers), so they decided to go back to January, 1941, to start the measurement. Since that date, the Cost of Living Index of the BLS had risen 15 per cent. The Board ruled that the steel workers were entitled only to the difference, namely, about 3 per cent above what they had already received in April, 1941. That decision started the controversy.

Wages and prices continued to creep upward, so in Act II, Congress passed the Stabilization Act in October, 1942, authorizing the President to stabilize wages, salaries, and prices at the levels of September 15, 1942. There were to be no further wage rate increases at all, except for certain inequalities, gross inequities, and substandard scales. These exceptions still left some leeway for wage adjustments. But in April, 1943, the President issued a "hold the line" order, which was designed to stop all upward movement. This persistent pressure finally resulted in the stabilization of hourly wage rates. Of course, earnings remained high, because there was widespread overtime at premium pay. However, the labor unions wanted the hourly rates to go up. They were in a favorable bargaining position, and they anticipated (correctly, as it turned out) that at the end of the war, the overtime and premium pay would evaporate, whereas hourly wage rates would be preserved.

During this period the union research statisticians in the AFL and the CIO (which at the time were separate and independent organizations) began making their own study of prices. Their theory was that price control was not working, while wage control was having the effect of cutting labor's real income. It was at this stage that the Bureau's price index was moved out to the center of the stage.

Thus far, these labor research groups had worked in an advisory capacity to the Bureau of Labor Statistics, which, in turn, was trying to adjust the price index to take account of quality deterioration, disappearance of items from the market, "trading up," and other wartime factors. Frequent conferences and exchanges of views and information took place between the labor advisory groups and the BLS, but under difficult circumstances and perhaps too slowly.

Meantime, the Bureau itself felt the need for an outside, objective determination of these technical issues of index-making. So, as it had done in the past, the Bureau turned to the American Statistical Association, and a committee, under the chairmanship of Frederick C. Mills of Columbia University, was appointed to review the index. After a review, which took place over the summer of 1943, the Mills Committee rendered its report in October. In brief, it vindicated the Bureau of Labor Statistics, saying that the index provided a trustworthy measure of price changes and, further, that many of the doubts and difficulties that had arisen were due to attempts to use the index "uncritically for purposes to which it is not adapted."

The Mills Committee report was made available to the War Labor Board and to the public. Commissioner Isador Lubin, who was serving on the White House staff, explained it to the President. Acting Commissioner Hinrichs hoped that the report would put an end to criticism of the index.

By this time, the wage dispute had reached the White House in full force. The curtain rose on Act III. Local pressures from the workers and their families were channeled up through the union leadership to the White House. The problem was wage stabilization, but the stumbling block was the index. The President decided that something broader than a statistical review of the index was needed. Accordingly, he proposed the appointment of a Presidential committee on the cost of living, consisting of members of the War Labor Board itself—two from labor, two from management, and the chairman, William H. Davis. That action was taken in late October, 1943. Within a few weeks the President's committee was faced with a resolution, adopted at the CIO annual convention, which urged the necessity of eliminating the "Little Steel formula," *plus* a program of demands by the Steelworkers Union for a general wage adjustment of seventeen cents an hour.

Chairman Davis interpreted the function of the President's committee to be to act as a fact-finding body to examine the Cost of Living Index and not to debate War Labor Board policy on wage controls. Accordingly, the meetings of the committee were focused on the index itself. The union members appointed technicians to develop the case against the index. The employer members later engaged their own statistical consultant. The committee met with Secretary of Labor Perkins, Assistant Secretary Daniel W. Tracy, and Acting Commissioner Hinrichs to decide upon the form of BLS participation. Secretary Perkins urged open hearings so that the BLS could get its case before the public, but Davis thought that newspaper publicity would only exaggerate the disagreements and serve no useful purpose. Likewise, he rejected the suggestion that a BLS representative should sit in at all the committee sessions. Under these conditions, Hinrichs and Mrs. Aryness Joy Wickens, then chief of the Prices and Cost of Living Division, presented the BLS case before the Committee.

Meanwhile, the labor members agreed to prepare a report on the BLS index for presentation to the committee. This took some weeks, so it was January 25, 1944, before the report was delivered. Then it turned out to be a new index presented as an alternative to the BLS index. It was based upon a multiplicity of secondary sources, including union food-price surveys in ten cities. That index showed that prices had risen 43.5 per cent from January, 1941, to December, 1943, while the BLS index showed only a 23.4 per cent rise. The report was accompanied by charges of politics and bad faith on the part of the BLS staff in trying to hold the index down. Finally, instead of being confined to Presidential committee hearings and debate, the report was released to the press.

The staff of BLS were surprised and dismayed by the tone and nature of the report. They had expected professional criticism, not a political attack. The staff was handicapped by the fact that there had been no opportunity to review the union document or even to obtain the charts and tables needed for an appraisal. Nevertheless, under pressure of time, Hinrichs and his assistants produced a review and appraisal, which disagreed with the union research estimate of the error in the index and which also tried to distinguish between the maintenance of an accurate statistical index and the application of the index to national policies by other agencies.

At this point, Chairman Davis made another move. On March 1, 1944, he appointed a technical committee, headed by Wesley C. Mitchell of Columbia University and director of the National Bureau of Economic Research, with two other members—Simon N. Kuznets of the University of Pennsylvania and Margaret G. Reid of Iowa State College. Both Kuznets and Reid were currently serving in government agencies in Washington.

While this committee was at work, a War Labor Board panel began public hearings on the Little Steel formula. A panel also held hearings on the basic steel case involving the demands of the Steelworkers Union. These two sets of hearings continued for several months, during which time the union index was used many times in support of labor's case.

In early June, the annual meeting of the Unions' Research Directors Conference took place, at which the BLS planned a discussion of the BLS review and appraisal. But George Meany appeared at the conference and made a direct personal criticism of the Acting Commissioner and his staff. As a result, Secretary of Labor Perkins ordered that the conferences with the union research directors be discontinued.

On June 22, the technical committee headed by Wesley Mitchell presented its report to the President's Committee of the War Labor Board, asserting first that the BLS had done a competent job in its price index work. Then, taking a new tack, the Committee made an official estimate of the amount of possible error in the BLS index, concluding that, instead of a discrepancy of 20 points as shown by the union index, a more likely estimate was 2.5 to 4 points. In taking this step, the Mitchell Committee provided the War Labor Board with some basis for a decision on wages. The Board decided that these percentage points should be added to the index for wage stabilization purposes. The Bureau of Labor Statistics in its monthly press releases continued to publish its own index on the same basis as before, but added a statement that

. . . the index does not show the full wartime effect on the cost of living of such factors as lowered quality, disappearance of low-priced goods, forced changes in housing, and eating away from home. Allowance should be made for a hidden increase of probably as much as 3 and cerainly not more than 4 percentage points.

Later, in 1945, the allowance was raised to 5 points. The statement continued to be published each month until it was eliminated in the January, 1947, index.

Meanwhile, the long delay had succeeded in holding the line on wages and prices, while the progress of the war had produced some changes in the economic outlook. The peak expansion in war production had been reached by the end of 1943, and some readjustments were already in process in 1944. On the military side, the successful Allied landing in Normandy in June turned people's attention toward the eventual postwar readjustment.

AFTERMATH

In retrospect, it is not difficult to point out how things might have been done differently. It seems that at times almost everyone blundered. The problem was that at every step of the way some things were being done for the first time. The War Labor Board certainly made the BLS bear the brunt of the attack. The BLS can be faulted for not being more alert to the warnings of the union statisticians. The Bureau was slow in making adjustments in the index. Nor does the staff seem to have had enough contact or influence with the administrative agencies. However, the Bureau did acquire public recognition for its service, and its reputation was enhanced, not undermined, by the conflict. The place of statistics in government policy-making was firmly established, and the accuracy and objectivity of the statistical agency was validated.

It is worthwhile to take a moment to look at the amazing statistical discrepancy. How could the union statisticians have found such a high cost-of-living increase? Despite all the conflicting reports on prices in numerous stores in various parts of the country (and outright errors in some price reports), there was no conceivable margin of error in BLS prices that could account for such a large difference. What the unions really came up with had many elements of an expenditure index, which took into account the rising expenditures of consumers with more money to spend. The concept of a price index is that it measures the effect of price changes, and of price changes only, on the cost of living. The index is designed to show the prices of identical goods and services of the same quality in successive periods. When a consumer decides to buy sirloin steak instead of round steak or hamburger, his cost of living will certainly go up, but it is not due to a rise in the prices of identical meats. He has raised his cost of living by raising his standard or level of living. The Consumer Price Index would show no change in prices for such a transaction.

What happened during World War II is now fairly clear. With full employment and much overtime at premium pay, the incomes of the working population rose sharply and persistently. Meantime, consumer goods were in short supply; new automobiles, for example, were practically nonexistent. High taxes and purchases of war bonds did not mop up all the funds available for spending. Some workers bought goods of better quality and rented better accommodations (sometimes because cheaper ones were not available). Consider how many of the millions of unemployed, living on WPA wages in 1939–40, were earning high wages in war industries in 1943. What happened was that the standard of living, the prevailing level of living, of the working population did in fact rise substantially, especially in the first years of the war. However, as full war mobilization was reached, consumer living standards had to decline. There simply were not enough consumer goods available to meet the demand. In that situation, some method had to be found to limit consumer expenditures; otherwise, the wage-price spiral would soon have begun to work.

Aside from providing a workable formula, the Mitchell Committee made one other important contribution. In order to keep the concept of the price index clear in the public's mind, the Committee suggested that the name should be changed. The Bureau of Labor Statistics was in favor of this idea, but Secretary Perkins was opposed to any change, so nothing was done about it at the time.

The death of President Roosevelt in April, 1945, brought a Cabinet change in the Labor Department. In a few months, Secretary Perkins resigned after serving twelve years as Secretary of Labor, and Judge Lewis B. Schwellenbach, a former senator from the state of Washington, was appointed by President Truman. At a press conference upon his accession, Secretary Schwellenbach announced that one of his first tasks would be to investigate the situation in the Bureau of Labor Statistics. The remark reverberated in the press, the staff of the Bureau was disturbed, and Acting Commissioner Hinrichs immediately turned in his resignation. A crisis threatened, which might have had widespread public repercussions, but the Secretary explained that his intent had been misinterpreted by the press, and he persuaded Hinrichs to withdraw his resignation.

Secretary Schwellenbach was able to resolve his difficulties with the BLS by changing the name of the index. In September, 1945, the new Secretary of Labor issued a statement affirming his confidence in the honesty and competence of the Bureau staff and announcing that the index would henceforth be named "Consumers' Price Index for Moderate Income Families in Large Cities." He stated that "this should end the confusion and controversy caused by misunderstanding of what the index is designed to measure." Thus ended the wartime controversy over the index.

THE PRICE INDEX IN THE KOREAN WAR

The outbreak in Korea came at a time when business recovery was getting under way following the business recession of 1949. However, the war came so suddenly and unexpectedly that it produced a speedy economic impact. The United Automobile Workers Union had renegotiated, in May, 1950, the widely known wage escalation contract that had attracted so much public attention two years before. At the time, other labor and management groups had taken a dim view of that contract, so there were very few followers. However, when the Korean outbreak came, masses of consumers remembered the shortages of World War II and rushed out to buy what they thought would be scarce commodities. The result was to send the Consumer Price Index sharply upward.

In anticipation of future wage and price controls, various economic groups began to take protective action. Businessmen raised prices so that they would be in good shape when price ceilings were set. On the labor front, there was a flood of contract reopenings for the purpose of negotiating escalation contracts based on the Consumer Price Index. The combination of these factors generated a wage-price spiral, which lifted prices nearly 10 per cent before ceilings and controls were imposed in February, 1951.

It was at this stage that a few members of the union research group, who had been active in the World War II controversy, decided upon a repeat performance. They began collecting prices and publishing an index showing increases far beyond those reported by the BLS index. This move attracted very little attention or support in the United States, but it triggered an international reaction. Isador Lubin, former Commissioner of Labor Statistics, was attending a meeting in Paris at which the Soviet representative cited the union index as evidence of how bad conditions were in the United States. Lubin cabled the Bureau for information on this new index, and the repercussions attracted the attention of Congress. The Education and Labor Committee of the House of Representatives appointed a subcommittee to conduct "a friendly investigation of the Consumer Price Index" and decided to hold public hearings and invite labor, management, and public groups to testify. The Commissioner and members of the BLS staff were invited first to present their account of how the index was made and what it was designed to measure. This presentation was followed by another week of hearings, at which many individuals and group representatives testified.

The hearings constituted a ringing endorsement of the Bureau's work on the index. Practically all who testified supported the Bureau. There were many suggestions for improvement, but none that challenged the Bureau's general principles. The subcommittee report, which was accepted by the committee as a whole, gave congressional approval and support to the Bureau and its staff. There was no further trouble with a competing index.

WHY THE DIFFERENCE?

The contrast between the two wartime episodes, less than ten years apart, raises the question of why things turned out so differently the second time, for the Bureau and for the country. Many factors combined to cause the difference. In the first place, the Bureau staff was more experienced. Except for the Commissioner, practically all the senior members of the staff had been through the fires in World War II. But this was a helpful rather than a decisive factor. Conditions during the Korean War were simply not the same.

It was a stroke of good fortune for the Bureau that Congress got into the problem at the beginning. This involvement provided the Bureau with an opportunity to present a positive picture of its activities, as well as to profit from whatever public support already existed. It is possible that earlier congressional interest and activity would have been helpful in World War II.

Then, too, the establishment in 1947 of two formal research advisory councils representing both labor and management undoubtedly had some influence on the outcome in 1951. The contacts of the Bureau with the labor and management groups were cemented by periodic meetings, as well as by established procedures. The assistance and support of the Business and

Labor Research Advisory councils was most impressive during the congressional hearings.

Another important factor was that in 1948 the CIO had ejected from their organization those unions that were under Communist leadership. It was these unions that sponsored the 1951 index, with the work being conducted by several of the researchers who had been active in World War II. But in 1951 neither the AFL nor the CIO wanted to lend any support to the projects or proposals of these left-wing unions.

Finally, the Korean War never reached anything like the dimensions of World War II. After the first surge of wages and prices, the economy remained quite stable for the remainder of the war. The extreme pressure that developed during World War II did not recur.

On balance, the outcome of the 1951 episode was due mostly to good fortune and circumstance, although some credit belonged to the Bureau staff, which had learned its lessons in public relations very well.

THE CONTROVERSY OF THE 1960's: UNEMPLOYMENT STATISTICS

In times of business recession, the statistics of unemployment get public attention and attract criticism. The brickbats come from both directions. To the labor groups the statistics are too low, failing to account for the "discouraged unemployed," "hidden unemployed," "partially unemployed." From employers, and frequently from the public, come comments such as "he doesn't want to work," "won't take a job," "prefers unemployment benefits." A citizen of Washington, D.C., wrote the Commissioner a letter several years ago arguing that "you should *not* count as unemployed any worker who won't take any job that he is physically able to do." This is the climate of opinion in which the controversy of the 1960's developed.

As in the case of the cost-of-living controversy, the plot developed slowly and reached an unexpected climax. As noted in Chapters I and II, the Labor Department and the Bureau of Labor Statistics acquired sole responsibility for the release and interpretation of labor force, employment, and unemployment statistics in 1959. The Bureau of the Census retained the responsibility for the collection and tabulation of the data. No longer were there joint releases to the press and the public by the secretaries of Commerce and Labor, nor were there two agencies to give their separate interpretations. The new system produced greater uniformity, but it also made the Department of Labor the responsible agency in the eyes of the public.

The problem began to unfold in the summer of 1960, when the economy passed its business peak and began to slide gently into a recession. The Presidential election was due in November. The Democratic candidate for President was campaigning on a platform of "getting the country moving again." The unemployment figures were a key statistic in the interpretation of the status of the economy.

Labor groups had been critical of "high levels of unemployment" for the past several years. With the election in the offing, they began to attack the interpretation of the unemployment situation being set forth each month in the Department of Labor press releases. Unemployment rises to a summer peak every June, when young people leave school and enter the labor force for the summer or longer. Those who do not get jobs frequently give up the search. In September, most of them return to school and unemployment drops to the low point of the year. However, it was the practice of the statistical agencies to present a "seasonally adjusted" unemployment rate, which irons out the seasonal rises and declines in unemployment and thus discloses the cyclical fluctuations and the long-run trend. In 1960, unemployment figures were declining each month from June to October. However, when the data were seasonally adjusted to allow for this decline, the adjusted unemploy-

ment rate was beginning to rise. Such was the economic background.

But the eventual attack on the figures came on an issue
much simpler and more readily understandable to the public.
The statistics of employment relate to the middle of the month,
and they are released to the public around the tenth of the
following month. The procedure at that time was for the BLS
to process and report as fast as it could, but there was no firm
date, and the statistics were published when they were ready.
Election day was Tuesday, November 7—too early for the
BLS to publish the October figures unless emergency measures
(Saturday and Sunday work) were taken, which might have
meant that figures could be made available by Monday eve-
ning. The decision of the Department was to release them at
the normal time, which, in that case, was Thursday, November
9. However, the basic tables were sent from the Census to the
BLS on Friday afternoon, and a few key figures were reported
to top officials in the Department of Labor, as well as to the
limited list of other officials entitled to receive them in advance. In some way, a hint concerning the data reached
George Meany, President of the AFL-CIO, who challenged
the Secretary of Labor to release them to the public. In some
former election years, there had been somewhat muted criticism to the effect that favorable unemployment figures were
issued in advance of the regular date. In 1960, the criticism
was the opposite—that they were being held up because they
were unfavorable.

In this the first act of the drama, the BLS was simply a by-
stander. The criticism was directed at the Department and the
Secretary. Within the Department, there was an investigation
of the source of the leak, but no culprit was ever found.

It is quite impossible to say whether the election was in any
way affected by this controversy. Since the unknown often
looms larger than the known, it could be that the impact on the
voters was somewhat greater than if the actual figures had

been made available. The Bureau staff had anticipated trouble and had recommended as far back as midsummer that a firm date for the public release of the October figures be announced in advance. However, the Secretary's judgment then was that this would only magnify the issue and create a problem where none existed.

When the Kennedy Administration took office in January, Secretary of Labor Goldberg took action against future repetition of the problem by instructing the Bureau of Labor Statistics to establish firm release dates a full year in advance, so that there would be no question about the possible withholding or advancing of information. There has been no difficulty on this score since.

ATTACK FROM ANOTHER DIRECTION

In February, 1961, the volume of unemployment rose to nearly 5.7 million—8.1 per cent of the labor force in actual figures and nearly 7 per cent on a seasonally adjusted basis. The low point of the business recession was reached in February, with both the seasonal and the cyclical peaks of unemployment coinciding. The new administration prepared to present a variety of new programs to deal with the unemployment problem.

Secretary of Labor Goldberg was a forceful and persuasive advocate, and many of the new programs involved the Department of Labor. As the custodian of the unemployment figures, he had the opportunity of relating the proposed programs to the nation's needs. If the tendency in the Eisenhower Administration had been to minimize the unemployment situation, the new tendency was to highlight it. At press conferences on manpower statistics, the Secretary would announce the figures and then proceed with an exposition of the Department's legislative program.

Once again it was a case of statistics' getting into the line of fire. Critics who do not like programs often attack statistics on which they are based. Before the summer was over, the *Reader's Digest* published an article on unemployment statistics. The theme and tone were almost exact replicas of those marking the attack on the price index in World War II. The argument, directed at the BLS and its unemployment statistics rather than at the remedial programs, was, first, that the Bureau was exaggerating the figures in order to serve the Department of Labor programs and, second, that the data themselves were wrong. The article was an attack on the integrity and the competence of the BLS staff.

The White House, the Department of Labor, and the Congress were all stirred into action. The Bureau's idea was to turn to the Congress, where such excellent results had been achieved in former crises. But Secretary Goldberg felt that something more positive, and of a longer range, was essential. On his advice, President Kennedy decided to appoint an expert committee of economists who could review the entire subject of labor force statistics, including the procedures of the agencies engaged in producing them. The Committee To Appraise Employment and Unemployment Statistics consisted of six well-known economists under the chairmanship of R. A. Gordon of the University of California at Berkeley. The Office of Statistical Standards of the Bureau of the Budget was designated to provide staff services. As soon as it was appointed, the Committee established contact with the Bureau of Labor Statistics and other statistical agencies for the purpose of obtaining detailed reports and analyses from each. The Gordon Committee did an intensive job; not until a year later, in September, 1962, were its report and recommendations published.

Meanwhile, in November, 1961, the congressional Joint Economic Committee appointed a subcommittee under the chairmanship of Senator William Proxmire of Wisconsin to hold hearings on the subject of unemployment statistics. Those hearings provided the first opportunity for the Bureau to present an official defense of its staff and its statistics. Once again, the Bureau had a stroke of good fortune. The author of the magazine article had failed to check it with the staff of the Bureau of Labor Statistics. In consequence, it contained a number of factual errors concerning the methods and procedures used in obtaining the statistics. Had the Commissioner, or any senior member of the staff, been presented with the text, he would have corrected the errors. As it turned out, it was not difficult to point out these errors to the congressional committee and thus to show that the criticism was not a well-done technical job. This lapse on the part of the writer undoubtedly contributed to a further result, namely, that neither he nor any other representative of the magazine appeared to testify at the hearings in response to the committee's request. The hearings turned out to be one-sided.

The Gordon Committee did a thorough and incisive job on the task assigned to it, and its report was a comprehensive masterpiece. Analytical papers prepared by the agencies were reviewed by the members of the Committee in their decision-making, and some were reproduced in the Committee's report. The Committee's work had both a short- and a long-run effect. Some recommendations could be adopted immediately by the agencies, and they were. Some required further tests and experimentation, which in turn required additional funds. A number of those recommendations also were eventually put into effect. The revised employment statistics of 1967 reflect the results of those recommendations. In pointing to the longer future, the Committee suggested that eventually the nation would have to do more in state and local areas. Nothing much has been accomplished yet in this respect, and the 1962 report indicated that it might be ten years before those objectives were achieved.

In any event, the Bureau of Labor Statistics came out of the controversy with a renewed reputation for integrity and competence. The statistics of labor force, employment, and unemployment have been greatly improved. Controversy does seem to be a roundabout and unpleasant way to achieve good results, but that is the way a democracy often works in taking into consideration divergent points of view. In the words of James Russell Lowell:

> Truth, crushed to earth, shall rise again.
> The eternal years of God are hers.
> But Error, wounded, writhes in pain
> And dies among his worshipers.

XIV

Forecasting the Future

Sometime in 1941, a feature writer for a popular magazine was writing a story about shipbuilding in one of the government's shipyards. Having been shown through the works, he interviewed the admiral in charge and asked some questions about the output of ships. The admiral fixed him with an eagle eye and thundered: "Do you want statistics or do you want ships?" The writer recorded the implied answer as evidence of the admiral's success in putting first things first.

But in fact the admiral was wrong. The nation needed both ships *and* statistics. The history of World War II, and of every war, is filled with unhappy examples of too much and too little, too soon and too late, too precise and too loose. It has been reported that the Army ended World War I with an unused stockpile of millions of bridles for horses. In 1918–20, there was a shortage of leather, and prices rose to high levels, helping to push the Cost of Living Index to new heights. The nation would have been better off if the Army had kept a better count of its bridles.

It is a truism to say that economics as a science is concerned with the balancing of demand and supply, with the maximizing of efficiency through producing the most goods and services with the least effort. And this balancing must be maintained over time, so that peaks of prosperity are not followed by troughs of depression, overemployment by unemployment. Citizens who stand in awe of the scientific achievements of the earth satellites, the probes of Mars, and the soft landing on the moon might well reflect on the achievements that will be required in order to solve the social and economic problems of our country and the world. In many ways, the human problems are more stubborn than the natural ones. Metals, machines, and electric power can be manipulated, transformed, and controlled; people cannot. The achievement of a rising standard of living, the provision of social security, and the solution of the problem of poverty will require all the knowledge and sophistication that have been put into our natural sciences.

In more mundane and more specific terms, the statistics necessary to serve as guides to well-being and good living have yet to be developed. We have done quite well in the last quarter century, but we have made only a beginning.

Consider the problem of economic stability—the avoidance of booms and depressions. In this respect, we have indeed achieved a revolution in thought since the Great Depression of the 1930's. At that time, we had neither the statistics nor the knowledge to enable us to do better. But we have learned from the experience. There has been no major depression since World War II, nor does one seem to be in sight. Our success so far can be attributed in part to our greatly improved economic statistics. Every month, our government (and the public also) takes stock of our latest statistics and attempts to interpret their meaning for policy guidance. The Bureau of Labor Statistics data on employment, wages, prices, and productivity are central to that decision-making.

MANPOWER PROJECTIONS

Let us take the problem of estimating for the young people of the nation the outlook for specific occupations. As the population and the economy expand with the years, there is an ever growing list of new occupations as well as the decline and disappearance of many once famous ones. If you look in the telephone book, you will find pages of Coopers, representing the survival in surnames of a skilled occupation that has almost disappeared from the occupational lists. Each new edition of the *Occupational Outlook Handbook* signals the imminent elimination of occupations and adds large numbers of new occupations requiring future manpower. The current edition describes for over 700 occupations "the nature of the work, places of employment, educational and training requirements for entry, and the job prospects for the next 10 years."

But how can we know what is going to happen ten years from now? Which occupations are going to expand their employment? Which are likely to decline? We read from time to time somber predictions that new technology is eliminating thousands of jobs. How do we know that new developments won't hit some of the most promising job prospects?

The answer, of course, is that we don't know—for sure. Certainty in a dynamic world simply does not exist. But does that mean we must throw up our hands? There are trends, probabilities, possibilities that can be weighed and balanced in arriving at some likely conclusions. Do you recall the old days when the Weather Bureau made a flat prediction for the next day—clear, cloudy, rain, snow, etc.? (I recall vividly an incident in Washington many years ago. The Weather Bureau predicted good weather on a day when Washington experienced a snowstorm. And that, of all the days in the year, was the day of the Bureau's appropriation hearing!) Nowadays you get from the Weather Bureau not a flat prediction but a probability estimate—"chance of rain, 90 per cent," "chance of snow, 20 per cent." This new method actually improves the accuracy of the weather predictions for the average citizen, because he is able to make better plans in the light of the probabilities that the Weather Bureau reveals to him.

So it is with the BLS and the occupational outlook. One cannot be sure of anything, but one can gauge the probabilities of many things.

In the beginning of its occupational outlook studies, the BLS relied heavily on the judgment of people connected with an industry or an occupation—businessmen, labor officials, engineers, economists, and others. In fact, the Bureau has always checked its findings with experts in the field. They are the people closest to the actual happenings and the ones most directly affected by what is happening.

But such people are not sure guides to the future. They may be deluded by their fears or by wishful thinking. Economic analysis can also make a contribution, and the Bureau staff has at its disposal the wealth of data provided by its statistical programs. One of the most firm and reliable projections in the economy is the over-all supply of labor. The decennial censuses give us a periodic cross-section of the population by age, sex, race, and other demographic characteristics. Since the United States has a relatively small amount of immigration and an even smaller amount of emigration, native birth and death rates determine our population growth. Furthermore, a labor market analyst has one big advantage in his projections of the supply side, namely, that the people who will be entering the labor force fifteen years from now have already been born. They can only be affected by death rates, which are very low.

But then comes the more difficult task—estimating how the supply of labor will find employment in industries and occupations. One good tool for this purpose is the analysis of interindustry relations.

FUTURE USE OF INTERINDUSTRY RELATIONS

The input-output table of interindustry relations is a statistical technique that is still in its infancy. The Office of Business Economics published in 1965 an 82-place input-output table. (In 1952, the BLS already had a 400-place table.) The OBE is ready to expand the present table, but the statistical agencies of the government must obtain the resources that will enable them to supply the data for it.

The input-output table in itself, as defined in Chapter III, is nothing more than a cross-classification table of purchases and sales among industries in the American economy. But it furnishes a framework from which vitally important analyses and projections can be made. The U.S. Department of Labor is interested in it for analyses of the prospective supply of and demand for labor. To achieve that, the current dollars of purchases and sales must be deflated for price increases so as to get a measure of real product. For this purpose, improved price statistics are needed, industry by industry. The price work needs to be expanded until every significant industry in the input-output table has its own price index.

The next step is to develop a labor requirements factor, which can translate the real product in each industry into the man-hours required to produce it. This requires periodic updating of productivity studies to show what are the labor requirements for a given volume of production at the current level of technological development in that industry. A more complex type of productivity study measures the range of man-hour requirements existing within the industry at any one time. When the range is wide—as when some firms in an industry produce, say, a dozen units of output with ten man-hours of labor, while other firms range as high as forty man-hours for the same product—the prospect is that the less advanced firms will either have to modernize or go out of business. From that type of study, the Labor Department can project the kinds of workers who are likely to be laid off in the future and also the skills that will be needed as advanced technology takes over the whole industry. Conversely, if the range in output per man-hour is comparatively narrow, it indicates that all employers are on a fairly even level and that no major technological revolution is in sight.

Input-output tables, with their companion data, as outlined above, can furnish a good foundation for both economic and labor force projections and hence projections of future economic growth. The BLS study *Projections, 1970* marks only the first step in a series of projections and analyses of economic growth, leading eventually to a determination of the policies, public and private, that can maximize the growth rate.

POVERTY

A national problem that will require intensive statistical study in future decades is poverty. With the standard of living of the average American rising steadily, why does a substantial fraction of the population share very little, if at all, in the general well-being? Sociological and psychological studies of human motivation and cultural patterns will be multiplied as the nation tackles this problem. Such studies are beyond the present scope of the Bureau of Labor Statistics. But foundation studies of the kinds conducted by the Bureau will be necessary.

For example, much more intensive and extensive studies must be made of family budgets for minimum and adequate standards of living. The four-person, middle-aged family and the elderly couple are not the only family types for which budget studies are needed. Especially urgent are studies in depth of the family throughout its life cycle—the young family in the twenties, the older family in the thirties, young single women beginning careers, and older women in their forties rejoining the labor force after a couple of decades of homemaking and child-rearing.

GUARANTEED INCOME?

The relationship between work and income will attract increasing public attention in coming decades. When Captain John Smith, in the Virginia Colony in 1608, said, "He who does not work shall not eat," he was addressing a class of cavalier families who in England had been accustomed to servants. In the harsh conditions of the Virginia wilderness, there was no place for such a luxury. Nowadays, in the economy of abundance, a school of thought has arisen that proposes that a minimum income be provided for every man, woman, and child without reference to work or service. The theory is that the spectacular revolution of automation and technology will make our economy so productive that everyone can enjoy a minimum standard of living, while leaving the necessary work to be done by those desiring higher standards or enjoying work for its own sake.

It is hard to imagine the Congress of 1968–69 legislating this theory into action. But that problem requires more attention than has so far been given to it. The nation has recognized that workers past retirement age have a right to income without work on the basis of their former contributions to the economy. We provide income to the permanently disabled and to widows with children. Young children, with or without parents, are considered to be worthy of support to maturity. But the thread of logic that runs through all of these is that their support has been earned by work or will eventually result in work. Substantial transfers of income to the poor cannot be made without some consideration of the effect upon work incentives.

But some of the anomalies of our present system are giving us pause. In the District of Columbia, an unemployed father (ineligible for unemployment insurance) had to desert his family in order for them to be eligible for public assistance. The system of welfare results in the creation of broken families. Again, a worker drawing unemployment insurance while out of work could take a temporary part-time job, but by so doing he would lose nearly all this unemployment insurance. So he avoids temporary and occasional work, although it would be income-producing to himself and to society.

The point is that our entire social security and welfare system needs reexamination. The relationship between work and income must undergo some drastic revisions. In the development of a new and better program, the research skills of the Bureau of Labor Statistics and other such statistical agencies will be needed.

SOCIAL INDICATORS

Federal agencies have already begun to work on the statistical needs of such a program. In 1966, John Gardner, Secretary of Health, Education, and Welfare, appointed the Advisory Panel on Social Indicators, consisting of sociologists, psychologists, economists, statisticians, and other professional groups. The objective was to plan for a "Social Report" of the President, which would be based upon series of social indicators designed to measure progress toward the economic and social well-being of the American people.

In 1967, Congress took notice of this subject. Hearings were scheduled by the Government Operations Committee under the chairmanship of Senator Fred Harris of Oklahoma. Senator Walter Mondale of Wyoming has introduced a bill providing for the creation of a council of social advisers, which would be the counterpart of the Council of Economic Advisers. Some of the witnesses at the hearings argued in favor of an enlarged Council of Economic Advisers with additional responsibilities. Others contended that the maintenance of economic growth and stability was enough of a task in itself and that the problems of poverty and welfare were sufficiently difficult to warrant the full-time attention of a separate coordinating federal agency.

INTERGOVERNMENTAL RELATIONSHIPS

The fundamental governmental problem in the United States is the federal-state-local relationship. In the economic and social advances of the last quarter century, the federal government has played the major role. Planning and programing have emanated from Washington, with the state and local governments receiving the benefits, but without local choice of methods. Furthermore, the federal government has the tax base and the resources to achieve results, while the states and localities are reaching the limit of their respective resources. The unfolding of this perspective led Walter Heller, then chairman of the Council of Economic Advisers, to propose federal-state revenue-sharing, with the federal government raising the funds by taxation and then rebating a proportion of the intake to the states in lump sums, which would permit the states to allocate the money as seemed best for each state. However, the cities of the nation have been less than enthusiastic about this plan, because they fear they would not get a fair share from their respective state governments. The explosion of the ghetto cities and the escalating problems of urban living make the problem of intergovernmental responsibilities the most urgent in the nation.

THE BLS AND SOCIAL CONTROL

Finally, technology itself may have to be brought under some form of social control. Modern technology, stimulated and energized by billions of dollars of research and development funds, has provided the tools for the abolition of poverty and the attainment of an economy of abundance. It has given us transistors, computers, satellites, and automated machinery for the expansion of knowledge and the production of wealth. But technology has its costs and its price. Americans possess nearly 100 million motor vehicles, and the air of our cities is polluted by exhaust gases. Our factories are marvelously productive, but our rivers are polluted with wastes. We have promoted the peaceful use of atomic energy, but our miners are subject to the risk of uranium poisoning. Some scientists argue that the American people will eventually be drowned in their own wastes.

What has happened is that the Congress, at the behest of the

American people, has lavished funds upon the natural sciences but has been penurious in supporting research in the social sciences. Natural science funds pay off in ways that can be readily identified; they deal with things more than with people. Social science deals primarily with people, who are harder to manage. We can put a satellite in orbit (by now almost routinely), but we can not raise the ghetto to the level of the suburbs. The United States is the richest nation in the world, but we have a poverty problem of enormous dimensions.

The urgency of the social problem and the logic of events will force a reconsideration of our national priorities and better regulation of technological advances. Money and thought will have to be devoted to the crisis of the cities. In this task, research and statistics will be essential. The BLS and other agencies of that type will be indispensable to the solution of these problems.

The future of the BLS itself will depend upon the continuation of the policies and principles that have served it so well in the past. This means the appointment in the future of commissioners who are competent, objective, and nonpolitical. It means recognition by the Department of Labor that the Bureau is *both* a service agency to the Department and a public service agency to the nation. It will require the continued recruitment of high-minded, dedicated young people who will do the work. It is to be hoped that enough of them will be attracted by the prospect.

A Career in Government, with Emphasis on the Bureau of Labor Statistics

Young people meditating on the choice of a career should give some thought to the opportunities in government service. In my own case, it was the best kind of luck that my first professional job after completing my graduate work was in government—and specifically in the Bureau of Labor Statistics. The Bureau is a fine place to work—it was forty years ago, and it is today. There is ample opportunity to exercise a wide variety of skills. If you like meeting people, you can work into a field-staff appointment calling on employers, store managers, union officials, and others, collecting data on prices, wage rates, earnings, union scales, consumer expenditures, etc. Such experience furnishes a firm foundation for more advanced analysis as the young social scientist works his way up the career ladder. One of my most valuable work experiences was the seven months I spent in the field in 1927 collecting information on output per man-hour in blast furnaces and steel works.

If you have a strong research bent, there are special studies in which the researcher concentrates on the analysis of a specific problem, the product of which usually becomes a bulletin or a BLS report. If you like to write, there are opportunities for articles in the *Monthly Labor Review* and in the other publications of the Bureau. It has been the policy of the Bureau to give personal credit to authors, and if you look through the publications of the Bureau or even the Bibliography of this book, you can note the extent to which articles and reports are signed and credited. The Bureau also encourages attendance and participation in the activities of professional associations, such as the American Statistical Association, the American Economic Association, the Industrial Relations Research Association, and, in fact, any of the social science associations.

In general, all positions in the Bureau, except that of the Commissioner himself, are under civil service. There are minor exceptions from time to time for strictly temporary employees or for those engaged in highly specialized projects. The Civil Service Commission is the agency that administers the civil service system; it furnishes the lists of candidates from which the Bureau makes its selections. The Commission periodically conducts entrance examinations open to all college graduates, such as Federal Service Entrance or Management Intern examinations. Anyone interested in government service should get information from the nearest Inter-Agency Boards of U.S. Civil Service Examiners, of which there are sixty-five offices throughout the country, at least one in every state and two or more in the more populous states. In addition, a young candidate can write to or visit the Bureau of Labor Statistics or the U.S. Department of Labor (or any of their regional offices), where the personnel directors can assist him or her in finding out how to qualify for appointment.

Not all employees of BLS are college graduates. There are plenty of openings for stenographers, typists, statistical clerks, research assistants, etc. In these occupations the turnover is high, because many of them are young women who eventually marry and then leave the service to rear a family—sometimes returning years later, when their children have grown.

There are many agencies in government similar to BLS in which a young person can find a satisfying career. Within the Department of Labor there are a number of bureaus and offices that use research workers as well as operating and administrative personnel. Among these are the Bureau of Employment Security, the Wage and Hour and Public Contracts Divisions, the Bureau of Labor Standards, the Women's Bureau, and many others.

Then there are agencies in other departments that have interesting programs and good prospects for employment. In several chapters in this book you have seen reference to the partnership in statistics between the Census Bureau and the BLS. The Census is a general purpose statistical agency, which services not only the Department of Commerce, in which it is located, but also many agencies throughout the government. I can mention also the Agricultural Economic Service, which performs similar functions in the Department of Agriculture. The Department of Health, Education, and Welfare has a very wide range of occupational requirements. In fact, every department in the federal government and most of the independent boards and commissions have some opportunities for social scientists.

Even more numerous and more spectacular openings are available to natural scientists. There are old-line agencies, such as the Bureau of Standards, the Food and Drug Administration, the National Institutes of Health, the Public Health Service, and scores of others. Then there are the newer agencies, such as the Atomic Energy Commission and the National Aviation and Space Agency.

Total civilian employment in the federal government in early 1968 amounted to about 2.75 million, in round numbers. These numbers include all grades of personnel from entry grades at the bottom to top supervisors and administrators. Of these, about 1.2 million are in the Department of Defense, where they perform functions of a civilian character much like those in other departments. The Post Office comes next in size, with a total of approximately 700,000 employees, mostly at Grades PFS-3 and PFS-4 (clerical in character). The Post Office is under a merit system of its own, in which it is serviced by the Civil Service Commission. Apart from Defense and Post Office, there are roughly 850,000 federal employees. The point is that there are ample and widespread opportunities for young people in the federal service.

APPENDIX B

Geographic Coverage of the Consumer Price Index

SEPARATE INDEXES PUBLISHED MONTHLY

Chicago, Ill.	New York, N.Y.–NE N.J.
Detroit, Mich.	Philadelphia, Pa.
Los Angeles–Long Beach, Calif.	U.S. city average

SEPARATE INDEXES PUBLISHED QUARTERLY

Jan.–Apr.–July–Oct.	Feb.–May–Aug.–Nov.	Mar.–June–Sept.–Dec.
Boston, Mass.	Buffalo, N.Y.	Atlanta, Ga.
Houston, Texas	Cleveland, Ohio	Baltimore, Md.
Minneapolis–St. Paul, Minn.	Dallas, Texas	Cincinnati, Ohio
	Milwaukee, Wis.	Honolulu, Hawaii
Pittsburgh, Pa.	San Diego, Calif.	Kansas City, Mo.
Portland, Ore.	Scranton, Pa.	St. Louis, Mo.
	Seattle, Wash.	San Francisco–Oakland, Calif.
	Washington, D.C.	

SEPARATE INDEXES PUBLISHED ANNUALLY

October   Anchorage and Fairbanks, Alaska
November   Juneau and Ketchikan, Alaska

REPRESENTED IN U.S. CITY AVERAGE BUT NOT PUBLISHED
SEPARATELY

Six Metropolitan Areas of 250,000–1,000,000 Population

Dayton, Ohio

Denver, Colo.

Hartford, Conn.

Indianapolis, Ind.

Nashville, Tenn.

Wichita, Kan.

Ten Metropolitan Areas of 50,000–250,000 Population

Austin, Texas

Bakersfield, Calif.

Baton Rouge, La.

Cedar Rapids, Iowa

Champaign–Urbana, Ill.

Durham, N.C.

Green Bay, Wis.

Lancaster, Pa.

Orlando, Fla.

Portland, Maine

Sixteen Cities of 2,500–50,000 Population

Crookston, Minn.

Devils Lake, N.D.

Findlay, Ohio

Florence, Ala.

Kingston, N.Y.

Klamath Falls, Ore.

Logansport, Ind.

Magnum, Okla.

Martinsville, Va.

McAllen, Texas

Millville, N.J.

Niles, Mich.

Orem, Utah

Southbridge, Mass.

Union, S.C.

Vicksburg, Miss.

APPENDIX C

Labor Research Advisory Council

Marvin Friedman (Chairman), Research Department, AFL-CIO
Otis Brubaker, United Steelworkers of America
Carrol L. Coburn, United Automobile Workers of America
George Cucich, Railway Employees' Department, AFL-CIO
Donald D. Danielson, United Brotherhood of Carpenters and Joiners of America
Milton Fried, Amalgamated Clothing Workers of America
Woodrow L. Ginsburg, Industrial Union Department, AFL-CIO
Nat Goldfinger, Research Department, AFL-CIO
Reese Hammond, International Union of Operating Engineers
Vernon Jirikowic, International Association of Machinists
William O. Kuhl, International Brotherhood of Boilermakers, Iron Shipbuilders, Blacksmiths, Forgers, and Helpers
Robert E. McMillen, United Association of Journeymen and Apprentices of the Plumbing and Pipe Fitting Industry of the United States and Canada
Abraham Morganstern, International Union of Electrical, Radio, and Machine Workers
James E. Noe, International Brotherhood of Electrical Workers
George Perkel, Textile Workers Union of America
Keith Prouty, Communications Workers of America
Boris Shishkin, AFL-CIO Housing Committee
Lazare Teper, International Ladies' Garment Workers' Union
Kenneth F. Thornbury, United Rubber, Cork, Linoleum, and Plastic Workers of America

Joint Labor Research Advisory Council, 1947–55

Standing Committee Cochairmen
- 1953–55 Bert Seidman, American Federation of Labor
- 1949–52 Margaret Scattergood, American Federation of Labor
- 1948–55 Albert Epstein, Railway Labor Executives' Association
- 1947–55 Katherine P. Ellickson, Congress of Industrial Organizations
- 1947–48 Glen K. Slaughter, American Federation of Labor

Labor Research Advisory Council, 1955–

Chairmen
- 1963– Marvin Friedman, American Federation of Labor and Congress of Industrial Organizations
- 1955–62 Bert Seidman, American Federation of Labor and Congress of Industrial Organizations

Executive Secretaries
- 1955– Joseph P. Goldberg
- 1953–54 David J. Saposs
- 1949–52 Morris Weisz
- 1947–48 David J. Saposs

APPENDIX D

Business Research Advisory Council

Randall T. Klemme, Northern Natural Gas Company
Anthony J. Nesti, National Electrical Manufacturers Association
Charles B. Reeder, E. I. du Pont de Nemours and Company, Inc.
Helen C. Richwine, The Rubber Manufacturers Association, Inc.
Paul F. Shaw, The Chase Manhattan Bank
David T. Shute, Liberty Mutual Insurance Company
Myron S. Silbert, Federated Department Stores, Inc.
William H. Smith, Federated Employers of the Bay Area
David G. Soash, Mechants and Manufacturers Association
Benjamin F. Stacey, The First National Bank of Boston
Leo Teplow, American Iron and Steel Institute
Brent T. Upson, General Motors Corporation
Theodore E. Veltfort, Copper and Brass Fabricators Council, Inc.
Cedric Wolfe, Metropolitan Life Insurance Company
C. Ashley Wright, Standard Oil Company (New Jersey)

Former CHAIRMEN

1948–49	Vincent P. Ahearn
1950–51	John C. Gebhart
1952	Robert W. Burgess
1953–54	Miles L. Colean
1955–Fiscal 1957	Martin R. Gainsbrugh
Fiscal 1958–59	Emerson P. Schmidt
Fiscal 1960–61	Leo Teplow
Fiscal 1962–63	George G. Hagedorn
Fiscal 1964–65	Lester S. Kellogg
Fiscal 1966–67	Myron S. Silbert

EXECUTIVE SECRETARIES

Kenneth G. Van Auken, Jr., 1963–
Herman B. Byer, 1948–63

Bibliography

BOOKS

DUNLOP, JOHN T. (ed.). *Automation and Technological Change.* (The American Assembly, Columbia University.) New York: Prentice-Hall, 1962.

HOWARD, DONALD S. *The WPA and Federal Relief Policy.* New York: Russell Sage Foundation, 1943.

KENDRICK, JOHN W. *Productivity Trends in the United States.* (National Bureau of Economic Research.) Princeton, N.J.: Princeton University Press, 1961.

LEIBY, JAMES. *Carroll Wright and Labor Reform: The Origin of Labor Statistics.* (Harvard Historical Monographs, XLVI.) Cambridge, Mass.: Harvard University Press, 1960.

LOMBARDI, JOHN. *Labor's Voice in the Cabinet: A History of the Department of Labor from Its Origin to 1921.* New York: Columbia University Press, 1942.

BUREAU PUBLICATIONS

The following periodicals, bulletins, and reports are published by the Government Printing Office for the Bureau of Labor Statistics. Most are available in depository libraries throughout the country, and many can be purchased through the Superintendent of Documents, Washington, D.C. 20402, or through the Bureau's regional offices. A few are on the BLS free list and are available from the Bureau until the supply is exhausted.

"A Look at Tomorrow's Jobs," (Reprint from the 1966–67 *Occupational Outlook Handbook.*) BLS Bulletin No. 1450–A. 1966.

"A Look Back, A Look Ahead," *Occupational Outlook Quarterly,* Vol. 9, No. 4 (December, 1965), 1–7.

Activities of the Bureau of Labor Statistics in World War II. (Historical Reports of War Administration, No. 1.), 1947.

America's Industrial and Occupational Manpower Requirements, 1964–75. 1966.

BOWDEN, WITT. *The Gift of Freedom: A Study of the Economic and Social Status of Wage Earners in the United States.* 1949.

The Bureau of Labor Statistics—Its History, Activities, and Organization. BLS Bulletin No. 319. 1922.

City Worker's Family Budget for a Moderate Living Standard, Autumn 1966. BLS Bulletin No. 1570–1. 1967.

The Consumer Price Index: A Short Description. 1967.

The Consumer Price Index: History and Techniques. BLS Bulletin No. 1517. 1967.

Employer Expenditures for Selected Supplementary Compensation Practices for Production and Related Workers; Composition of Payroll Hours: Manufacturing Industries, 1962. BLS Bulletin No. 1428. 1965.

Employment and Earnings Statistics for States and Areas, 1939–67. BLS Bulletin No. 1370–5. 1966.

Employment and Earnings Statistics for the United States, 1909–68. BLS Bulletin No. 1312–6. 1968.

"Estimating Equivalent Incomes or Budget Costs by Family Type," *Report of the Advisory Committee on Standard Budget Research.* June, 1963.

GREENBERG, LEON. *Data for Measurement of Industrial Productivity in the United States.* 1965.

Handbook of Labor Statistics. BLS Bulletin No. 1600. 1968.

Handbook of Methods for Surveys and Studies. BLS Bulletin No. 1458. 1966.

Health Manpower, 1966–75: A Study of Requirements and Supply. BLS Report No. 323. 1967.

How the Government Measures Unemployment. BLS Report No. 312. 1967.

LEVINE, MORTON, and MURPHY, LUDMILLA K. *Looking Ahead to a Career.* 1967.

Major BLS Programs. A Summary of Their Characteristics. 1968.

MITCHELL, WESLEY C. *Index Numbers of Wholesale Prices in the United States and Foreign Countries.* BLS Bulletin No. 284. 1921.

The Negroes in the United States: Their Economic and Social Situation. BLS Bulletin No. 1511. 1966.

Occupational Employment Statistics, 1960–66. BLS Bulletin No. 1579. 1968.

Occupational Outlook Handbook, 1968–69 Edition. BLS Bulletin No. 1550. 1968.

Projections 1970. Interindustry Relationships, Potential Demand, and Employment. BLS Bulletin No. 1536. 1967.

Retired Couple's Budget for a Moderate Living Standard, Autumn 1966. BLS Bulletin No. 1570–4. 1968.

Social and Economic Conditions of Negroes in the United States. BLS Report No. 332; Census Report P–23, No. 24. 1967.

Technological Trends in Major American Industries. BLS Bulletin No. 1474. 1966.

Thirteenth Annual Report of the Commissioner of Labor, 1898. (*Hand and Machine Labor,* Vol. I.) 1899.

Tomorrow's Manpower Needs: National Manpower Projections and a Guide to Their Use as a Tool in Developing State and Area Manpower Projections. 1968.

TREIRES, JAMES J. "The Occupational Outlook Handbook Through Five Editions," *Occupational Outlook Quarterly,* Vol. 5, No. 4 (December, 1961), 3–8.

Wage Calendar, 1968. BLS Bulletin No. 1593. 1968.

Workers' Budgets in the U.S.: City Families and Single Persons, 1946 and 1947. BLS Bulletin No. 927. 1948.

OTHER PUBLICATIONS

ARNOW, KATHRYN SMUL. "The Attack on the Cost of Living Index," *The Inter-University Case Program.* Indianapolis, Ind.: Bobbs-Merrill Company, Inc., 1952.

BARRINGTON ASSOCIATES. *Effects of the 1966 New York City Transit Strike on the Travel Behavior of Regular Transit Users.* New York: N.Y.C. Transit Authority, 1967.

BRADY, DOROTHY S., and WILLIAMS, FAITH M. "Advances in the Techniques of Measuring and Estimating Consumer Expenditures," *Journal of Farm Economics* (May, 1945), 315–44.

CLAGUE, EWAN. "Effects of Technological Change on Occupational Employment Patterns in the United States," *Manpower Implications of Automation.* (U.S. Department of Labor.) Washington, D.C.: Government Printing Office, 1964, 29–38.

CLORETY, JOSEPH A. "Consumption Statistics: A Technical Comment," *How American Buying Habits Change.* (U.S. Department of Labor.) Washington, D.C.: Government Printing Office, 1959, 217–42.

Consumers' Price Index. (Report No. 2 of a Special Subcommittee of the Committee on Education and Labor, House of Representatives, 82d Cong., 1st sess.) Washington, D.C.: Government Printing Office, 1951.

DOUTY, H. M. "Trends in Labor Compensation in the U.S., 1946–66," *Labor Issues in Perspective.* (U.S. Department of Labor.) Washington, D.C.: Government Printing Office, 1967.

EVANS, W. D., and HOFFENBERG, MARVIN. "Input-Output Relations and Appraisal," *Studies in Income and Wealth.* (National Bureau of Economic Research, Vol. 18.) 1955.

Government Price Statistics: Hearings. Parts 1 and 2. (Joint Economic Committee, 87 Cong., 1st sess.) Washington, D.C.: Government Printing Office, 1961.

GREENBERG, LEON. "Technological Change, Productivity, and Employment in the United States," *Manpower Implications of Automa-*

tion. (U.S. Department of Labor.) Washington, D.C.: Government Printing Office, 1964, 1–14.

GREENBERG, LEON, and MARK, J. A. *Sector Changes in Unit Labor Costs.* (Conference on Income and Wealth, National Bureau of Economic Research.) Washington, D.C.: Government Printing Office, 1966.

Hearings on Employment and Unemployment. (Joint Economic Committee, December 18–20, 1961.) Washington, D.C.: Government Printing Office, 1962.

Manpower—Challenge of the Sixties. (U.S. Department of Labor.) Washington, D.C.: Government Printing Office, 1960.

Measuring Employment and Unemployment. (President's Committee to Appraise Employment and Unemployment Statistics.) Washington, D.C.: Government Printing Office, 1962.

WOLFBEIN, SEYMOUR L. "The Pace of Technological Change and the Factors Affecting It." *Manpower Implications of Automation.* (U.S Department of Labor.) Washington, D.C.: Government Printing Office, 1964, 15–28.

MONTHLY LABOR REVIEW

The following articles appeared in the *Monthly Labor Review,* which can be found in most libraries and can be ordered from the Superintendent of Documents, Washington, D.C. 20402. (Subscription price, $7.50 per year; single copies, 75 cents each.)

ALTERMAN, JACK. "Interindustry Employment Requirements." Vol. 88, No. 7 (July, 1965), 841–50.

BLOCH, JOSEPH W. "Union Contracts—A New Series of Studies." Vol. 87, No.10 (October, 1964), 1184–85.

BRACKETT, JEAN C. "Intercity Differences in Family Food Budget Costs." Vol. 86, No. 10 (October, 1963), 1189–94.

COOPER, SOPHIA, and JOHNSTON, DENIS F. "Labor Force Projections for 1970–80." Vol. 88, No. 2 (February, 1965), 129–40.

CUNNINGHAM, FRANCIS S. "The Use of Price Indexes in Escalator Contracts." Vol. 86, No. 8 (August, 1963), 948–52.

DAVIS, WILLIAM, and DAVID, LILY MARY. "Pattern of Wage and Benefit Changes in Manufacturing." Vol. 91, No. 2 (February, 1968), 40–48.

DIVISION OF MANPOWER AND EMPLOYMENT STATISTICS. "The Calculation and Uses of Spendable Earnings Series." Vol. 89, No. 4 (April, 1966), 405–9.

EVANS, W. DUANE, CORNFIELD, JEROME, and HOFFENBERG, MARVIN. "Full Employment Patterns, 1950." Part I: Vol. 64, No. 2 (February, 1947), 163–90. Part II: Vol. 64, No. 3 (March, 1947), 420–32.

"50 Years' Progress of American Labor." The Thirty-fifth Anniversary Issue. Vol. 71, No. 1 (July, 1950).

GOLDSTEIN, HAROLD. "BLS Occupational Trend Projections: An Appraisal." Vol. 86, No. 10 (October, 1963), 1135–38.

HENLE, PETER. "Recent Growth of Paid Leisure for U.S. Workers." Vol. 85, No. 3 (March, 1962), 249–57.

HOOVER, ETHEL D. "The CPI and Problems of Quality Change." Vol. 84, No. 11 (November, 1961), 1175–85.

JAFFE, SIDNEY A. "The Statistical Structure of the Revised CPI." Vol. 87, No. 8 (August, 1964), 916–24.

"Labor in the South." Special Issue. Vol. 63, No. 4 (October, 1946).

"Labor in the South." Special Issue. Vol. 91, No. 3 (March, 1968).

LAMALE, HELEN. "Poverty: The Word and the Reality." Vol. 88, No. 7 (July, 1965), 822–27.

MARK, JEROME A. "Industry Indexes of Output per Man-Hour." Vol. 85, No. 11 (November, 1962), 1269–73.

MYERS, ROBERT J., and CHANDLER, JOHN H. "International Comparisons of Unemployment." Vol. 85, No. 8 (August, 1962), 857–64; and Vol. 85, No. 9 (September, 1962), 969–74.

MYERS, ROBERT J., and SWERDLOFF, SOL. "Seasonality and Construction." Vol. 90, No. 9 (September, 1967), 1–8.

PERRELLA, VERA C. "Women and the Labor Force." Vol. 91, No. 2 (February, 1968), 1–12.

SALT, ALLAN F. "Estimated Need for Skilled Workers, 1965–75." Vol. 89, No. 4 (April, 1966), 365–71.

STERN, BORIS. "Displacement of Labor by Machinery in the Glass Industry." Vol. 24, No. 4 (April, 1927), 1–13.

"Worker Security in a Changing Economy." Special issue in honor of the Fiftieth Anniversary of the U.S. Department of Labor. Vol. 86, No. 6 (June, 1963).

Index